A GENERATION OF SPANISH POETS

1920–1936

C. B. MORRIS

Senior Lecturer in Spanish
University of Hull

CAMBRIDGE

AT THE UNIVERSITY PRESS

1969

Published by the Syndics of the Cambridge University Press
Bentley House, 200 Euston Road, London N.W.1
American Branch: 32 East 57th Street, New York, N.Y.10022

© Cambridge University Press 1969

Library of Congress Catalogue Card Number: 69-11270
Standard Book Number: 521 07381 2

Printed in Great Britain
at the University Printing House, Cambridge
(Brooke Crutchley, University Printer)

FOR BARBARA AND PHILIP

CONTENTS

PLATES

ACKNOWLEDGEMENTS

To thank those who have helped me in the preparation of this book is less a duty than an inadequate recognition of advice and assistance freely given and all too readily requested. For financial help enabling me to work in Spain I am indebted to the Sir Ernest Cassell Educational Trust and particularly to the University of Hull, whose generosity enabled me to visit Spain several times and to collect material patiently sought and put at my disposal by the helpful staff of its Library. For the photographs reproduced in this book I am grateful to Don Jorge Guillén, Don Miguel Prados and Don José Vergés Matas, who generously gave me copies of photographs published by Ediciones Destino, Barcelona, in Don José Luis Cano's *García Lorca. Biografía ilustrada* (1962). As well as sending me useful bibliographical material, Srta Paloma Altolaguirre allowed me to quote from her father's poetry and to reproduce the photograph that appeared in the homage dedicated to him in 1960 by *Caracola*, a copy of which was kindly given to me by Don Carlos Altolaguirre. Professor Carlos Blanco Aguinaga selflessly put at my disposal unpublished notes of Emilio Prados which, now kept at the Library of Congress, Washington, are reserved for his exclusive use till November 1969. I am grateful to Don Miguel Prados for permission to consult these notes and to quote from his brother's works. I am indebted to Don Rafael Alberti, Don Vicente Aleixandre and Don Jorge Guillén for so readily allowing me to draw on their works; to Doña Isabel García Lorca for authorizing my quotations from her brother's writings; to Don Jaime Salinas for permission to reproduce his father's works; and to the Fondo de Cultura Económica, Mexico, for letting me quote from Cernuda's poetry. Professor G. W. Ribbans, editor of the *Bulletin of Hispanic Studies*, has kindly let me utilize material which I published originally in that journal. Mr R. A. Cardwell, Dr D. R. Harris and Mr R. M. Price have affably sought references and provided information; Don Antonio Rodríguez Moñino ended my search for the elusive second (1936) edition of Guillén's *Cántico* by lending me a copy. I am most grateful to my colleague Miss Margaret Wilson for her comments

ACKNOWLEDGEMENTS

on several sections of this book, and to the staff of the Cambridge University Press for expert guidance. My last thanks go to two secretaries on whose sunny patience and nimble fingers I came to depend heavily: Miss Patricia M. Foster, and her predecessor as secretary to the Department of Spanish in the University of Hull, Mrs Zuzan J. Lakin. Mrs Lakin helped me to prepare the foundations of this book, sifting much material and typing many notes. When Miss Foster succeeded her, she devoted herself with characteristic care and amiability to typing the several drafts of this book, preparing the final version for the press and helping me to compile the index; to her I owe a great deal.

February 1969   C.B.M.

'THE BRILLIANT PLEIAD'

A little group of wise hearts is better than a wilderness of fools.
John Ruskin, *Crown of Wild Olive*

The contributors to the lively magazine *Lola*, which appeared in Spain in 1928 and 1929, ended their collective pieces with a signature as playful as it was appropriate: 'The Brilliant Pleiad'. My aim in borrowing this label is to celebrate a unique generation of poets and not to compete with the names by which it is generally known: 'The Generation of 1927', 'The Generation of 1925' and 'The Generation of the Dictatorship'. It is easier to dismiss the last two for capriciousness and to criticize the first for magnifying the significance of Luis de Góngora's tercentenary than to find a better label. As Jorge Guillén has wisely pointed out, 'Any name seeking to give unity to a historical period is the invention of posterity... No label is convincing...'[1]

What matters is less an apt and generally acceptable name than the existence of a group of distinguished and distinctive poets who were never fused by a programme into a clearly defined school. The novels, short stories, memoirs, plays and critical essays which I list in the appendix provide ample evidence of the enterprise and versatility which made the poetry of this generation admirably varied in theme, mood, form and language. Rafael Alberti (1902–) in particular moved with masterful ease from manner to manner; his first works, *Marinero en tierra* (1924) and *La amante* (1925), identified him as a poet who, absorbed in Spanish poetry of the sixteenth and seventeenth centuries, could skilfully emulate the verbal artifice of Góngora and the buoyant lyricism of Spain's popular songs.

It was in *La amante* that Alberti radiated most infectiously the joy which was the mainspring of the ecstatic but precise *Cántico* (1928) of Jorge Guillén (1893–) and which Federico García Lorca (1898–1936) expressed in an equally strong echo of Spain's popular poetry in *Primeras canciones* (1922) and *Canciones* (1921–4).

Until the emotional disturbances which preceded and erupted in *Poeta en Nueva York* (1929–30), Lorca transposed into captivating rhythms and striking verbal pictures the contact of his senses with the superficially attractive world around him: the picturesque landscape of his native Andalusia in *Poema del cante jondo* (1921) and the flamboyant gipsy life in *Romancero gitano* (1924–7).

A roughly simultaneous emotional and spiritual crisis released Alberti from the stranglehold of formal and linguistic beauty which, according to his own recollections, almost petrified his feelings in *Cal y canto* (1926–7),[1] where, in a dazzling display of the techniques he learned from Góngora, he gave elegant shape and expression to the technical innovations delighting people in the 1920s. In *Sobre los ángeles* (1927–8) and *Sermones y moradas* (1929–30) he was forced to express a complex and indefinable crisis in dense images, which challenge our imaginations as forcefully as those of Lorca's *Poeta en Nueva York* and Vicente Aleixandre's *Pasión de la tierra* (1928–9), *Espadas como labios* (1930–1) and *La destrucción o el amor* (1932–3). The formal moulds which Aleixandre (1898–   ) adopted in *Ámbito* (1924–7) could no longer contain his rapturous, excited visions of the oneness of the universe, which spilt into a breathless, proliferating parade of visions and images.

After choosing the discipline of verse patterns in *Perfil del aire* (1927) and *Égloga, elegía, oda* (1927–8), Luis Cernuda (1902–63) relaxed the form of his poems at the same time that he accepted in *Un río, un amor* (1929) and *Los placeres prohibidos* (1931) the stimulus of surrealist freedom in order to describe his bitterness in and alienation from a world he found hostile. With his active imagination and constant search for new techniques, Cernuda described solitude in a much more varied and graphic way than Pedro Salinas (1892–1951), Emilio Prados (1899–1962) and Manuel Altolaguirre (1905–59), who remained as faithful to their manners as they did to their dominant preoccupations. With his playful visions, verbal games and carefully cultivated colloquial style, Salinas viewed life—in *Seguro azar* (1924–8) and *Fábula y signo* (1931) especially—with more humour and humanity than Altolaguirre, who narrated his loneliness in sober, uncoloured statements which changed little from *Las islas invitadas y otros poemas* (1926) to *Nuevos poemas de las islas invitadas* (1936). Because he reacted against it or created new visions of it, Salinas was more aware of the outside world than Prados, whose ecstatic repetitions and exclamations—particularly in *Cuerpo perseguido* (1927–8)—plotted a relentless flight from the body into an exclusive world of private thoughts and sensations.

'The Brilliant Pleiad' abounded in numbers as well as in achievements; although Alberti, Aleixandre, Altolaguirre, Cernuda, Lorca, Guillén, Prados and Salinas stood out as its most accomplished poets and so dominate the pages of this book, they were surrounded by writers who helped to reflect or mould the tastes and techniques of their age. For that reason, the poetry of the eight poets I single out for special attention will be seen not detached from but in conjunction with the work of Dámaso Alonso, Mauricio Bacarisse, José Bergamín, Juan Chabás, Juan-José Domenchina, Antonio Espina, Pedro Garfias, Ernesto Giménez Caballero, José María Hinojosa, Vicente Huidobro, Juan Larrea, José Moreno Villa, Guillermo de Torre and Gerardo Diego, whose effortlessly varied and fluent poetry carried less weight than his collaboration in the homage to Góngora, his publication of the magazines *Carmen* and *Lola* and his compilation in 1932 of his famous anthology, *Poesía española 1915–1931*.

With his passion for Góngora on the one hand and his fondness for French poetry on the other, Diego illustrates the open-mindedness of a generation of poets not hamstrung by doctrinaire tastes who looked backwards to Spain's literature and outwards to Europe, particularly France. The frequent mentions of and tributes to Baudelaire and Rimbaud, for example, are not invitations to trace their mark on the poetry of this generation, but a pointer to spiritual affinities and technical models which matter more than verbal reminiscences. While Baudelaire's *Les fleurs du mal* impressed Guillén as 'an organic unity',[1] it marked for Alberti the influx into modern poetry of 'The disagreeable, the ugly, the wounding, the cruel, the fetid, the atrocious.'[2] Fond of the 'ascetic sparseness' of Pierre Reverdy, Cernuda censured the devotees of Paul Valéry, who included Guillén, as 'snobs'.[3] What is

3

clear is that the poets of this generation, whether they read because they wanted to or, in the case of university teachers like Dámaso Alonso, Cernuda, Guillén and Salinas, because they needed to, illustrated in their works and exhibited in their reminiscences, statements and critical essays a vigorous curiosity and a breadth of tastes that were by no means uniform.

This generation found in Spanish poetry much to admire and emulate. Proud of a hispanic pedigree that started in the thirteenth century, Guillén has written that the 'fathers' of his generation are to be found 'from Gonzalo de Berceo to Rubén Darío and his descendants...Góngora did not exclude St John of the Cross or Lope—or Bécquer'.[1] When Alberti needed a model of lyrical gaiety, he turned enthusiastically to the prolific poet and play-wright Lope de Vega (1562–1635), who reproduced in many of his poems and plays the simple words and lively rhythms of popular songs. When Alberti sought a poetic ancestor of the malaise he recorded in *Sobre los ángeles*, he resorted to Gustavo Adolfo Bécquer (1836–76), whose *rimas* were of a fragile, tender and time-less simplicity, and whose legends were the products of a 'lucid somnambulism'[2] foreshadowing the twentieth-century interest in mental freedom.

Sensitive to 'the verbal matter, the cadence and the rhythm' of Rubén Darío's poetry,[3] Aleixandre felt at the beginning of his career the explosive impact of the Nicaraguan diplomat and jour-nalist, who from his first visit to Spain in 1892 stimulated by his pen and by his presence a new passion for poetry, which had stag-nated in Spain in the late nineteenth century in the prim and pedestrian verses of Ramón de Campoamor (1817–1901) and Gaspar Núñez de Arce (1834–1903). Obsessed with 'the nobility of Art',[4] Darío (1867–1916) described in the exuberant language and resonant lines of *Azul* (1888) and *Prosas profanas* (1896) an aristocratic fairy-tale world peopled with mythological figures and adorned with what Cernuda censured as 'objects and things he considered previously "poetic": roses, swans, champagne, stars, peacocks, malachite, princesses, pearls, marchionesses, etc.'[5]

Darío's vigorous revitalization of Spanish poetry and his bold liberties with the metres and accentuation of verse marked him as a revolutionary whose achievements and aims set a standard for and challenged the sensibilities of the three figures who were in turn to become the spiritual mentors of a generation: Miguel de Unamuno (1864–1936), Antonio Machado (1875–1939) and Juan Ramón Jiménez (1881–1958).

Jiménez's letters to Darío, whom he praised in 1904 as 'the only great poet at present in Spain',[1] demonstrated his respect for the conscious artistry and complete professionalism of Darío, whose dislike of Jiménez's melancholy did not prevent him from recognizing his delicate sensibility or admiring his pure perceptions. Jiménez and Antonio Machado accepted the stimulus and patronage of Darío without harm to their temperaments or their poetic integrity. Although Darío urged Jiménez in 1903 to 'conquer life',[2] Jiménez withdrew from life in order to immunize his sensations and perceptions against human contact. And, unlike the flamboyantly virile pose maintained by Darío, Machado opted for a rugged honesty, a candid intimacy which expressed his deep thoughts and authentic feelings in solemn rhythms and clear, sober language unrelieved by metaphor or image. Machado did not shrink from presenting himself in his writings as a lonely, crumpled figure because, as he wrote to Jiménez in 1903 or 1904, 'that is what I am'.[3]

As the title *Campos de Castilla* (1912) suggests, Machado was more open to and aware of the concrete world than Jiménez. Less interested in capturing sensations than in expressing feelings, thoughts and opinions, he created two academic figures, Abel Martín and Juan de Mairena, who explored in two books the meditative and epigrammatic vein which makes of Machado's poetry a bleakly moving narrative of one man's passage through life and meditations on time.

That most of the poets starting their careers in the 1920s looked up to Jiménez, Machado and Unamuno as poetic patrons is shown by Guillén's reminiscence that 'We admired Machado, Jiménez and Unamuno without reserve.'[4] Alberti, who resolved in 'Con él' of *Marinero en tierra* to sail from his birthplace, Puerto de Santa María, to Jiménez's home in Palos de Moguer, has described Jiménez and Machado as 'the poets most respected by recent generations of Spaniards.'[1] What Alberti's generation admired in Jiménez and Machado was their spiritual integrity and their complete dedication to the craft and calling of poetry. Altolaguirre, who wrote to Jiménez of his respect, debt and 'true silent friendship',[2] enclosed himself as tightly as his master in a cocoon of pure and private sensations. Salinas found in Jiménez an 'authentic poet'[3] who sought before him to ignore the body; Salinas's decision in *Fábula y signo* to

> Dejarte. Te dejaré
> como olvidada
> y pensando en otras cosas
> para no pensar en ti,
> pero pensándote a ti,*   (p. 97)

duplicates the posture adopted by Jiménez, who stated in *Eternidades* (1916–17) that

> Ante mí estás, sí.
> Mas me olvido de ti
> pensando en ti.†[4]

The 'solitary pilgrim' who appeared in Dámaso Alonso's *Poemas puros. Poemillas de la ciudad* (1921),[5] where roses wither and a fountain slowly drips, perpetuated the sadness of Machado, whose 'caravanas de tristeza' moving through *Soledades* (1899–1907) reappeared in a poem Lorca wrote in 1918, 'Éste es el prólogo':

> En los libros de versos,
> entre rosas de sangre,
> van pasando las tristes
> y eternas caravanas...‡   (p. 508)

And when in *Libro de poemas* Lorca went

> ...camino de la tarde,
> entre flores de la huerta,

---

* Leave you. I shall leave you as if forgotten and think of other things not to think of you, but thinking you.
† Before me you stand, yes. But I forget you by thinking of you.
‡ In books of verses, among roses of blood, the sad and eternal caravans pass by.

                    dejando sobre el camino
                    el agua de mi tristeza,*   (p. 111)

or introduced into his poems a cricket, a water wheel, a poplar tree
or a fading evening, he used the objects and settings favoured by
Machado to create what the latter called a 'spectral background
of generic and familiar images' against which to project his
melancholy.[1]

When Lorca and his companions plumbed their imaginations to
seek a manner that was personal and distinctive, their coining of
images was interpreted by Unamuno as a pursuit of 'facile difficulty'[2] and by Machado as a betrayal of the intuition and human
emotion essential in his view to the writing of poetry. Machado's
acrid censure of 'the motley images of the very new poets',[3]
which was in keeping with his assault on baroque poetry in *Abel
Martín*,[4] revealed his failure to understand that the young poets
for whom the early 1920s were a time of apprenticeship and experiment reacted to a complex of stimuli in which Góngora did
not exclude Juan Ramón Jiménez, Max Jacob or James Joyce.
While in *Romancero gitano* and *Cal y canto* Lorca and Alberti
responded to the challenge of Góngora's poetry and emulated his
technique of ennobling the commonplace, they were led by their
own geniuses to write works that were individual and unmis-
takably theirs; Alberti required native talent to transform a
moving train into a 'Galope de las férreas amazonas'† (p. 212);
Lorca needed authentic imaginative power to visualize feverish
kisses as
                    avispas y vientecillos
                    en doble enjambre de flautas.‡   (p. 394)

It was a profusion of images such as these that helped to make
this generation into what Salinas once called a generation born
'under a lyrical star'.[5] The magazines which sprang up and died so
fast in the 1920s that in a tart verse Unamuno explained every fire
he saw as the quick extinction of a periodical[6] made lyrical fervour

---

* journeying towards the evening, among flowers of the fields, leaving the waters
  of my sadness on the way.
† Gallop of the iron amazons.
‡ wasps and breezes in a double swarm of flutes.

and imaginative vitality into a national phenomenon whose growth was unstemmed by the disapproval of older critics like Eduardo Gómez de Baquero, who railed against 'a taste for cheap imagery'.[1] Madrid was only one centre of poetic activity; *Índice* (1921–2), published by Juan Ramón Jiménez, *La Gaceta Literaria* (1927–32) and *Los Cuatro Vientos* (1933) were accompanied in the provinces by *Alfar* (1921–5) in Corunna; *La Verdad* (1923–7) and *Verso y Prosa* (1927–8) in Murcia; *Mediodía* (1926–9) in Seville; *L'Amic de les Arts* (1926–8) in Sitges; *Papel de Aleluyas* (1927–8) in Huelva; *Gallo* (1928), published in Granada by Lorca; *Carmen* and its 'friend and supplement' *Lola* (1928–9), published in Gijón by Gerardo Diego; and, perhaps the most important of all, *Litoral* (1927–9), published in Málaga by Altolaguirre and Prados, whom Alberti has celebrated as 'the solitary heroes of the printing press'.[2] That their press was, as Altolaguirre has written, 'a real corner of poetry'[3] is amply demonstrated by the series of supplements whose titles are now part of the poetic history of a generation; among the first series appeared Alberti's *La amante*, Aleixandre's *Ámbito*, Altolaguirre's *Ejemplo*, Bergamín's *Caracteres*, Cernuda's *Perfil del aire*, Lorca's *Canciones*, Hinojosa's *La rosa de los vientos* and Prados's *Vuelta*.

Guillén's description of *Verso y Prosa* in a letter to Lorca of 12 December 1926 as 'an exercise of friendship'[4] suggests that, apart from channelling into print the poetic fervour of a generation, magazines like *Verso y Prosa* and *Litoral* fertilized ideas and established personal contacts which were frequently to harden into firm friendships, attested by volleys of dedications and recorded in letters, tributes and reminiscences. The almost proverbial friendship of Altolaguirre and Prados was celebrated playfully by Lorca in one of his fanciful short plays, *La doncella, el marinero y el estudiante* (1928), when in a stage direction he introduced the two poets 'flour-white with fear of the sea' (p. 813); it was commemorated in a grimmer context by Altolaguirre, who in a chapter of his unpublished novel recalled his interrogation in France after his flight from Spain in 1939:

> One of the members of the tribunal knew me.
> He uttered my name. He asked me about my best friend...
> —Do you know where your friend Emilio Prados is?[5]

When Guillén ended a letter to Lorca of 19 February 1926: 'Always yours, in Poetry and in Friendship',[1] he signalled an intimacy and a common dedication to poetry prevented by the savagery unleashed by the Civil War from enduring as long as the deep friendship of Guillén and Salinas. Even Cernuda, whose pathological shyness made personal contact difficult, found in Altolaguirre and Aleixandre, who were themselves firm friends, the comradeship and understanding he needed. Altolaguirre's wife, Concha Méndez, has recalled that Cernuda was 'like a brother of ours whom we saw daily for years and years'.[2] Cernuda's closeness to Aleixandre made him a frequent visitor to the latter's house, which was a hospitable place in which to talk, recite or listen to Lorca at the piano; it was a focal point of poetic fervour as lively and informal as the Residencia de Estudiantes, administered by the Institución Libre de Enseñanza, which counted among its residents at different times Lorca, Prados, Moreno Villa, Buñuel and Dalí. Alberti, who remembered many years later Lorca's spellbinding recital of his 'Romance sonámbulo' during their first meeting at the Residencia, has paid tribute to it as a 'house of culture', a 'retreat of poets' who exchanged ideas and enthusiasms, recited new poems, aired their poetic discoveries and listened to lectures by such distinguished men as Paul Claudel, Paul Valéry, Louis Aragon and Paul Eluard.[3]

Such a web of contacts provided stimuli to poetic activity more amiable, informal and unpredictable than any manifesto. As Guillén has recalled, 'There was no program, there was no manifesto attacking or defending fixed positions. There were dialogues, letters, dinners, walks, and friendship under the bright light of Madrid...'[4] Each poet maintained his individuality and displayed a distinctive manner despite frequent meetings and such communal activities as the homage to Góngora instigated by Alberti, Dámaso Alonso, Diego, Guillén, Lorca and Salinas, and the visit to the Ateneo of Seville made in December 1927 by Alberti, Bergamín, Chabás, Diego, Guillén and Lorca. The liberal use of the adjective *putrefacto*, invented by Dalí or Lorca, demonstrated a youthful zest perfectly compatible with a readiness to acknowledge literary debts and revere spiritual and poetic mentors. It was with playful mischief rather than malice that Lorca would repeat the line of Rubén Darío: 'Que púberes canéforas te ofrenden el acanto'* only to say: 'The only word I understand in all that is *que*.'[1]

José Ortega y Gasset's attack in *La deshumanización del arte*, written in 1925, on the cult of sport in life and literature, which in his view caused in poetry 'the superior algebra of metaphors',[2] was based on a valid diagnosis of the first half of the 1920s, when most poets of the younger generation seemed keen to display their imaginative litheness. Had Ortega turned particularly to the poetry of Alberti, Cernuda and Lorca four years later, he would have observed in their use of images the interplay of emotion and imagination which he could have diagnosed as *la rehumanización del arte*. But it was precisely Alberti's response in *Sobre los ángeles* to the personal pressures inside him that provoked Juan Ramón Jiménez's vicious assault in 1930 on his 'magic wand' and 'disjointed prattling'.[3] Jiménez's reluctance to allow the younger poets to develop in fidelity to their own temperaments and personalities made him swing from patronage to open hostility. Despite his claim in a letter to Alberti written about 1945 that his estrangement from the younger poets after 1927 was 'not my fault',[4] his refusal to take part in the homage to Góngora and his belief that Alberti was wasting his time on his nonsense play, *La pájara pinta* (1925), pointed to a queen-bee mentality which detached him from the younger poets as much as their growing assurance and individuality removed them from his spiritual control. Years later Alberti asked himself whether Jiménez was afraid of 'perhaps losing the baton and suddenly finding himself alone, without an orchestra, tracing signs in the air of an empty room?'[5]

With majestic fickleness Jiménez made waspish attacks on writers to whom he had earlier paid lyrical tributes. His description of Salinas in 1923 as 'a smiling, fair and ruddy' poet whose *Presagios* he exalted as 'a most beautiful mound of human fruit of shining gold and rich shadow', changed in his letters into bitter sniping at 'the opportunist'.[6] The affable formulas of 'My dear poet' and 'Your friend always' with which he began and ended his letter to Guillén of 7 August 1932 changed on 27 June 1933 into

* For pubescent canephores offer unto you the acanthus.

the cold, curt words of the telegram which started the feud he was to maintain against Guillén until his death: 'Poem and friendship are withdrawn today.'[1] The lyrical letter he wrote to Alberti in 1925 to express his delight at *Marinero en tierra* was followed in 1929 or 1930 by a barbed note in which he demonstrated his displeasure with the slapstick tributes to the silent cinema comics which were to form part of *Yo era un tonto y lo que he visto me ha hecho dos tontos* (1929):

For a year you have been telling us in *La Gaceta Literaria* that you were a fool. I thought that, since you were so happy with and proud of your discovery, you would also like me to tell you about it.

In any case you write that you are a fool. I have the right to believe it and to repeat it. Don't you think so?[2]

What alienated the sympathy and devotion of several poets of this generation was Jiménez's inability to realize that respect for his poetic zeal did not imply automatic obeisance to his every whim or conflict with the new impulses and infectious 'isms' which in the 1920s, according to Alberti, 'infiltrated everywhere, succeeded one another in such sudden waves, like seismic tremors, that it was more than difficult to emerge unscathed from their ceaseless ebb and flow'.[3] One of the 'isms' which appealed to Alberti at the beginning of his career was *ultraísmo*, which, paralysed into an absurd and hollow rhetoric by its technical vocabulary, its wildly spiralling lines and its breathless exaltation of machinery, aimed to coin what Guillermo de Torre defined as 'double, triple and multiple images'[4] as relentlessly as Gerardo Diego, who in his first work called appropriately *Imagen* (1922) advocated as the basis of *creacionismo* the 'Multiple image'.[5]

As Torre, Diego and many other minor poets who grouped themselves under the banners of *ultraísmo* or *creacionismo* coined their images with tireless enthusiasm, they continued and provoked in Spain the poetic ferment which had been fostered in Italy and France by such movements as futurism and Dada, whose revolutionary fervour was partly recorded in Spanish magazines in the years immediately before and after 1920. Marinetti's rabid declarations, which reached a Spanish audience in 1909 and 1911,[6] anticipated *ultraísmo*'s anti-sentimentality and cult of the machine with their advocacy of war as a social hygiene, their hostility to woman and exaltation of mechanical beauty. In 1919 *Cervantes* published Tristan Tzara's 'Proclama sin pretensión. Dada 1919' and Diego's 'Posibilidades creacionistas', as well as pieces on or by Apollinaire, Jacob and Supervielle. In the same year there appeared in *Grecia* pieces on or by Apollinaire, Cendrars, Reverdy, Tzara and Jacob, whose *Coup de dés* Guillermo de Torre translated into Spanish in 1924 under the title of *El cubilete de dados*.

As I shall show in chapter 2, Jacob's insistence that 'art is purely a "distraction"'[1] was echoed in Spain by Dámaso Alonso, Bergamín, Espina, Giménez Caballero and Ramón Gómez de la Serna and illustrated on the cinema screen by the clowning of the idolized comics. The articles written by Bacarisse in *España* in 1920 and 1921 and the reports and reviews which appeared frequently in *La Gaceta Literaria* signalled a deep curiosity in a new art form that, finding a focal point in the Cineclub of Madrid, offered in its rapid flow of visions a technique which challenged Alberti in particular to create in *Cal y canto* images 'that at times, in the same poem, would succeed one another with cinematographic speed'.[2]

But Cernuda's use of two film titles in *Un río, un amor* to head poems of sadness suggested that all was not high spirits and play in the poetry of the 1920s. Although several images of Altolaguirre and Prados and the interest Cernuda showed in surrealism indicate that these three poets were not immune to new fashions and techniques, they kept sternly and soberly aloof both from the games in poetry and prose with which Guillén began his career in 1919 and 1920 and from the displays of ingenuity which Salinas made consistently in his poetry, prose and plays. And just as the anguish which led to and exploded in Lorca's *Poeta en Nueva York* banished the gaiety he paraded in *Canciones* and *Romancero gitano*, so did coincidental personal crises force Alberti to look at rather than away from himself as he did in the poetry preceding *Sobre los ángeles*. Deeply shaken by the emotional and spiritual malaise he recorded in *Sobre los ángeles* and *Sermones y moradas*, Alberti fell an easy victim to the political fever of the 1930s which began with

Alfonso XIII's dismissal of Primo de Rivera in 1930; his facile writings in support of the Republic and of communism, which justify sadly his awareness that 'One must not seek great civic poets in Spain,'[1] reflect little honour on a poet who debased his skills by putting his pen to the service of a political cause.

With their differences of technique, language, mood and intention the poetic works written between 1920 and 1936 made this a period whose density and richness it is difficult, if not impossible, to encompass in one book. A detailed study of the poetry written by this generation after the Civil War would have made this book unwieldy and weakened its purpose: to present the major phases and cross-currents of a tightly knit and highly articulate generation of poets as they moved in the sixteen years on which I focus from apprenticeship to maturity. The eight major poets of this generation, together with its many minor ones, move in and out of the five chapters, each of which deals with a specific trend or theme; in chapter 1, 'Old Poetry, New Poets', I examine the fervent interest shown by most members of this generation in Spain's poetic past. In chapter 2, 'The Game of Poetry', I look in particular at those lighthearted writings of Alberti, Lorca, Guillén and Salinas that reflected the energy, playfulness and experimental fervour of the Jazz Age. In chapter 3, 'In Praise of Creation', I concentrate on the vigorous exaltation of life sung by Guillén in *Cántico* and echoed by Aleixandre in *Ámbito*. In chapter 4, 'The Closed Door', I consider the cult of solitude maintained by Altolaguirre, Cernuda, Prados and Salinas. In chapter 5, 'The Broken Rhythm', I look at those works in which Alberti, Aleixandre, Cernuda and Lorca, led by choice—as in Aleixandre's case—or forced by stress —as in the others—, erupted into images so profuse and overlaid that *Sermones y moradas*, *Pasión de la tierra* and *Poeta en Nueva York* are three of the most demanding works in twentieth-century Spanish poetry. In an epilogue, 'After the War', I glance briefly at the poetry written mostly in exile by a generation dispersed by the Civil War.

It is not my aim to examine every aspect of every poet of a generation so productive that, as the following list shows, its eight leading writers alone produced from 1920 to 1936 over forty books of poetry which, in the cases of Lorca, Guillén and Salinas particularly, have received generous critical attention. I list as separate items two titles which I consider as distinct and clearly distinguishable works: *Perfil del aire*, and the mature and assured version which Cernuda reconstituted in 1936 under the title of *Primeras poesías*. Although I mention in my list both the 1928 and the 1936 editions of *Cántico*, I shall refer in chapter 3 to the poems contained in the earlier edition, which are reinforced by the poems of the elegant but almost completely inaccessible later one.

Most of the following titles, which catalogue the activities of a dynamic generation, will recur with varying degrees of frequency in the five chapters:

ALBERTI	*Marinero en tierra*	1924
	La amante	1925
	El alba del alhelí	1925–6
	Cal y canto	1926–7
	Sobre los ángeles	1927–8
	Yo era un tonto y lo que he visto me ha hecho dos tontos	1929
	Sermones y moradas	1929–30
	Verte y no verte	1934
ALEIXANDRE	*Ámbito*	1924–7
	Pasión de la tierra	1928–9
	Espadas como labios	1930–1
	La destrucción o el amor	1932–3
	Mundo a solas	1934–6
ALTOLAGUIRRE	*Las islas invitadas y otros poemas*	1926
	Ejemplo	1927
	Poesía	1930–1
	Soledades juntas	1931
	La lenta libertad	1936
	Nuevos poemas de las islas invitadas	1936
CERNUDA	*Perfil del aire*	1927
	Primeras poesías	1924–7
		[according to Cernuda]

	Égloga, elegía, oda	1927–8
	Un río, un amor	1929
	Los placeres prohibidos	1931
	Donde habite el olvido	1932–3
	Invocaciones	1934–5
GARCÍA LORCA	*Libro de poemas*	1921
	Poema del cante jondo	1921
	Primeras canciones	1922
	Canciones	1921–4
	Romancero gitano	1924–7
	Poeta en Nueva York	1929–30
	Llanto por Ignacio Sánchez Mejías	1935
	Seis poemas galegos	1935
	Diván del Tamarit	1936
GUILLÉN	*Cántico* [1st edition]	1928
	Cántico [2nd edition]	1936
PRADOS	*Tiempo*	1923–5
	El misterio del agua	1926–7
	Memoria de poesía	1926–7
	Cuerpo perseguido	1927–8
	La voz cautiva	1933–4
	Andando, andando por el mundo	1934–5
SALINAS	*Presagios*	1923
	Seguro azar	1924–8
	Fábula y signo	1931
	La voz a ti debida	1933
	Razón de amor	1936

Unless otherwise stated, the page references embedded in the text are to the following editions:

Alberti, *Poesías completas* (Buenos Aires, 1961)
Aleixandre, *Poesías completas* (Madrid, 1960)
Altolaguirre, *Poesías completas* (Mexico, 1960)
Cernuda, *La realidad y el deseo*, 3rd ed. (Mexico, 1958)
García Lorca, *Obras completas*, 3rd ed. (Madrid, 1957)

Guillén, *Cántico* (Paris, 1962; reprint of 1st ed., Madrid, 1928)
Prados, *Antología* (Buenos Aires, 1954)
Salinas, *Poesías completas* (Madrid, 1955)
All other references will be specified in the notes.

I have provided at the foot of the page a prose gloss in English of every poetry quotation. As it is less important that the prose extracts from essays, letters and reminiscences, etc., should remain in the original, I have tried to avoid the cumbrous weight of an English translation of every Spanish phrase and sentence by rendering all the prose quotations directly into English; references to these quotations are given in the notes. Readers will find in the glossary definitions of the Spanish technical terms I use.

OLD POETRY, NEW POETS

...l'influence...ne crée rien: elle éveille.

André Gide, *Prétextes*

It takes no sharp vision or skilled powers of detection to note the vigorous revival of Spain's poetic past in Spanish poetry of the 1920s and 1930s. To read Spanish poetry of this period is to rediscover a rich compendium of poetic traditions, for concentrated in two decades was a wide range of forms, metres, techniques, diction and imagery that owed their new life to Spain's poetic heritage. The exuberant language and dislocated syntax of much of Góngora's verse was reborn along with the limpid elegance of Garcilaso; the brief and seemingly effortless lyrics of Gil Vicente and Spain's sixteenth-century song books stood side by side with rigid and demanding moulds like the tercet, *décima* and sonnet. And even the genre of the *auto* was resurrected by Alberti, who has stated that when he wrote *El hombre deshabitado* in 1930 he followed 'the aesthetic and the technique of the *autos sacramentales*'.[1]

Alberti's confession is not unique, for he and other poets of his generation acknowledged their debts with pride in their country's literature. With the list of poets he included in the 'Poética' he wrote in 1934, Alberti recited his poetic pedigree and chanted a litany of tribute at the same time:

The poets who have helped me, and whom I continue to admire deeply, have been Gil Vicente, the anonymous poets of Spain's *Cancionero* and *Romancero*, Garcilaso, Góngora, Lope, Bécquer, Baudelaire, Juan Ramón Jiménez and Antonio Machado.[2]

Guillén has acknowledged that lines of Quevedo 'clearly influence my attitude and my writing'.[3] Salinas singled out Quevedo and Lope de Vega as two of his favourite poets.[4] And in an essay where Cernuda employed his favourite technique of talking about himself in the third person, he paraded his reading and admitted his debts as candidly as Alberti:

His tradition was integrated not only by Góngora, but also by Manrique, and Garcilaso, and Aldana, and Fray Luis de León, and St John of the Cross, and Quevedo and Calderón. Traces of all these can be found in the poetry of Cernuda.[1]

Although magazines like *Índice* and *Carmen* reflected and fostered the interest the poets of this generation showed in such marginal Golden Age figures as Juan de Jáuregui, Francisco de Rioja, Pedro Espinosa and Pedro Soto de Rojas,[2] it was a select group of major Golden Age poets who were most warmly and consistently honoured with pen and with voice; it was the names of Lope de Vega, Garcilaso de la Vega, Luis de León and Góngora that recurred most frequently in the lectures, tributes and critical essays of Alberti, Cernuda, Lorca, Guillén and Salinas.[3] Although he regarded Lorca and Fernando de Villalón as also descended from Lope, Alberti considered himself to be 'the nearest, something like a nephew of Lope'.[4] Lorca proved his kinship with Lope by including three of his plays in the repertory of La Barraca, the student drama group which under his direction toured Spain from 1932 to 1936.[5] When Salinas chose the phrase 'la voz a ti debida' from Garcilaso's second eclogue as a title for his major work, he was paying an implicit tribute to a poet revered by Cernuda, whose own eclogue in *Égloga, elegía, oda* was the direct result of what he called 'My love and admiration for Garcilaso (the Spanish poet who is dearest to me)...'[6] Alberti's regard for Garcilaso was just as deep and steadfast; in an edition of Garcilaso's poetry published in Buenos Aires in 1946 he reproduced as 'Homenajes' the two poems he had written years previously: the sad and bitter 'Elegía a Garcilaso', which belongs to *Sermones y moradas*, and the simple, light-hearted tribute he included in *Marinero en tierra*:

> Si Garcilaso volviera,
> yo sería su escudero;
> que buen caballero era...* (p. 69)

Although his poetry seems to have had little impact on the poets of this generation, Luis de León was honoured in 1928 by *Carmen*. Devoting its double number 3–4 'To the Master Fray

---

* If Garcilaso were to return, I would be his squire; for he was a good knight.

Luis de León', *Carmen* reproduced three of León's poems, printed essays by J. M. de Cossío, Gerardo Diego and J. M. Quiroga Plá, and published the tributes of nine poets who offered León 'a garland of ardent poetic good will'. The 'Soledad' which Lorca wrote in his honour is the most striking tribute of this homage because it is written in the *lira* which León used more than any other form and which is most often associated with his name. Lorca's poem is, to quote the first line of the second stanza, a 'Soledad con estilo', for it could have been written by a poet who spent all his life composing *liras*. Lorca's mastery of this stanza form allowed him to write a gentle and elegant poem whose melody is tranquil and whose structure is effortlessly direct:

> En la curva del río
> el doble cisne su blancura canta.
> Húmeda voz sin frío
> fluye de su garganta,
> y por los juncos rueda y se levanta.* (p. 542)

Lorca's use of the *lira* illustrates one feature of the poetry of this generation which Gerardo Diego defined in an essay written in 1927 as 'La vuelta a la estrofa'. Rejecting Benjamín Jarnés's accusation that the return to the stanza was 'the return of the vanquished', Diego proclaimed defiantly that 'We make *décimas*, we make sonnets, we make *liras* because we want to.'[1] Guillén confirmed the popularity of the sonnet with his recollection years later that 'These Spaniards could write sonnets with complete freedom, whenever they "felt like it" poetically.'[2] 'These Spaniards' included Alberti, Altolaguirre, Cernuda, Diego, Lorca and Guillén himself; and even Salinas—whose indifference to verse-forms tempts us to use the question and answer found in his *Víspera del gozo*: 'Prose or poetry? One doesn't know—included three sonnets in *Presagios* and published another as early as 1916.[3]

The elegant sonnets of *Marinero en tierra*, which Alberti constructed with hendecasyllables or alexandrines, heralded his pursuit of formal beauty which is so striking a feature of *Cal y canto*,

---

* At the bend of the river the swan, doubled by its reflection, sings its whiteness. A liquid voice untouched by cold flows from its throat and rolls and rises through the reeds.

where he tried so hard to chisel fine images and sculpture elegant ballads, sonnets, madrigals and tercets that the challenge of architectural elegance squeezed out and fossilized his emotions. His admission that in *Cal y canto* 'formal beauty took hold of me until it almost petrified my feelings'[1] is matched by Cernuda's recognition that the technically demanding moulds he used in *Égloga*, *elegía*, *oda* were 'exercises' which, although beneficial to his poetic development, nevertheless excluded 'a live and essential part of me'.[2]

Although Cernuda's choice of the eclogue and ode, with their intricate rhyme schemes and interplay of hendecasyllables and heptasyllables, revealed a greater ambition and technical expertise than he displayed in *Perfil del aire*, the sonnets, *décimas* and quatrains which compose his first work amply prove Diego's contention that 'Cernuda, in the stanza, lives like a fish in water.'[3] His use of the *décima* in particular helped to reinstate a form whose popularity in the sixteenth and seventeenth centuries was attested by Lope's tribute in his *Laurel de Apolo*:

> ¡ Qué breve laberinto !
> ¡ Qué dulce y elegante… !*[4]

This neat, concise and streamlined form found favour both with Prados, Guillén and Lorca, whose *décimas* mentioned in his letter to Guillén of 28 March 1927 have not survived,[5] and with marginal figures like Max Aub, Bergamín, Domenchina and Diego, who praised Góngora's *décimas* as 'these tiny marvels of a Swiss watchmaker.'[6]

What Cernuda and Guillén in particular did with the *décima* was to expunge the frivolity and sententiousness found in many Golden Age examples. Instead of using the *décima*, as Góngora did, for light-hearted occasional pieces about 'a little dog which died when a lady's husband was absent',[7] Cernuda observed the canon Lope laid down in his *Arte nuevo de hacer comedias* that 'Décimas are good for complaints.'[8] Poem XXII of *Primeras poesías* shows that Cernuda was projecting within the *décima* a mood and a vision of himself:

* What a concise labyrinth ! How elegant and sweet !

En soledad. No se siente
El mundo, que un muro sella;
La lámpara abre su huella
Sobre el diván indolente.
Acogida está la frente
Al regazo del hastío.
¿ Qué ausencia, qué desvarío
A la belleza hizo ajena?
Tu juventud nula, en pena
De un blanco papel vacío.*   (p. 23)

Proud of his ability to compose *décimas*, Cernuda pointed out
that 'Many of the *décimas* written by Guillén are not strictly
décimas.'[1] And he was right, for of the seventeen *décimas* published
in the first edition of *Cántico* seven only conform to the authentically Spanish rhyme scheme of the *décima espinela* (a b b a a c c
d d c), and ten follow the foreign pattern used, for example, by
Valéry (a b a b c c d e e d). Guillén's use of both schemes shows
his love of what one critic has called 'consciously cultivated geometric proportions'[2] which contain his visions of the world as
something whole, precise, interlocking and beautiful. What dis-
tinguishes his *décimas* from those of Cernuda is their greater
fluidity and speed; by reducing the number of pauses, Guillén
quickened the tempo and set the *décima* free within its precise
limits. 'La cabeza', which follows the traditional pattern, flow
into movement after the fourth line:

¡ Tierno canto de la frente,
Batido por tanta onda !
La palma presume monda
La calavera inminente.
Si la tez dice que miente
El tacto en ese barrunto
Porque a un gran primor en punto,
Ápice de su matiz,

---

* In solitude. Sealed by a wall, the world cannot be heard; the lamp leaves its
shadow on the languid divan. The brow nestles in the lap of weariness. What
absence, what delirium alienated beauty? Your empty youth, condemned to a
sheet of blank white paper.

Conduce la piel feliz,
Palpa el hueso ya difunto.* (p. 69)

But the traditional verse forms of Spanish poetry were not always revived with such earnestness or respect. When 'fray *Luis de Pato*' set out in his satire published in *Lola* in 1928 (nos. 3–4) to obey *Lola*'s aim of laughing 'at all that is laughable and of debunking the Spanish literary establishment',[1] it was the *lira*—studded with lines of Luis de León—that he chose for his deflation of Antonio Espina, Fernando Vela, Guillermo de Torre, Giménez Caballero and Ortega y Gasset. And when an anonymous writer, adapting *chicle* (chewing-gum) to make his pseudonym 'Chiclet', lampooned Ortega and his periodical *El espectador* in the first number of *Lola*, he revived the scurrilousness of many Golden Age *letrillas* with his gruesome verses on 'El espectorador y la saliva'.

The satires of 'Chiclet' and 'Fray Luis de Pato' were symptoms of the tension between the older generation and the young writers whose independence was brought to the surface and sharpened by the tercentenary of Góngora in 1927. When Juan Ramón Jiménez, Unamuno and Valle-Inclán declined the invitation to pay homage to Góngora, they thrust Góngora into the centre of a literary battle in which the old guard faced the new militant partisans of a poet they considered unjustly slighted and neglected. With defiant possessiveness Góngora was championed as 'our don Luis de Góngora', as Guillén wrote when he sent Lorca the *décima* he composed in Góngora's honour;[2] on the other hand, the once revered Juan Ramón Jiménez, who signed his sharp refusal and his sour attack on Diego and the 'Revista de Desoriente' with the initials 'K.Q.X.', was now ridiculed as 'Kuan Qamón Ximénez'.

The ambitious plans to honour Góngora were recorded, together with a sober balance-sheet of modest achievement, by Diego in his 'Crónica del centenario de Góngora (1627–1927)'.[3] What Diego made clear in these accounts is that the celebrations in Góngora's honour had a serious as well as a frivolous side; the

* Tender rock of the brow, beaten by so many waves! The palm already senses the bareness of the impending skull. If the skin says that the hand is wrong in that conjecture because the happy flesh leads to a pointed splendour, the peak of its hue, it feels the already dead bone.

tercentenary was to be marked by 'all sorts of serious and frivolous youthful manifestations'. The earnest tributes aimed to be comprehensive: twelve volumes of Góngora's poetry were to be published by the Revista de Occidente; a play by Góngora was to be performed; there would be a *verbena andaluza*; a concert, for which Falla wrote his *Soneto a Córdoba*; and an exhibition of drawings to which Dalí and Joan Gris promised contributions. However, Diego's chronicle showed that achievements did not measure up to their joint plans or his private hopes; Dámaso Alonso published his famous edition of the *Soledades*; José María de Cossío published his edition of Góngora's *romances*; Diego produced his *Antología poética en honor de Góngora*; but, as Diego tartly observed, Salinas and Guillén will finish their editions of the *Sonetos* and *Octavas* in 2027—in time for the quater-centenary. Had the realization of all these plans depended on Diego's energy and enthusiasm, everything would have been achieved; as it is, he appears as the secretary, the chronicler, the promoter penning verse to urge his companions to get on with their tasks.[1]

That Góngora was a pretext for youthful ferment and light-hearted protest was shown by the *auto de fe* which, according to Diego's report, took place on 23 May 1927 at a place he refused to name. The tribunal was formed by 'the three greatest devotees of Góngora': Dámaso Alonso, Alberti and—immodestly—himself; the subdeacons and acolytes were José María de Cossío, Buñuel, Bergamín and Chabás. Their first sentence was imposed on three dummies made by Moreno Villa, which represented the three enemies of Góngora who therefore deserved to burn: 'The mole-like scholar, the marmot professor and the crustacean academician.' The next victims were a pile of books, burned on two bonfires which Dámaso Alonso claimed many years later did not really exist,[2] and Jorge Guillén, 'excommunicated' by the tribunal for not attending the ceremony. On the following day, however, the revellers turned exuberance to veneration when they attended 'a solemn requiem mass for the soul of don Luis'.

Although 1927 was a year of youthful combat in which a great but neglected poet was justly rehabilitated, it is a misleading date, for it suggests a sudden and unpredictable rediscovery of

Góngora's poetry. The homages published in *La Gaceta Literaria, Litoral, Lola* and *Verso y Prosa*, together with Dámaso Alonso's brilliant study of the *Soledades*, signalled the climax of devotion and interest which had already inspired the pioneer critical works of Alfonso Reyes and Lucien-Paul Thomas and which were sporadically apparent in Spanish literary magazines of the 1920s.[1] It is as wrong to visualize 1927 as a magic, electrifying date as it is to think that Góngora influenced all the poets of this generation in the same degree; with his passionate absorption of Góngora's poetry and skilful imitation of his style, Alberti stands a long way from Cernuda, who immunized himself against what he regarded as the two main pitfalls of Spanish poetry in the 1920s: 'the folkloric and the pedantic'.[2]

Cernuda's hostility to popular poetry was a symptom of the spasmodic way in which Spain's poetic past relives in the twentieth century. Like the enthusiasm for Góngora, the interest in popular poetry swung between extremes. At the one end was the aloof Cernuda, who believed that 'the imitation of a supposedly "popular" poetry' cannot express 'the very depths' of a poet;[3] in the middle were Altolaguirre, Prados and Salinas, whose use of popular poetry was sporadic rather than systematic; and at the opposite end were Alberti and Lorca, who revived and emulated with loving skill Spain's popular lyrics, which had been tirelessly collected by such devotees as Dámaso Ledesma, Francisco Rodríguez Marín and Antonio Machado y Álvarez.

The number of Spain's ballads and popular lyrics is so vast that one anonymous poet aptly likened their profusion to a fountain:

> De cantares bonitos
> tengo una fuente;
> cuando quiero cantares,
> le doy corriente.*[4]

Spain's popular songs have been conserved by a happy partnership of voice and pen: people have kept singing them, poets have heard or read them, and collectors have copied them. When in the twentieth century Alberti and Lorca were penetrated by the lively

---

* I have a fountain brimming with pretty songs; when I want songs, I let it flow.

spirit and simple melodies of popular poetry, they repeated the process of revitalization which in the fifteenth century made Santillana introduce a popular *villancico* into his *serranillas*, and which in the sixteenth and seventeenth centuries made Gil Vicente and Lope de Vega put into their plays the songs and dances of the people.

The most musically appealing type of Spain's traditional songs is the *villancico*, a lyrical statement or exclamation that was glossed in several stanzas and rounded off by all or part of the *villancico* repeated as a refrain. The simple lyrics and refrains of Spain's *villancicos* were frequently deployed in parallel lines, which provided a rhythmic measure to the dances which were performed in Castile around 1500 to the accompaniment of parallel songs.[1] And just as the parallel lines regulated the dancers' steps, so do they still captivate the reader by impressing on his ears and putting before his eyes one or two recurrent elements:

> Alta estaba la peña,
> nace la malva en ella.

> Alta estaba la peña
> riberas del río;
> nace la malva en ella,
> y el trébol florido.[*2]

Parallelism in the Castilian *villancicos* was more dramatic and vigorously rhythmic than in the Portuguese *cantigas de amigo*, in which the carefully organized lines ensnare the reader within a web of sentimental and syntactic variations. However, the decrease in the seventeenth century in the social activities of dancing and singing reduced the popularity of the *villancicos*, which retreated before the growth of such art forms as the *letrilla*, the *glosa* and the *copla*, which engendered many of the *coplas* of modern times.

All that survives of many *villancicos* is the detached, isolated exclamation, which expresses freshly and simply an undeveloped moment of emotion. This brief emotion could be aroused by

---

* The rock was high, the mallow is born in it.
  The rock was high on the banks of the river; the mallow is born in it, and the flowering clover.

many things, like the gleeful prospect of enjoying the feast of
San Juan:

> Mañana de San Juan, mozas;
> vámonos a coger rosas.*1

Or the anonymous poet would pay simple tribute to a woman:

> Ojos garzos ha la niña:
> ¿quién se los namoraría?†2

Or the dark-skinned girl who recurs frequently in these poems
would wistfully lament her complexion:

> Criéme en aldea,
> híceme morena;
> si en villa me criara,
> más bonica fuera.‡3

Or the coming of day could be celebrated in a joyous rhythmic
chant:

> Ya viene el día
> con el alegría,
> ya viene el sol
> con el resplandor.§4

What is obvious from these few examples is that the appeal of
poems in which parallelism, repetition, alliteration and onomato-
poeia are salient features is hauntingly musical; that there are so
many lullabies among Spain's popular lyrics is a pointer to their
musical nature, as Lorca recognized in his lecture on 'Las nanas
infantiles'. Alberti's praise in his lectures on popular poetry of the
lullabies of Gil Vicente and Lope de Vega was part of his enthusiastic championing of two poets who, like Alberti and Lorca
in the twentieth century, contributed in their day to the vigorous
revival of popular lyrics. The boatman who appears in *Marinero en
tierra* (p. 36) signals his reverence for the 'marvellous Gil Vicente'5
as simply as 'los tréboles del soto' found in *La amante* (p. 106) and

---

* It is the morning of San Juan, lasses; let us go and pick roses.
† The girl has blue eyes; who would fall in love with them?
‡ I was brought up in a village, I became dark-skinned; if I had been brought up
in a town, I would have been prettier.
§ The day comes with joy, the sun comes with splendour.

the play he wrote in 1946, *El trébol florido*, reveal his worship of Lope, who fascinated him with this refrain:

> Trébole, ¡ ay Jesús, cómo huele !
> Trébole, ¡ ay Jesús, qué olor !*1

But Lope de Vega was not by any means the first to sing to the clover, which had already inspired this Asturian song:

> A coger el trébole
> la noche de San Juan,†

and this *villancico*:

> Trébol, florido trébol,
> trébol florido.‡2

By using a lyrical motif which appealed to him, Lope exploited and kept alive the songs and rhythms of the people. Like Gil Vicente and many anonymous poets before him, he placed many of his songs where they belonged: in the countryside. He sang various rustic labours; he praised the birds, trees and rivers; and he exalted with a gay simplicity the 'atmospheric happiness' which was to fill Guillén three centuries later:3

> En las mañanicas
> del mes de mayo
> cantan los ruiseñores,
> retumba el campo.§4

The fact that the *trébol* refrain which Alberti attributed to Lope was sung by other, anonymous, poets underlines the popular pedigree of this *villancico* and shows that it belongs to no single author; like all authentic popular poems it is, to use Alberti's apt phrase, 'the property of no-one and of everyone'.5

In both of his lectures on popular poetry Alberti recalled how he once heard four lines of 'Joselito en su gloria', of his own *El alba del alhelí*, sung in a tavern in the Triana district of Seville; what he did not tell us, however, is whether the four lines he heard were

---

* The clover, oh how it smells ! The clover, oh what fragrance !
† Let us pick the clover on Midsummer night.
‡ Clover, flowering clover.
§ In the mornings of the month of May the nightingales sing and the countryside resounds.

exactly the lines he had written. It would be surprising if they were, for the common man instinctively scents and quickly purges any artificiality within a poem. Nevertheless, Alberti could well congratulate himself that four lines which he had written were adopted and treated as authentically popular, for, as Manuel Machado neatly explained in *Sevilla* (1920),

> Hasta que el pueblo las canta,
> las coplas, coplas no son;
> y cuando las canta el pueblo,
> ya nadie sabe el autor.*[1]

Manuel Machado's flamboyant pride in Andalusia led him in 1912 to write a poetic tribute to its songs, *Cante hondo*, which was surpassed in 1921 by Lorca's eulogy, *Poema del cante jondo*. Andalusian popular poetry is one of deep and grave feelings; its many finely turned lines and beautiful images have nothing to do with the pastiche glitter of what Alberti termed derisively 'the recent Andalusian *costumbrismo* or picturesqueness'.[2] In his lecture on 'El cante jondo' Lorca neatly summarized its main themes as pain, grief, love and death (p. 1520); in his poem 'La copla andaluza' of *Cante hondo* Manuel Machado was more melodramatic and explicit:

> Dice de ojos negros
> y de rojos labios;
> de venganza, de olvido, de ausencia,
> de amor y de engaño...

> Y de desengaño.
> De males y bienes,
> de esperanza, de celos..., de cosas
> de hombres y mujeres.†[3]

The characteristically Castilian popular verse forms are the *villancico* and the *seguidilla*, although the *seguidilla* is also used in

---

* Until the people sings them folk-songs are not folk-songs; and when the people sings them, no-one knows who wrote them.
† It tells of dark eyes and of red lips; of vengeance, of forgetfulness, of absence, of love and deceit...
   And of disillusion. Of fortunes and misfortunes, of hope, of jealousy..., of things between men and women.

1 Lorca and Alberti in 1927

Andalusia; the octosyllabic quatrain is common to both Castile and Andalusia, and is known in the latter as the *copla*. An authentically Andalusian form matching the *copla* in popularity is the *solear*, composed of three octosyllables whose first and third lines are linked by rhyme or assonance. Much Andalusian song has a gravity which in this *solear* of neglect and unrequited love heralds personal tragedy:

> Tu orbío me tiene loca:
> cuando me siento a comé,
> no me para ná en la boca.*[1]

At times the anonymous Andalusian poet comments tartly on human failings:

> Er tambor es tu retrato;
> que mete mucho ruío,
> y si se mira por dentro,
> se encuentra que está basío.†[2]

At others he sings an elegant tribute to a woman's beauty, as in this *seguidilla*:

> La iglesia se ilumina
> cuando tú entras
> y se yena de flores
> donde te sientas.
> Y cuando sales,
> se rebisten de luto
> tos los artares.‡[3]

The popular poetry of Andalusia was fortunate to attract such devoted admirers as Antonio Machado y Álvarez, the father of Antonio and Manuel Machado, and Francisco Rodríguez Marín, who gathered many songs of the region in his *Cantos populares españoles* and *El alma de Andalucía en sus mejores coplas amorosas*. While Manuel Machado recorded in his poems the sensual appeal of Andalusia, his brother echoed the earnestness of its verse in epigrams that, like this *solear*, offer sober comment and advice:

* Your neglect of me drives me to madness; when I sit down to eat, nothing stays in my mouth.
† The drum is your portrait; for it makes a lot of noise, and if one looks inside one sees that it is empty.
‡ The church lights up when you enter and fills with flowers where you sit. And when you leave all the altars are covered in mourning.

> Despacito y buena letra:
> el hacer las cosas bien
> importa más que el hacerlas.*[1]

Antonio Machado's belief that 'the people makes true poetry'[2] was one that Alberti seemed firmly to oppose when he stated that 'My early poetry has nothing, or very little, to do with the people...More with the learned tradition.'[3] His first three books were written in a range of styles and were derived from a variety of sources that embraced Lope de Vega, Gil Vicente, Espinosa, Garcilaso and Góngora on the one side and, on the other, Rodríguez Marín's anthology of *Cantos populares españoles*, which provided him, for example, with the speckled hen who is the central character of his *La pájara pinta* (1925) and offered him 'el hacha de la envidia' as the metaphoric basis of his 'El ángel envidioso'.[4] The elegant naiads and sirens of cultured verse mix with the simple boatmen of popular lyrics and 'el perro de San Roque' of childhood song.[5] But whatever style he adopted and whatever source he drew on, Alberti was a conscious artist; while Rodríguez Marín thought that the cultured poet writing popular poems became a poet of the people, Alberti maintained that the successful popular poet is really a cultured writer who, like the anonymous author of the famous song 'Las tres morillas de Jaén', 'has a consciousness of his art, a musical feeling for rhythm and language, a preoccupation with form, etc.'[6]

Although *Marinero en tierra* and *El alba del alhelí* show that Alberti descended from what he called in his first work 'la estirpe gongorina' (p. 30), they also prove with *La amante* that he had absorbed the songs of Gil Vicente and Lope de Vega, whose simple rhythms he captured with such skill that Ernesto Halffter set to music 'Mi corza' from *Marinero en tierra*. 'Mi corza' and 'Zarza florida', from *La amante*, were the two poems that Alberti singled out and recited in both of his lectures on popular poetry as examples of his debt to and recreation of popular lyrics. When he quoted as an epigraph to 'Mi corza' the first line of a poem he read in Asenjo Barbieri's *Cancionero musical de los siglos*

---

* Slowly and in a clear hand: doing things well matters more than doing them.

XV y XVI, he acknowledged his debt to the collection as a whole and to the poem in particular, which is a perfect specimen of a simple theme presented in a few quiet and melodious moments:

> En Ávila, mis ojos,
> Dentro en Ávila.
>
> En Ávila del Río
> Mataron á mi amigo,
> Dentro en Ávila.*[1]

Although in Alberti's poem it is the fawn that is killed and not the lover, he has kept the pathos and tenderness of his model by contrasting the purity of the defenceless white fawn with the quick savagery of the fleeing wolves:

> Mi corza, buen amigo,
> mi corza blanca.
>
> Los lobos la mataron
> al pie del agua.
>
> Los lobos, buen amigo,
> que huyeron por el río.
>
> Los lobos la mataron
> dentro del agua.†   (p. 35)

Alberti's use of short lines and assonance, his simple diction and his repetition within a confined area of the few words and lines basic to his theme, show that he had mastered the art of creating melody out of very little. His ear was attuned to catching rhythms which he recorded with the devices of popular poetry. In some of his poems he beat out a regular tempo by ending his lines with words stressed on the last syllable; in others, following the example of anonymous poets who would write lines like:

> pisá, amigo, el polvó,
> tan menudó,‡[2]

* In Ávila, my love, there within Ávila.
  In Ávila del Río they killed my lover, there within Ávila.
† My fawn, good lover, my white fawn.
  The wolves killed it at the water's edge.
  The wolves, good lover, which fled through the river.
  The wolves killed it in the water.
‡ tread, my love, the dust so fine.

he moved the stress to the last syllable in order to maintain the regularity of the rhythm; he ended his beautifully melodious 'Nana del niño muerto', in which he introduced the boatman of popular song, with 'miraló':

> Barquero yo de este barco,
> sí, barquero yo.
>
> Aunque no tenga dinero,
> sí, barquero yo.
>
> Rema, niño, mi remero.
> No te canses, no.
>
> Mira ya el puerto lunero,
> mira, miraló.* (p. 36)

Marinero en tierra is the first of Alberti's tributes to the seas of Andalusia, which aroused in him a passion that moved him to write *Ora marítima* some thirty years later. Like the anonymous poets who began their songs by addressing their mothers in lines like 'Irme quiero, madre...' and 'Madre, la mi madre...',[1] Alberti appealed touchingly to his mother to put on him 'la blusa azul, y la cinta milagrera sobre el pecho' which he found in a poem of Juan Ramón Jiménez and which he used as an epigraph to his own song:

> —Madre, vísteme a la usanza
> de las tierras marineras:
> el pantalón de campana,
> la blusa azul ultramar
> y la cinta milagrera.† (p. 71)

Even in *La amante*, where Alberti recorded buoyantly his journey by car from the centre to the north of Spain, the thought that he was approaching another sea quickened his pulse and revived his passion which no amount of travelling on land could diminish. After celebrating the things he has seen and heard in Castile, he

* I am the boatman of this boat, the boatman am I, yes.
  Although I have no money, the boatman am I, yes.
  Row, child, my rower. Do not tire, no.
  Look there is the teasing port. Look, look at it now.
† Mother, dress me in the manner of the sea-faring lands: bell-bottom trousers, ultramarine blue sailor-blouse and the guardian sash.

suddenly insists in a kind of parallel balance-sheet that this region is inferior to his own Andalusia for the simple reason that it has no sea:

> Castilla tiene castillos,
> pero no tiene una mar.
>
> Pero sí una estepa grande,
> mi amor, donde guerrear.
>
> Mi pueblo tiene castillos,
> pero también una mar.
>
> Una mar de añil y grande,
> mi amor, donde guerrear.* (p. 104)

Just as in a poem of *Marinero en tierra* Alberti urged the balcony of his house to be a 'torreón de navío' (p. 58), so in 'Medina de Pomar' he races, with a breathless urgency conveyed in the poem's insistent exclamations and commands, to the top of the tower to try to catch sight of the sea:

> ¡ A las altas torres altas
> de Medina de Pomar !
>
> ¡ Al aire azul de la almena,
> a ver si ya se ve el mar !
>
> ¡ A las torres, mi morena!† (p. 106)

With its description of the sea as an orchard containing a little green siren, 'Madrigal del peine perdido' takes us back to the zestful underwater world of *Marinero en tierra*, which in 'Pregón submarino' was a submarine garden inhabited by a female gardener. The playfully diminutive 'sirenita verde' (p. 116), along with 'el niño chiquitito' appearing in 'Nana. Quintanar de la Sierra' (p. 98), are games in the frolics Alberti presented in *La amante*. What he offered us in this work was a simple travelogue in

---

* Castile has castles, but it does not have a sea.
  But it does have, my love, a vast plain on which to wage war.
  My region has castles, but it also has a sea.
  A great blue sea, my love, on which to wage war.
† To the tall, tall towers of Medina de Pomar !
  To the blue air of the battlements, to see if the sea can be seen !
  To the towers, my dark-haired love !

which he plotted with brief lyrical notes a route through the north of Spain, including Burgos, where he arrived, according to Salinas's reminiscence, 'ruddy with the expectation and haste of a lover on his way to a tryst'.[1] Alberti's journey is clearly signposted, for the titles of most of his verses are place names, some of which are resonant little poems in themselves; 'De Guzmiel de Hizán a Gumiel del Mercado', 'De Aranda de Duero a Peñaranda de Duero', 'De Canicosa de la Sierra a Santo Domingo de Silos' and 'De Laredo a Castro Urdiales' suggest that he was as fascinated by the noble ring of Spanish place names as Unamuno, who hymned them in lists like:

> Ávila, Málaga, Cáceres,—Játiva, Mérida, Córdoba,
> Ciudad Rodrigo, Sepúlveda,—Úbeda, Arévalo, Frómista...[2]

In *La amante* Alberti, like Gil Vicente and Lope de Vega, takes us out of the city and invigorates us with bracing Castilian air. He describes the simple pleasures of a lighthearted outdoor adventure which he was determined would not be jeopardized by sentimental complications. An anonymous poet offered the choice of marriage or cohabitation:

> Si te pluguiere, señora,
> conmigo te llevaría,
> si quieres por mujer
> o si quieres por amiga.*[3]

Alberti, however, offered only one option; the first poem of the book allows no misunderstanding and cautiously insures against unwanted emotional problems:

> Por amiga, por amiga.
> Sólo por amiga.
>
> Por amante, por querida.
> Sólo por querida.
>
> Por esposa, no.
> Sólo por amiga.†   (p. 89)

* If it would please you, my lady, I would take you with me as my wife, if you wish, or, if you wish, as my mistress.

† As my mistress, as my mistress. Only as my mistress.
  As my lover, as my paramour. Only as my lover.
  Not as my wife. Only as my mistress.

What mattered to Alberti was that someone shared his enjoyment of the simple things he saw and heard on his journey: clover; dawn; cocks crowing; the wind shaking leaves; a bridge; a mule; a carter; a grandmother among her hens with her grandson up a tree:

> Sí, nada más que la abuela,
> la abuela entre las gallinas,
> y el nieto subido a un árbol.
> Sí, nada más.*   (pp. 98–9)

'Sí, nada más' is a humble formula of satisfaction, a tribute to the simple joys which Gil Vicente, Lope de Vega and many anonymous poets had celebrated before him, and a symptom of the emotional limpidity which Alberti conveyed in regular forms, short metres and everyday diction. That this is a poetry of lyrical suggestions and skilfully contrived rhythms is shown by the beautifully compact and moving 'Zarza florida (Sierra de Guadarrama)', whose theme of death among the roses has been hauntingly treated by an anonymous poet:

> Dentro en el vergel
> Moriré.
> Dentro en el rosal
> Matarm' han.
>
> Yo m'iba, mi madre,
> Las rosas coger;
> Hallé mis amores
> Dentro en el vergel.
> Dentro del rosal
> Matarm' han.†¹

In Alberti's poem the search for and the discovery of the badly wounded girl moves slowly within the 'zarza florida' and the 'rosal', which provide both a natural setting and a rhythmic framework. To achieve the tenderness and restraint of this poem Alberti relied on deft touches, like the repetition of 'hallé la cinta

---

* Yes, nothing more than the grandmother, the grandmother among the hens, and the grandson up a tree. Yes, nothing more.
† I shall die in the garden. They will kill me in the rose-bush.
  I was going, o mother, to pick roses; I found my love in the garden. They will kill me in the rose-bush.

prendida' and the poignant contrast between 'sin vida' and 'mi vida' on the one hand and between the dying girl and the flowering bramble on the other:

> Zarza florida.
> Rosal sin vida.
>
> Salí de mi casa, amante,
> por ir al campo a buscarte.
>
> Y en una zarza florida
> hallé la cinta prendida,
> de tu delantal, mi vida.
>
> Hallé tu cinta prendida,
> y más allá, mi querida,
> te encontré muy mal herida
> bajo del rosal, mi vida.
>
> Zarza florida.
> Rosal sin vida.
> Bajo del rosal sin vida.* (p. 90)

It was in *La amante*, where he kept his imagination in check and his language under control, that Alberti came nearest to recreating and emulating the emotional simplicity and lyrical directness of Spain's popular poetry. His next work, *El alba del alhelí*, is an uneasy blend of the popular and the stylized, for although he still used a wide range of popular verse forms, his themes owed little to popular tradition. What is immediately apparent is that the poems of *El alba del alhelí* have more narrative than musical appeal. Alberti was by now less interested in trapping a moment or an impression in a few lyrical words than in developing a potentially dramatic situation; for example, with their sections and changes of perspective, 'La maldecida', 'La encerrada' and 'El prisionero' treat dramatically the theme of seclusion suggested to him by his

---

* Flowering bramble. Lifeless rose-bush.
  I left my house, my love, to go and seek you in the country.
  And I found trapped on a flowering bramble the ribbon of your apron, my life.
  I found your trapped ribbon, and further on, my love, I found you very badly
    wounded under the rose-bush, my life.
  Flowering bramble. Lifeless rose-bush. Lifeless under the rose-bush.

discovery when he visited Rute in 1926 that a woman was shut away in the neighbouring house.

Alberti also enlarged in poems like 'El Niño de la Palma', 'El tonto de Rafael' and 'A Jean Cassou' the vein of fantasy which had led him in *Marinero en tierra* to write such poems as 'Madrigal de Blanca-Nieve' and 'Madrigal dramática de Ardiente-y-fría'. But what was playfully imaginative in his first work became in *El alba del alhelí* deformed and burlesque; his self-portrait in particular reveals vivacity of mind and tongue:

> Por las calles, ¿ quién aquél?
> ¡ El tonto de Rafael !
>
> Tonto llovido del cielo,
> del limbo, sin un ochavo.
> Mal pollito colipavo,
> sin plumas, digo, sin pelo.* (p. 180)

In one of his lectures on popular poetry Alberti rejected the critical commonplace that he and other poets of his generation were influenced by the French surrealists, claiming instead that 'the exaltation of the illogical, the subconscious, the sexually monstrous, dreams and the absurd' existed before Louis Aragon and André Breton based their theories and manifestos on them.[1] When Lorca made Cristóbal say to the Mother in his farce *Retablillo de San Cristóbal* (1931):

> Y usted es vieja
> que se limpia el culito con una teja,† (p. 940)

he showed that he too was attracted to the 'marvellous lists, songs, strange rhymes' which Alberti postulated as the source of 'Spanish surrealism':[2] Cristóbal's insult derives from the nonsense rhyme that, opening with the 'Last night, the night before' formula found in the jingles of British schoolchildren,[3] Alberti recited in his lecture on popular poetry:

---

* Who is that walking through the streets? That fool Raphael !
  A fool rained from heaven, from limbo, without a cent. A bad little cock with a big fat tail, with no feathers, with no hair.
† And you are an old woman who wipes her little bottom with a tile.

Antier noche y anoche
Parió Joroba
Veinticinco ratones
Y una paloma.
La paloma tenía un molino,
Donde Jorobita molía su trigo.
Detrás del molino había una vieja,
Limpiándose el c...con una teja.
Detrás de la vieja había un viejo,
Limpiándose el c...con un pellejo...*[1]

That Alberti was drawn like Lorca to this vein of absurdity in Spanish popular poetry is apparent from a poem of *Marinero en tierra*, 'De 2 a 3', whose structure and playfulness derived from the genre of fanciful catalogue poems; in the song of the moon Alberti let his humour and his imagination unwind in a series of eccentric elements which he rounded off with a group of those meaningless but musical words he strung together so persistently in *La pájara pinta*, a work compounded almost entirely of nonsense words and the quaint jingles sung by children:

—Una niña chica,
sin cuna, jugando.
La Virgen María
la está custodiando.

Tres gatitos grises
y un mirlo enlutado,
la araña hilandera
y el pez colorado.

Un blanco elefante
y un pardo camello,
y toda la flora del aire
y toda la fauna del cielo.

Tín,
tín,

---

* Last night and the night before Joroba gave birth to twenty-five mice and a dove. The dove had a mill where little Joroba ground her wheat. Behind the mill there was an old woman, wiping her bottom with a tile. Behind the old woman there was an old man, wiping his bottom with a wine-skin.

tán:
    las tres, en la vaquería.

Tón,
tón,
tán:
    las tres, en la prioral.*   (p. 44)

Alberti clearly enjoyed having fun with words; the frisky rhythms and deft verbal games found in 'El Niño de la Palma' of *El alba del alhelí* justify its subtitle of 'Chuflillas', which he derived from the *chufla*, an Andalusian song and dance in tango rhythm, and *chuflar*, which in Andalusia means 'to jest'. Alberti is teasing us with words and tempo just as the bullfighter taunted the bull to fight:

¡Qué alegría !
¡ Cógeme, torillo fiero !
¡Qué salero !†   (p. 179)

The Giralda and the Virgen de la Macarena found in 'Joselito en su gloria' of the same work confirm that we are in Andalusia. Although his poetry is less organically linked to his native region than Lorca's *Poema del cante jondo* and *Romancero gitano*, Alberti the dutiful Andalusian has swollen the large body of poems that celebrate Seville and its river with a fervour exemplified by Lope:

Río de Sevilla,
¡ cuán bien pareces,
con galeras blancas
y ramos verdes !‡¹

In the conversation of Joselito and Seville, Alberti has evoked with a nostalgia which war and exile will make authentic the city's

---

* A little girl playing without a cradle. The Virgin Mary is watching over her.
  Three grey kittens and a blackbird in mourning, the spinning spider and the goldfish.
  A white elephant and a brown camel, and all the flora of the air and all the fauna of the heaven.
  Tin, tin, tan: three o'clock in the dairy.
  Ton, ton, tan: three o'clock in the priory.
† What joy ! Catch me, fierce little bull ! What nimbleness !
‡ River of Seville, how fine you look, with white galleys and green boughs !

olive groves and orange blossoms and the Guadalquivir with its ships and its sailors:

> Tu río, de tanta pena,
> deshoja sus olivares
> y riega los azahares
> de su frente, por la arena.
>
> —Díle adiós, torero mío,
> díle adiós a mis veleros
> y adiós a mis marineros,
> que ya no quiero ser río.*   (p. 176)

When Alberti introduced into 'Mala ráfaga' of *Marinero en tierra* the peculiarly Andalusian description of waves as 'red oxen' (p. 64), he offered a clue to his regional origin which is reinforced by the number of *coplas* and *soleares* he composed in his first three books, some of which may be echoes of 'the songs and ballads of the south' his mother sang to him when he was a child.[1] In his lecture on Lope de Vega Alberti mentioned the existence in Altolaguirre's poetry of a popular strain that derived not from Lope but from the Andalusian *copla*; his poetry is, stated Alberti, 'full of echoes of *soleares*'.[2] The first *solear* of the poem he quoted, 'Miradas' of *Poesía*, is a grave and melancholy recasting of some famous lines of Jorge Manrique, to which I shall return later in this chapter:

> Ojos de puente los míos
> por donde pasan las aguas
> que van a dar al olvido.†   (p. 73)

Altolaguirre and Prados, who also penned grave *soleares*, were cocooned so soberly within their solitude and melancholy that they eased the sobriety and tension of their poems with few light rhythms. Although in two poems of *Tiempo* Prados used refrains as short and simple as

---

* From so much grief, your river strips its olive groves and, along its shores, waters the orange blossoms of its brow.
  Say farewell, my bullfighter, say farewell to my sailing boats and farewell to my sailors, for I no longer want to be a river.
† My eyes are the arches of a bridge through which run the waters which will flow into oblivion.

> Cielo gris.
> Suelo rojo...,*

and

> Luna en el cielo.
> Luna en el suelo,† (p. 11)

later, in *Memoria de poesía*, the parallelistic refrains he used in
'Fuentes de bautismo' are not a joyful chorus but a mournful
litany; in his solemn chant of

> En el nombre del Padre
> —¡ sangre viva en las sienes !—.
> En el nombre del Hijo
> —¡ sangre viva en las sienes !—,‡ (p. 66)

he kept the technique but not the spritely rhythm of such lively
anonymous poems as:

> La que bien quiero,
> anda, amor,
> de la mano me la llevo,
> anda, amor,
> y ¿ por qué no me la beso ?,
> anda, amor,
> porque soy mochacho y necio,
> y anda, amor.§[1]

Altolaguirre's use of parallelism and refrains was even rarer;
when he repeated 'Yo y mi sombra' in 'Playa' of *Las islas invitadas* (p. 21), he was simply insisting on his own solitude. Nothing
excited him; the anonymous poet sang with speed and zest:

> Mira que te mira, mira,
> mira que te mira Dios.‖[2]

In his 'Romance de la luna, luna' Lorca chanted playfully that

---

* Grey heavens. Red earth.
† Moon in the heavens. Moon on the earth.
‡ In the name of the Father—live blood on the temples ! In the name of the Son—
live blood on the temples !—.
§ The girl I really love, come, my love, I take by the hand, come, my love, and
why do I not kiss her ?, come, my love, because I am a lad and a fool, so come,
my love.
‖ Look, God is looking at you, looking at you, look, God is looking at you [now].

> El niño la mira, mira.
> El niño la está mirando.* (p. 353)

And in 'Amor de miramelindo' of *Marinero en tierra* Alberti toyed with the words *mirar, me, mi* and *lindo* in a light-hearted verbal romp:

> —Miramelindo, mi amor,
> mírame qué linda estoy.† (p. 42)

But Altolaguirre quelled the rhythmic glee of these word games with a slow and ponderous statement:

> Miran profundos, me miran,
> me están mirando por dentro.‡ (p. 51)

The tempo of Salinas's repetitions is much quicker, especially when, as in these lines of *Razón de amor*, he played with a word as dominant in his thoughts and writings as *querer*:

> Lo que queremos nos quiere,
> aunque no quiera querernos.§ (p. 225)

As I shall try and show in chapter 4, Salinas used love as a kind of exercise which kept him mentally agile; as his mind darted in and out of paradoxes, so do his words chase round in games like this one of *La voz a ti debida*:

> ¡ Cuánto tiempo fuiste dos !
> Querías y no querías.
> No eras como tu querer,
> ni tu querer como tú.‖ (p. 230)

Salinas's conceits and paradoxes, often based on the insistent repetition of a single word, owed more to popular than to cultured tradition. His sport with *querer* was as lithe as that of the anonymous poets who often used the word to construct paradoxes as rhythmic as:

* The child looks at her, looks at her. The child is looking at her.
† Miramelindo, my love, look and see how pretty I am.
‡ They look so deep, they look at me, they are looking deep inside me.
§ What we love loves us, although it does not want to love us.
‖How long were you two ! You loved and you did not love. You were not like your love, nor was your love like you.

Quiero y no quiero querer,
Y estoy sin querer queriendo.*1

When in *Presagios* he swore 'fidelidad...de veleta' (p. 37) to his
amada, his promise to be as faithful as a weather-vane is as pungent
as those traditional poems where the weather-vane was used as
a symbol of fickleness:

Me dijistes veleta,
Por lo mudable;
Si yo soy la veleta,
Tú eres el aire.
Que la veleta,
Si el aire no la mueve,
Siempre está quieta.†2

The traditional distinction between the *ojos del alma* and *ojos del
cuerpo* was maintained by Salinas, whose motto could be a line of
Razón de amor: 'visiones y no miradas' (p. 253). When he claimed
to see what was invisible, like the 'artificial princesa' imprisoned
in the electric light bulb in *Seguro azar* (p. 71), Salinas was reviving
the *ver–no ver* conceit with which Spain's popular and cultured
poets had played. Quevedo's statement that

...vi donde el mismo ver
fue ocasión para cegar...,‡3

is as paradoxical as an anonymous author's avowal that

si os miro, me dejáis ciego,
y estoy ciego, si no os miro.§4

Salinas's denial of sight and his determination to visualize things
in his imagination is an important feature of his writings. His anti-
theses between seeing and not seeing are as ingenious and crisp as
his traditional prototypes; his statement in *Fábula y signo* that

* I love and do not want to love, and I am, without wanting to, loving.
† You called me the weather-vane, because of my fickleness. If I am the weather-
vane, you are the air. For the weather-vane, if the air does not move it, is always
still.
‡ I saw where the very act of seeing could make one blind.
§ if I look at you, you leave me blind, and I am blind, if I do not look at you.

> Si esto que ahora vuelvo a ver
> yo no lo vi nunca, no*   (p. 100)

jolts the reader as sharply as his description of his *amada* in *La voz a ti debida* as:

> ciega
> de mirar, sin ver nada,
> y querer lo que ve.†   (pp. 147-8)

To judge from these similarities alone, Salinas owed a lot to popular poetry; the *querer* and *ver* conceits provided him with a succinct ready-made expression of consistently held attitudes to love and to the world. And when he defined love in *Seguro azar* as:

> Amor: distancias, vaivén
> sin parar,‡   (p. 64)

he echoed the end of a *seguidilla* in which an anonymous poet had already thought of the same definition:

> ¡ Oh, amor supremo,
> Todo tú eres distancias,
> Todo tú extremos !§[1]

As if to commemorate the time he spent teaching at the University of Seville, in 'Sur, con viento' of *Seguro azar* Salinas sang to a city that has provoked many poets to equally lyrical hyperbole:

> ¡ Ay, Sevilla, Sevilla,
> guerrera mala, dime
> por qué todas las tardes
> tantas saetas me las clavas,
> rebrillo de azulejos,
> desde tus espadañas !
> ¡ Ay, Sevilla, Sevilla !‖   (p. 77)

But the lilting melody of such lines of *Presagios* as

---

* If this which I now see again I never saw before.

† blind from looking, without seeing anything, and loving what she sees.

‡ Love: distances, ceaseless fluctuation.

§ Oh! supreme love, you are all distances, you are all extremes!

‖ Oh, Seville, Seville, bad warrior-woman, tell me why every evening from your belfries you pierce me with your arrows, which are the glittering tiles! Oh, Seville, Seville!

¡ Ay, Sevilla, Sevilla,
quiéreme por amigo !*   (p. 77)

and

El río va a su negocio
corre que te correrás†   (p. 43)

is as rare in Salinas's poetry as this play of words from *Canciones* is
in Lorca:

¡ Ay, que trabajo me cuesta
quererte como te quiero !‡   (p. 308)

Just as Salinas owed these playful rhythms and lyrical tributes to
popular poetry, so did Lorca borrow this play of words from an
anonymous *copla*:

Cuando te oigo mentar
M'entra er suó de la muerte;
¡Bárgame Dios, compañera,
Lo que me cuesta er quererte !§¹

Salinas's tribute to Seville is an isolated expression of gratitude;
Andalusia was so deeply rooted in Lorca and his writings that
Guillén wisely urged him in his letter of 5 October 1926 to 'leave
Andalusia (which is deep inside you), go away, try and change'.²
It was in *Poema del cante jondo* that Lorca was most completely and
enthusiastically committed to his native region. Although the
book deals with one area and is therefore limited in range, the
atmosphere Lorca absorbed and reproduced offers the poetic thrill
which Manuel Machado's well-meaning but flaccid *Cante hondo*
fails to excite. In *Libro de poemas* Lorca merely affirmed that Andalusia 'sufre pasiones gigantes y calla'‖ (p. 30); in *Poema del cante
jondo*, however, he did not make statements but illustrated these
passions and communicated their atmosphere. His skill at creating
an atmosphere, which he exploited fully in works as distinct as
Romancero gitano and *Poeta en Nueva York*, makes us feel that
Andalusia, with its plaintive guitars, dim lamps and sinister

* Oh, Seville, Seville, take me as your lover.
† The river runs on to its duty, runs as fast as running can.
‡ Oh, what trouble it costs me to love you as I love you !
§ When I hear you mentioned, I break out in a deathly sweat; God help me,
comrade, what it costs me to love you !
‖ suffers gigantic passions and keeps silent.

cloaked men, is a place of mystery, of the unexpected, where horsemen gallop without motive or destination. In 'Camino' the alternation of long and short lines, and the strong stress placed, as in many popular poems, on the final syllable of every even line, create a purposeful, regular rhythm which emphasises that nothing will deflect these riders from their course:

> Cien jinetes enlutados,
> ¿ dónde irán,
> por el cielo yacente
> del naranjal?
> Ni a Córdoba ni a Sevilla
> llegarán...*   (p. 241)

But Lorca admired the beauty as well as the mysteriousness and latent violence of Andalusia. His songs to Seville and the Guadalquivir in *Poema del cante jondo* belong to the tradition which links poets as remote in time and manner as Lope de Vega and Antonio Machado, who exclaimed in *Nuevas canciones* (1917–30):

> ¡ Oh Guadalquivir !
> Te vi en Cazorla nacer;
> hoy, en Sanlúcar morir.†¹

In 'Baladilla de los tres ríos' Lorca exalted the superiority of the Guadalquivir over the Dauro and Genil in *coplas* divided into contrasting couplets and linked by a light and haunting refrain:

> El río Guadalquivir
> va entre naranjos y olivos.
> Los dos ríos de Granada
> bajan de la nieve al trigo.
>
> ¡ *Ay, amor*
> *que se fue y no vino!*
>
> . . . .
> Para los barcos de vela
> Sevilla tiene un camino;

---

* One hundred horsemen in mourning, where will they ride, through the lowering sky of the orange-grove? Neither Seville nor Córdoba will they reach.

† O Guadalquivir! I saw you rise in Cazorla and end in Sanlúcar today.

por el agua de Granada
sólo reman los suspiros.

¡ *Ay, amor*
que se fue y no vino!*   (p. 223)

And in 'Sevilla' he imagined like Salinas that the city's towers
were shooting arrows at him, one of which is the revered Guadalquivir itself:

Sevilla es una torre
llena de arqueros finos.

. . . .

Bajo el arco del cielo,
sobre su llano limpio,
dispara la constante
saeta de su río.†   (pp. 236–7)

Although Andalusia provided Lorca with ready-made themes
and a setting, he drew on sources other than purely local ones;
when he dedicated 'Serenata' in *Canciones* to Lope de Vega he
pointed to one of them; when he started 'Balada de la placeta' of
Libro de poemas with 'Cantan los niños...' he indicated another.
That lines, topics, images and characters of popular poetry are an
organic part of his work has been amply demonstrated by Daniel
Devoto, whose thorough and comprehensive investigation of the
traditional elements in Lorca's plays and poems has revealed the
sources of many lines and images.[1] Like Alberti, Lorca was fascinated by the techniques of popular poetry; in the light-hearted
Primeras canciones and *Canciones* especially, he used parallelism,
repetition and refrains as eagerly as he played rhythmic verbal
games like:

. . .la noche platinoche,
noche que noche nochera.‡   (p. 382)

---

* The river Guadalquivir flows amid orange-trees and olive-trees.
   The two rivers of Granada descend from the snow to the wheat.
   Oh, love which went and did not return!
   Seville has a passage for sailing boats; only sighs can row through the water of
      Granada.
   Oh, love which went and did not return!
† Seville is a tower full of pointed archers.
   Beneath the arch of heaven, over its limpid plain, it shoots the constant arrow
      of its river.
‡ the silver-nighted night, a night as deep as the deepest night.

Such titles as 'Variación' in *Primeras canciones* and 'Balanza' in *Canciones* hint at his fondness for the regular patterns and rhythmic possibilities of parallel lines; in 'Variación' he presented in the first two couplets a neat and skilful interplay of air, water, foliage and stars, and introduced in the last variation a woman who harmonizes effortlessly with these elements:

> El remanso del aire
> bajo la rama del eco.
>
> El remanso del agua
> bajo fronda de luceros.
>
> El remanso de tu boca
> bajo espesura de besos.*   (p. 274)

When Lorca contained his humour and fantasy within a parallelistic framework the result is playful and musical, as in 'Naranja y limón' of *Canciones*; here he devised a poetic game in which the orange and the lemon are a simple refrain linking the motifs of sun, water and 'la blanca niña', whom he had already introduced into 'Balada de un día de julio' of *Libro de poemas* (p. 148) and whom he had encountered in traditional poems like this *villancico*:

> ¿Quién tendrá alegría
> sin la blanca niña?†¹

Lorca's use of the orange and lemon has given this poem both a musical unity and a symbolic framework, for Spanish popular tradition generally associates these fruits with love. Just as children chant a rhythmic accompaniment to their games, so did Lorca play with the orange and lemon as he divided his song into neatly measured stages:

> Naranja y limón.
>
> ¡ Ay de la niña
> del mal amor !
>
> Limón y naranja.

---

* The pool of the air beneath the echo's branch.
The pool of the water beneath the foliage of stars.
The pool of your mouth beneath the thicket of kisses.
† Who can be happy without the snowy-white girl?

¡ Ay de la niña,
de la niña blanca!

Limón.

(Cómo brillaba
el sol.)

Naranja.

(En las chinas
del agua.)*   (p. 320)

The games Lorca played in 'Galán' and 'Cortaron tres árboles'
point to the candour that let him get on well with children, as
Guillén has recalled.[1] In the second poem he systematically eliminated items in a series: first there were three trees, then there
were two, then one, then none. In 'Galán' he followed, as Alberti
did in 'De 2 a 3', the pattern of those childhood songs that link and
compile a list of elements:

Ni que te vayas, ni que vengas,
con llave cierro la puerta.

Con llave de plata fina.
Atada con una cinta.

En la cinta hay un letrero:
'Mi corazón está lejos.'†   (p. 310)

Lorca's fondness for children was matched by his enthusiasm for
their songs. With the first line of 'Balada de la placeta' in *Libro de
poemas*, 'Cantan los niños' (p. 177), he revealed disarmingly the
source of the refrain which runs through the poem:

* Orange and lemon.
  Alas for the girl thwarted in love!
  Lemon and orange.
  Alas for the girl, the snowy-white girl!
  Lemon.
  (How the sun shone!)
  Orange.
  (On the pebbles in the water.)
† Whether you come or whether you go, I lock the door with a key.
  With a key of fine silver. Tied with a ribbon.
  On the ribbon there is a sign: 'My heart is far away.'

¡ Arroyo claro,
fuente serena !*1

And, as Devoto has shown, motifs and lines of childhood rhymes
are an integral part of 'Balada triste' in *Libro de poemas*, where
Lorca referred on several occasions to legends and fairy tales. His
statement that

Fui también caballero
una tarde fresquita de mayo,†

and his question:

¿Quién será la que coge los claveles
y las rosas de mayo?‡   (p. 119)

clearly derived from this *rima infantil*:

Una tarde
fresquita de mayo
cogí mi caballo
y me fuí a pasear...
Yo la vi que cogía una rosa,
yo la vi que cogía un clavel...§2

And the 'arroyo imaginario' he mentioned at the end of the
second stanza, where he lost 'la sortija de mi dicha' (p. 119), has
been identified by Devoto as 'el arroyo de Santa Clara' into which
an anonymous poet accidentally dropped a ring:

Al pasar el arroyo
de Santa Clara
se me cayó el anillo
dentro del agua.‖3

Although Lorca's poetry clearly reflects his fondness for children's rhymes, it also contains elements taken or adapted from a
wide range of popular poems which sometimes attracted him
with strange lines and images. The curious statement he made in
'Adelina de paseo' of *Canciones* that 'La mar no tiene naranjas'

---

* Clear stream, tranquil fountain !
† I was also a horseman one fresh evening in May.
‡ Who can she be, the one picking the carnations and roses of May?
§ One fresh evening in May I took my horse and went for a ride. I saw her
picking a rose, I saw her picking a carnation.
‖ As I passed by the stream of Saint Clare my ring dropped in the water.

(p. 305) is clarified only when we realize that he condensed two lines of a popular *copla*:

> A la mar fui por naranjas,
> Cosa que la mar no tiene... *1

Like Gil Vicente, Lope de Vega and many anonymous poets, Lorca exalted with simple words and simple refrains the freshness of nature, celebrating with a playful zest the things and people he saw, like the trees and the oxen, the reaper, the hunter and the shepherd, who appears in the first two of the 'Cuatro baladas amarillas' as the 'pastorcillo' found frequently in popular poems (p. 276). 'Cazador' is a poem which in its touching simplicity recalls Alberti's 'Zarza florida'; its last two lines, which exactly parallel the first two, not only close the poem into a compact unit, but deepen the pathos aroused by the sudden wounding of the doves in the one brief stanza: at one moment they were in the air; the next moment they are on the ground:

> ¡ Alto pinar !
> Cuatro palomas por el aire van.
>
> Cuatro palomas
> vuelan y tornan.
> Llevan heridas
> sus cuatro sombras.
>
> ¡ Bajo pinar !
> Cuatro palomas en la tierra están.†   (p. 293)

Two of the elemental delights of nature praised by popular poets and particularly by Lope de Vega are the fountain and the stream. When in 'Balada de un día de julio' Lorca made the 'blanca niña' sing:

> —Vengo de los amores
> y de las fuentes,‡   (p. 148)

---

* I went to the sea for oranges, something the sea does not have.
† Lofty pine grove! Four doves fly through the air.
  Four doves fly and turn. They carry their four wounded shadows.
  Low pine grove! Four doves are on the ground.
‡ I come from love and from the fountains.

he was reviving the motif of the joyful fountain which Lope had treated with gay simplicity:

> A los verdes prados
> baja la niña,
> ríense las fuentes
> las aves silban.*[1]

That the fountain is traditionally visualized as a place of delight is shown by the recurrence in anonymous poems and in Lope's songs of lines like 'Ríense las fuentes' and 'Y el agua se va riendo'.[2] Lorca revived this topic in 'Agua, ¿dónde vas?...' of *Canciones* when, using the archaic gerund of *reír*, he made the water say:

> Riyendo voy por el río
> a las orillas del mar.†
> (p. 344)

Lorca's love of popular lyrics is also apparent in his *Romancero gitano*, where he elaborated traditional motifs and introduced into his ballads lines and images from popular songs. The sinister opening of 'Muerto de amor':

> ¿Qué es aquello que reluce
> por los altos corredores?‡
> (p. 377)

repeated the question found in religious *coplas* like:

> ¿Qué es aquello que reluce
> En aquel monte florido?
> Es Jesús de Nazareno,
> Que con la cruz se ha caído.§[3]

And in the 'Romance de la Guardia Civil española' the place where the gipsies gather after the attack—'En el portal de Belén' (p. 384)—is the setting of this playfully irreverent anonymous song:

> En el portal de Belén
> Gitanillos han entrado

* The girl goes down to the green meadows, the fountains laugh, the birds whistle.   † I go laughing through the river to the shores of the sea.
‡ What is that shining along the lofty corridors?
§ What is that shining on that flowering mountain? It is Jesus of Nazareth who has fallen with the cross.

Y al Niño recién-nacido
Los pañales le han robado.*[1]

Although Lorca claimed in one of his letters to Guillén that
'Preciosa y el aire' was 'a myth invented by me',[2] the 'viento-
hombron't of his ballad, whom he mischievously described as
'el viento verde',‡ is with its erotic urges and obviously phallic
'espada caliente'§ descended from the wind which in popular
lyrics strains to 'deflower' young girls:

No vayas solita al campo
Cuando sople el aire recio;
Porque las niñas son flores
Que hasta las deshoja el viento.||[3]

And the starting-point of 'La casada infiel' was not real life but a
literary attitude; like anonymous poets before him, Lorca was
posing as a man of the world whose motto of sex without strings
made him welcome the unfaithful wife as an ideal partner for his
adventures. The closing lines of the ballad, in which the 'gitano
legítimo' explains that

...no quise enamorarme
porque teniendo marido
me dijo que era mozuela
cuando la llevaba al río,¶   (p. 364)

echo the cautious decision of an anonymous poet:

No quiero amor con casada;
Que me ha dicho una viuda
Que a quien de ajeno se viste
En la calle lo desnudan.**[4]

With his lavish use in *Romancero gitano* of images and rhythmic
games, Lorca did in the twentieth century what Lope de Vega and

---

* In the doorway at Bethlehem gipsies have gathered and have stolen the napkins
from the new-born child.
† giant-wind.   ‡ the lascivious wind.   § burning sword.
|| Do not go alone to the fields when the wind blows hard, for girls are flowers
which are stripped even by the wind.
¶ I did not want to fall in love because, as she had a husband, she told me she was
a maiden when I took her to the river.
** I do not want love with a married woman; for a widow has told me that he
who dresses in another man's clothes gets stripped of them in the street.

Góngora did in the sixteenth and seventeenth centuries: he embellished and lyricized a form that in the hands of the anonymous balladeers had contained many concise, emotionally restrained and metrically regular accounts of historical events and fictional happenings. The vogue enjoyed by the *romance* in the Golden Age is matched by its vigorous revival in the 1920s and 1930s. Articles on 'Figuras del romancero' published in *Cervantes* in 1919 anticipated the widespread enthusiasm for the *romance*, which crystallized in Lorca's *Romancero gitano* and Fernando Villalón's *Romances del 800* (1927). From Lorca, who absorbed and utilized the ballads he read in Spain's *romanceros* and those he heard sung around him, to Altolaguirre, who used the ballad's octosyllabic metre blandly and undistinctively to narrate not an event but a mood, many major and minor figures resuscitated a form that has recorded changing tastes and styles so accurately that, as Salinas has aptly observed, its history is the history of Spanish literature.[1]

As Alberti acknowledged in his lectures on popular poetry, it was Juan Ramón Jiménez and Antonio Machado who helped to revitalize the *romance* in the twentieth century. The episodic structure, narrative purpose, sober diction and emotional restraint of Machado's 'La tierra de Alvargonzález', which appeared in *Campos de Castilla* (1907–17), made it closer in spirit, style and intention to the traditional *romancero* than Jiménez's ballads, which were frozen into immobility by his obsession with his sadness. While Machado aimed to involve the reader in his long, chill tale of murder, curse and retribution, Jiménez set out to paralyse him in a symbolic setting, like 'the holy garden of the soul' found in *Rimas de sombra* (1900–2):

> ¡Qué triste es tener sin flores
> el santo jardín del alma,
> soñar con almas en flor,
> soñar con sonrisas plácidas,
> con ojos dulces, con tardes
> de primaveras fantásticas!... [*2]

---

* How sad it is to have bare of flowers the holy garden of the soul, to dream of souls in flower, to dream of placid smiles, of gentle eyes, of evenings of fantastic spring-times!

As absorbed in himself as Jiménez, Altolaguirre rested his *romances* on little other than his states of mind. With their neat structure, measured tempo, sober diction and sparse images, they were in his hands one more conveniently regular vehicle for the unhurried, uncomplicated and uncoloured personal statements which I shall consider in chapter 4. Prados also expressed his major themes in his *romances*, which were less frequent and much more vibrant than those of Altolaguirre. The idea of escape and detachment so excited Prados that it generated within him an energy which dictated his liberal use of enjambment, exclamation and short, staccato lines and which made him race in one *romance* of *Cuerpo perseguido* over a sentence sixteen lines long (p. 90). And another ballad of the same work is a recital of impressions ejaculated so breathlessly that in Prados's hands the *romance* became a rapid narrative of instantaneous feelings and strange, unsifted impressions:

> ¡Qué quebrar de plumas
> cruza la voz del Espacio!
> ¡Qué ramalazos de risas
> quedan del viento colgando!
> ¡Qué campanadas de altura!
> ¡Qué temblor de espejo abajo!*   (p. 100)

In three of the five ballads of *Ámbito*—'Cinemática', 'Íntegra' and 'Cruzada'—Aleixandre was led by an even greater fervour to fragment his lines more violently than Prados. The title 'Íntegra' is delightfully ironic when one realizes that spurts of sound and splinters of syntax compose one part of the poem; and the furore of hiatuses, exclamations, dots, questions and parenthetic stage settings makes 'Cruzada' taxing to the eye, disturbing to the ear and demanding of attention:

> —¿Es tiempo?
> ¡Oh si ya lo fuera!—(*Venas*
> *de noche*).—¡Qué frío!—(*Y siento*
> *casi quieta la flúida*

---

* What a noise of breaking feathers crosses the voice of Space!
  What lashes of laughter remain dangling from the wind!
  What tolling bells on high! What shimmering mirror below!

> *verdad.*)—Algo; lo primero
> quisiera…—(*Avanza la noche*
> *muda.*)—O si no, aquel lucero
> tan puro; algo…—(*Menea*
> *la brisa nocturna tiemblos*
> *de luz.*)—¡ Dámelo ! ¿ No oyes?—
> (*Se turba el aire*).—¡ Lo quiero !—*   (p. 125)

Aleixandre's ballads reveal that he did not share Guillén's ability to discipline his strong feelings. Although 'Agosto' and 'Luz' are more fluid and relaxed, 'Cinemática', 'Íntegra' and 'Cruzada' show that in *Ámbito* the *romance* was bursting at its seams; as I shall indicate in chapter 5, the impulses and surges which Aleixandre contained only with effort in *Ámbito* forced him in subsequent works to shatter the trammels of form and burst into a free and uninhibited expression.

While Aleixandre's raptures led to ruptures, Guillén made a perfect match of technique and emotion in *Cántico*, whose successive editions signalled his growing fondness for the *romance*. The four examples which appeared in the 1936 edition are controlled, like the poetry of *Cántico*, by what Guillén has called in one of them, 'Redondez', a '¡ Fatalidad de armonía !'[1] which dictated their neat and rounded shape: 'El aparecido' has seventy lines; 'Festividad', which appeared in the 1928 edition, and 'Ardor' have forty lines; and 'Redondez' contains twenty lines. With their disciplined joy, these four ballads have a quality which Guillén defined in 'El aparecido' as '¡ Tersura en acción !'[2] Both the intensity of his emotions and his ruthless exclusion of any element that could weaken their power made these *romances* as taut and concentrated as the blue sky in 'Redondez', where he gazes at the sky and thinks of the energy which comes from it:

> Restituído a su altura
> Más cóncava, más unida,
> Sin conversiones de nubes

---

* Is it time? Oh if it were ! (Veins of night.) How cold ! (And I sense that the fluid truth is almost still.) Something; the first thing I would like. (The night moves dumbly on.) Or if not, that star so pure; something… (The night breeze stirs shimmers of light.) Give it to me ! Don't you hear? (The air is troubled.) I want it !

Ni flotación de calina,
El firmamento derrama,
Ya invasor, una energía
Que llega de puro azul
Hasta las manos ariscas.
Tiende el puro azul, el duro,
Su redondez, ¡ Bien cobija !
Y cabecean los chopos
En un islote de brisa
Que va infundiendo a la hoja
Movilidad, compañía,
Situadas, penetradas
Por el mismo azul de arriba.
Azul que es poder, azul
Abarcador de la vida,
Sacro azul irresistible:
Fatalidad de armonía.*[1]

After mentioning 'su altura' in the first line, he leads us to 'El firmamento' in line 5, to the key word 'energía' in line 6, and in line 7 to 'azul', which he then repeats five times in the remaining thirteen lines. Just as 'redondez' in line 10 restates the setting established in 'altura' and 'firmamento', so does the 'islote de brisa' moving the trees exemplify the energy he imagined flowing from above. The last four lines of the poem, which are an ecstatic tribute to the dynamic, enfolding blue sky, not only condense the previous sixteen lines but provide a vigorous and satisfying climax to a ballad that, like others of Guillén, is taut in structure, terse in diction and sure in movement.

As Salinas has pointed out, Guillén brought two innovations to the *romance*: he split it into a series of 'multiple incidents', and deployed it in such a way that the spaces on the printed page show the reader where he must pause.[2] One of the four ballads in the

---

* Restored to its most concave, most compact, height, clear of masking clouds and drifting haze, the heavens like an invader pour forth an energy which comes from the pure blue to the haughty hands. The pure, hard blue tenses its round-ness: how well does it shelter us! And the poplars nod in an islet of breeze which infuses into the leaf movement and company, which are positioned and penetrated by the same blue from above. Blue that is power, blue that embraces life, sacred irresistible blue whose destiny is harmony.

1936 edition, 'Ardor', indicates that Guillén was not content with maintaining the rhythmic and structural regularity he observed in 'Festividad', for example, whose even tempo and strong stresses at the end of each line are undisturbed by the enjambment:

> La acumulación triunfal
> En la mañana festiva
> Hinche de celeste azul
> La blancura de la brisa.*[1]

In 'Ardor' he created a spasmodic, unpredictable rhythm as he suddenly braked or raced to the next line:

> Ardor. Cornetines suenan
> Tercos, y en las sombras chispas
> Estallan. Huele a un metal
> Envolvente. Moles. Vibran.
> Extramuros despoblados
> En torno a casas henchidas
> De reclusión y de siesta.
> En sí la luz se encarniza.
> ¿Para quién el sol? Se juntan
> Los sueños de las avispas.†[2]

The excitement which Guillén communicated in his ballads is a long way from the sober melancholy which Altolaguirre related in his. The four terse, controlled and confident specimens included in the 1936 edition of *Cántico* show that in his exploration of the rhythmic and structural possibilities of the *romance* Guillén had matured considerably since 1921, when he published in *Índice* under the title of 'Poniente de bronce' two sing-song, melodramatic ballads which he has excluded from all his subsequent collections. The bells ringing at sunset awoke in him two different moods crudely represented by black and green; in 'Bronce verde' he heard in their persistent peals his determination to conquer death;

---

* The triumphal accumulation in the festive morning swells the whiteness of the breeze with celestial blue.
† Heat. Cornets stubbornly sound, and in the shadows sparks flash. It smells of an enveloping metal. Huge shapes. Uninhabited spaces vibrate around houses swollen with seclusion and sleep. The light rages within itself. For whom is the sun? The dreams of the wasps unite.

in 'Bronce negro' the bells intoned a melancholy message and created a sepulchral atmosphere also evoked by Juan Ramón Jiménez in *Jardines lejanos* (1903–4):

> Viento negro, luna blanca.
> Noche de Todos los Santos.
> Frío. Las campanas todas
> de la tierra están doblando.*[1]

In 'Bronce negro' the bells, whose monotonous ringing is represented by ham-handed repetitions, toll a dirge to lost illusions:

> ¿Por quién, por quién sollozáis,
> campanas de bronce negro?
> . . . .
> Campanas en el ocaso,
> campanas de bronce negro,
> doblad, doblad lentas, lentas
> por todos mis sueños muertos...†[2]

Like Jiménez and Guillén, Lorca heard in the tolling bells a doleful confirmation of and accompaniment to his adolescent sadness; in a *romance* of *Libro de poemas* written according to him in December 1918, 'Canción menor', he imagined himself wandering through the streets in a twilight setting whose sentimentality matched his tearfulness:

> Las campanas
> también me dicen adiós
> y los árboles se besan
> en el crepúsculo. Yo
> voy llorando por la calle,
> grotesco y sin solución...‡   (p. 112)

When he told Guillén in a letter of 2 March 1926 of his ambition to 'make the ballad as tightly knit and solid as a stone',[3] Lorca

---

* Black wind, white moon. All Saints' Night. Cold. All the bells on the earth are tolling.
† For whom, for whom do you weep, bells of black bronze?
  Bells in the sunset, bells of black bronze, toll, toll slowly, slowly, for all my dead dreams.
‡ The bells also bid me farewell. And the trees kiss in the twilight. I go weeping along the street, grotesque and hopeless.

seemed to acknowledge that the ballads he wrote before *Roman-cero gitano* were neither firmly constructed nor tersely expressed. In 'Encrucijada' of *Libro de poemas* he tried so hard to exalt sorrow as a theme of poetry that his banal expression is relieved only by his strained and eccentric description of grief as 'sticky':

> ¡ Oh, qué dolor el dolor
> antiguo de la poesía,
> este dolor pegajoso
> tan lejos del agua limpia !*   (p. 181)

However, 'pegajoso' suggests that in the *romances* and other poems of *Libro de poemas* Lorca was seeking a mode of expression that would appeal to the reader's imagination and involve his senses; in 'El diamante' his playful visions of corpses playing cards and young poplars reciting their lessons are let down only by a sentence of sentimental doggerel which shows that his touch was still erratic:

> Los chopos niños recitan
> su cartilla; es el maestro
> un chopo antiguo que mueve
> tranquilo sus brazos muertos.
> Ahora en el monte lejano
> jugarán todos los muertos
> a la baraja. ¡ Es tan triste
> la vida en el cementerio !†   (p. 137)

The slack and plaintive ballads of *Libro de poemas* were a useful factor in Lorca's poetic development; he let his fantasy train and experiment in them and he learned how to master a form which he would use in his plays and to perfection in his *Romancero gitano*. And when in the several *romances* of *Canciones* he explored his fantasy instead of exposing his feelings, he was clearly moving towards the unreal world of his gipsy ballads. In 'Nocturnos de la ventana' he invented a little myth about the death of 'una niña de agua' who is unable to hear the call of a fish or the wind:

* Oh, what grief is the old grief of poetry, this sticky grief so far from clean water !
† The infant poplars read from their spelling-book; the master is an old poplar who quietly waves his dead arms. Now on the distant mountain all the dead will be playing cards. Life is so sad in the cemetery !

> Al estanque se le ha muerto
> hoy una niña de agua.
> Está fuera del estanque,
> sobre el suelo amortajada.
>
> De la cabeza a sus muslos
> un pez la cruza, llamándola.
> El viento le dice 'niña',
> mas no pueden despertarla.*   (p. 297)

And 'Arbolé, arbolé...', where Lorca brought to life the passionate wind who was to pursue Preciosa in *Romancero gitano*, shows how near he had come to his ideal of the 'tightly-knit ballad' after the tearful *romances* of *Libro de poemas*; the series of fanciful episodes occurring between morning and night lifts us outside reality and Lorca's emotions and gives a simple pattern and a firm development to the poem, dominated and unified by the presence of the disdainful 'niña del bello rostro' and the amorous attentions of the wind:

> La niña de bello rostro
> está cogiendo aceituna.
> El viento, galán de torres,
> la prende por la cintura.
> Pasaron cuatro jinetes,
> sobre jacas andaluzas
> con trajes de azul y verde,
> con largas capas oscuras.
> 'Vente a Granada, muchacha.'
> La niña no los escucha.
> Pasaron tres torerillos
> delgaditos de cintura,
> con trajes color naranja
> y espada de plata antigua.
> 'Vente a Sevilla, muchacha.'
> La niña no los escucha.
> Cuando la tarde se puso

---

* One of the pool's water-girls has died today. She is outside the pool, lying on the ground in her shroud.
  A fish swims over her from her head to her thighs, calling her. The wind says 'girl' to her, but they cannot awake her.

morada, con luz difusa,
pasó un joven que llevaba
rosas y mirtos de luna.
'Vente a Granada, muchacha.'
Y la niña no lo escucha.
La niña del bello rostro
sigue cogiendo aceituna,
con el brazo gris del viento
ceñido por la cintura.* (pp. 309–10)

The simple tale imagined and related in this ballad clearly heralded the myths which Lorca spun in *Romancero gitano* around people: gipsies and the Civil Guard, which have replaced the warring armies and epic heroes of whom he would have read in Spain's fifteenth- and sixteenth-century *romances*; the faithless wife, who may have been put in his mind by the song of the mule driver who accompanied Lorca and his brother Francisco during an excursion to the Sierra Nevada:

Y yo que me la llevé al río
creyendo que era mozuela,
pero tenía marido.†1

And Lorca may have been led to write his *romance* 'Thamár y Amnón' by a recollection of an oral ballad in which, surprisingly, Amnon is not murdered by Absalom but forced to marry the half-sister he had raped; Lorca's stark statements that

Ya la coge del cabello,
ya la camisa la rasga‡ (p. 394)

---

* The girl with the beautiful face is picking olives. The wind, a gallant haunting high towers, takes her by the waist. Four horsemen passed by on Andalusian steeds with suits of blue and green and long dark capes. 'Come to Granada, lass.' The girl does not listen to them. Three little bullfighters with slim waists passed by with orange-coloured suits and swords of old silver. 'Come to Seville, lass.' The girl does not listen to them. When the evening became purple, with a diffuse light, a youth passed by carrying roses and myrtles of the moon. 'Come to Granada, lass.' And the girl does not listen to him. The girl with the beautiful face carries on picking olives, with the grey arm of the wind entwined around her waist.

† And I took her to the river thinking that she was a maiden, but she had a husband.

‡ Now he pulls her by the hair, now he tears her shift.

echo the bleak and brutal precision with which in the oral ballad
Amnon prepared his rape:

> La agarró de la muñeca,
> la tumbó sobre la cama;
> la puso un puñal al pecho
> para que no diga nada;
> una pelota en la boca
> para que no diga palabra.*[1]

That Lorca was emulating the capricious fantasy which in some
oral ballads creates complications that have to be resolved by the
intercession of the Pope or the Virgin Mary, is apparent in his
definition of 'Preciosa y el aire' as 'a myth invented by me'.[2] His
statement that the passionate encounter related in 'La casada infiel'
took place on 'la noche de Santiago', St James's Day, followed the
custom of many anonymous balladeers, whose habit of specifying
time and place to give their narrative a spurious authenticity was
parodied by Lorca himself in an ironically precise *romance* of his
farce *La zapatera prodigiosa* (1930):

> Un lunes por la mañana
> a eso de las once y media...†   (p. 871)

Essential to the fabric of Lorca's *romances* are his evocations of
atmosphere, which remind us, as if it were necessary, that the
world of the gipsy ballads is one of lyrical fantasy. Lorca's description of *Romancero gitano* in 1931 as 'an Andalusian song in which
the gipsies serve as a refrain' (p. 1609) made it clear that he looked
on his protagonists not as real people but as a pretext, a peg from
which to hang his poems. Dalí's comment that the 'Romance
sonámbulo' 'seems to have an argument, but doesn't'[3] pointed to
Lorca's ability to suspend the reader within a setting where actions
and events are few. All he presented in 'La monja gitana' was a
nun whose secret thoughts of the outside world related her to the
girls who complained in traditional songs that 'No quiero ser

---

* He seized her by the wrist, he threw her on the bed; he put a dagger to her
breast to stop her saying anything; [he put] a ball in her mouth to stop her
saying a word.
† One Monday morning at about half-past eleven...

monja, no...';*[1] 'Muerto de amor' rests only on the sinister lights gleaming 'por los altos corredores', whose potential mystery had already attracted Lorca in the second poem of 'Palimpsestos' in *Primeras canciones*:

> Por los altos corredores
> se pasean dos señores.† (p. 279)

And Lorca made the intense heat and parched, scarred earth not incidental to but an integral part of 'Thamár y Amnón', because they frame and complement Amnon's feverish lust for his sister; the jangling 'nervios de metal' of the electric atmosphere correspond with Amnon's twitches, his feverishly restless eyes and his agitated kisses.

Lorca's fusion of atmosphere and action was as unobtrusive as his mixture of the old and the new, which he acknowledged as a feature of *Romancero gitano* when he told Guillén in his letter of 2 March 1926 that the work was compounded of 'New themes and old suggestions.'[2] Unlike Quevedo, who set out to parody and debunk traditional ballads, Lorca was moved by his love of 'old suggestions' to introduce smoothly and elegantly into his poems details and devices of the traditional *romances*. From the latter he learned how to open a ballad with a magnetic first line; the simple repetition of 'Doliente estaba, doliente'‡ was matched centuries later by Lorca's 'Verde que te quiero verde',§ just as Doña Urraca's shout of '¡Afuera, afuera, Rodrigo!'‖[3] provided a dramatic opening paralleled by 'Muerto de amor', which is begun by an ominous question made even more mysterious by the irrelevant reply:

> ¿Qué es aquello que reluce
> por los altos corredores?
> Cierra la puerta, hijo mío,
> acaban de dar las once.¶ (p. 377)

---

* I do not want to be a nun, no.
† Two gentlemen walk through the lofty corridors.
‡ Suffering he was, suffering. § Green, I love you, green.
‖ Away, away, Rodrigo!
¶ What is that shining along the lofty corridors? Close the door, my son, it has just struck eleven.

When the adventurous protagonist of an oral ballad ended his tale of progressive familiarity with two women, he recounted their precise preparations for the amorous climax in a series of antithetical lines:

ellas quitan la su saya
y yo el mi pantalón;
ellas quitan su camisa,
y yo el mi camisón.*[1]

When Lorca echoed these stages of rhythmic disrobing in 'La casada infiel', he too was attracted by a technique that allowed him and many balladeers before him to make melodiously balanced recitals of details:

Yo me quité la corbata.
Ella se quitó el vestido.
Yo, el cinturón con revólver.
Ella, sus cuatro corpiños.† (p. 363)

That Lorca had a sharp eye for an attractive detail is shown by the elements he borrowed quite unselfconsciously from the written and oral ballads. Like the beds of many fine ladies in the *romances*, the bed in which the mortally wounded hero of 'Romance sonámbulo' wants to die is covered with cambric sheets;[2] the three hundred wounds from which he bleeds to death are as imposingly lavish as the three hundred knights accompanying Fernán González, the three hundred ladies attending Doña Alda and the princess Claraniña, and the jewelled finery of Conde Claros, who had

And the

trescientas piedras preciosas
al derredor del collar.‡[3]

Siete gritos, siete sangres,
siete adormideras dobles§ (p. 378)

which appear in 'Muerto de amor' may be a resonant echo of a number repeated obsessively in oral ballads, where the lives of

---

* they take off their dress, and I take off my trousers; they take off their shift, and I take off my shirt.
† I took off my tie. She took off her dress. I took off my revolver belt. She took off her four bodices.
‡ three hundred precious stones around his collar.
§ Seven shouts, seven bloods, seven double poppies.

man and beast are regulated by the figure seven; characters wander
for seven years through seven kingdoms and die of seven wounds;
in one ballad dogs

> Han andado siete leguas,
> pasaron siete colladas,
> y al cabo de las siete leguas,
> la loba iba cansada.*[1]

The anonymous ballads contain the prototypes of several of the
characters Lorca introduced into *Romancero gitano*. While Soledad
Montoya has the dark skin of the many disgruntled and resentful
morenas of popular verse, her lonely wanderings 'por el monte
oscuro' duplicate those of a sad princess condemned to roam 'los
siete años / sola en esta montiña'.†[2] And the figures who in several
traditional ballads were *emplazados*, given a fixed term of life
by Death itself, were the ancestors of Lorca's El Amargo in his
'Romance del emplazado' and of Alberti's protagonist in his
unpublished and now lost play *El enamorado y la muerte*.[3] When
the cards told El Amargo that

> ...dentro de dos meses
> yacerás amortajado,‡   (p. 380)

they echoed the chill prophecy with which Death doomed a
nameless lover in the 'Romance del enamorado y la muerte':

> ¡ Un día no puede ser,
> una hora tienes de vida !§[4]

Lorca's ballads diverged from those of the *romancero* and moved
closer to those of Lope de Vega and Góngora in what Salinas
called their 'lyrical aggression'.[5] Lorca lingered over details mentioned only perfunctorily by the anonymous poets; in a traditional
ballad the 'mucha sangre derramada' was a raw statement of fact;[6]
in 'Reyerta' Lorca used synaesthesia to transform blood into a
sinuous gore which seems to moan its own elegy:

---

* They have travelled seven leagues, they passed seven hillocks, and at the end of
  seven leagues, the she-wolf was tired.
† seven years alone in this mountain.
‡ within two months you will lie in your shroud.
§ A day it cannot be, an hour you have to live !

> Sangre resbalada gime
> muda canción de serpiente.*　　　　(p. 357)

The whiteness of a woman's skin, which an anonymous poet praised simply when he wrote that

> Blanca sois, señora mía,
> más que el rayo del sol,†1

was inflated by Lorca and Góngora into a pretext for elegant exercises like this gallant tribute of Góngora:

> Con su garganta y su pecho
> no tienen que competir
> el nácar del mar del Sur,
> la plata del Potosí.‡2

When Lorca extolled the whiteness of the unfaithful wife, he resorted in equally hyperbolic lines not to metals and snow, but to flowers, glass and moonlight:

> Ni nardos ni caracolas
> tienen el cutis tan fino,
> ni los cristales con luna
> relumbran con ese brillo.§　　　　(p. 363)

The trees and flowers which decorate and brighten his gipsy poems—from the 'polisón de nardos' of the first to the 'coral de rosas y dalias' of the last—give the work a lushness which takes it away from the stark *romances* of tradition and near to the opulent ballads of Lope and Góngora. When Lorca described gun-flashes in 'Romance de la Guardia Civil española' as 'rosas de pólvora negra'‖ (p. 385), his linking of objects as normally incompatible as roses and gunpowder invites us to see something beautiful in explosions and offers us an insight as original as Góngora's description of water beating against the shore as 'pólvora de las piedras'.¶3

---

* Trickling blood moans a silent serpent's song.
† You are white, my lady, whiter than the sunbeam.
‡ Neither the mother-of-pearl from the Pacific Ocean nor the silver from Potosí can compete with her throat and breast.
§ Neither spikenards nor myrtles have such a fine skin, nor does the moon playing on glass glitter with that sheen.
‖ roses of black gunpowder.　　　　¶ gunpowder of the stones.

To create these unusual images both poets made their fantasy take the 'equestrian leap' between 'two opposing worlds' which Lorca in his essay on Góngora's imagery regarded as an acrobatic act essential to the coining of metaphors and to the pursuit of 'new beauty' (pp. 69, 72). The mental leaps between garlic, silver and the moon enabled him to describe the latter in 'Muerto de amor' as an 'Ajo de agónica plata'* (p. 377); and when he imagined in 'Romance sonámbulo' that

> Mil panderos de cristal
> herían la madrugada,† (p. 360)

he associated tambourines, glass and the dawn to record an original vision of dew glittering at daybreak as he obeyed with his appeal to the eyes and the ears the principle he established in his lecture on Góngora's imagery: 'A poet must be master of the five senses. The five senses, in this order: sight, touch, hearing, smell and taste. To be able to be the owner of the most beautiful images he must open doors of communication in all of them and very often must superimpose their sensations and even disguise their natures' (pp. 70–1).

By linking and interlocking the five senses in his ballads, Lorca brought the reader's own senses into play, involved him in a complex of new sensations that are as strange to experience as they were to create; his poetic diagnosis of Amnon's torment as

> Yedra del escalofrío
> cubre su carne quemada‡ (p. 393)

gives us with the feverish skin something whose heat we can easily experience and in the ivy something which we can readily visualize as it chokes and covers Amnon. And Lorca's observation after the rape that

> Corales tibios dibujan
> arroyos en rubio mapa§ (p. 394)

---

* Garlic of dying silver.
† A thousand tambourines of glass wounded the dawn.
‡ Like the ivy the shudder creeps over his burning flesh.
§ Warm corals trace streams on the blond map.

transports us from violent and sordid reality on gently sounding lines in which the crimson pattern on the white sheet is an elegy in simple colours to the still warm blood of Tamar's lost virginity.

What Lorca managed to do in 'Thamár y Amnón' was to blunt the horror of a brother lusting for and ravishing his sister with elegant images which detach us from reality. When the anonymous authors of Spain's ballads wanted to narrate an erotic episode they either used the stark, down-to-earth verb *folgar*, to sport, or merely reported in a bluntly factual way that

> de la cintura abajo
> como hombre y mujer se han.*[1]

Whereas in a typically grotesque *romance* Quevedo presented a man swimming in a sea of flesh,[2] Lorca's determination to exalt and not degrade made him present love-making in 'La casada infiel' as a ride on horseback; although the horse and horse-riding are obviously erotic symbols—as *Bodas de sangre* and *La casa de Bernarda Alba* clearly show—, Lorca tempered their eroticism by his description of the woman in all her whiteness as a 'potra de nácar':

> Aquella noche corrí
> el mejor de los caminos,
> montado en potra de nácar
> sin bridas y sin estribos.†   (p. 363)

Referring to the lost 'Soledad' which Lorca was writing in homage to Góngora, Guillén praised his friend in his letter of 25 February 1927 for his self-discipline and infallible instinct in knowing just when to stop: 'what I like most is the point of *gongorismo* where you stop: the right point—with echoes and analogies—but without a too narrow formal imitation'.[3] Guillén could never have paid the same tribute to Alberti's 'Soledad tercera (Paráfrasis incompleta)' or to his tortured and contorted *romances*, which show that Alberti was to Lorca what Quevedo was to Lope de Vega and Góngora. The eight ballads of *Cal y canto* are as aggressive as the satirical *romances* of Quevedo, whose cult of

---

* from the waist down they possess each other as man and woman.
† That night I rode the best road of all, mounted on a filly of mother-of-pearl without bridle and without stirrups.

the grotesque and determination to mock led him to adopt a waggish, inflated tone. While Góngora gallantly likened a woman's lips to a ruby and her breath to the jasmine,[1] Quevedo highlighted a woman's enormous nose in unkindly hyperbolic lines:

> promontorio de la cara,
> pirámide del ingenio,
> pabellón de las palabras,
> zaquizamí del aliento.[*2]

And when Quevedo began a *romance* with

> Helas, helas por do vienen
> la Corruja y la Carrasca,[†3]

he abused our automatically attentive response to a traditionally ensnaring first line by introducing not a figure of epic legend but a pair of whores whose names are grimly euphonious. Just as Quevedo aimed to shock us by composing ballads about drunks, bald heads, prostitutes, cats on the rooftops and scabies, so does Alberti challenge our sensibility by dealing with a drunken sailor in 'Romance que perdió el barco' and cooking in 'Metamorfosis y ascensión'. And in lines both ironic and fanciful Alberti imagined in 'Mi entierro (Naturaleza muerta)' his own funeral as an absurd spectacle full of eccentric details: the dead poet, dressed as a grocer, with chickpeas rattling in his coffin and lentils rolling in his pocket, is mourned by people as different as the Archbishop on one side and tramdrivers on the other:

> Vestido ya de tendero
> de tienda de ultramarinos
> (baila el garbanzo en mi caja,
> la lenteja, en mi bolsillo;
> cien coches de punto, en fila;
> en un taxi, el Arzobispo;
> la Academia de la Lengua,
> sin habla, en su velocípedo),

---

* promontory of the face, pyramid of the intelligence, pavilion of words, garret of breath.
† Here they come, here they come, La Corruja and La Carrasca.

me lloran los tranviarios
—timbres en el equilibrio
de la tarde—los fumistas
y los serenos del frío.* (p. 230)

The thought of something as august as the Spanish Academy perched on a velocipede would undoubtedly have amused Quevedo, who took a savage pleasure in deflating the pompous. With such a detail Alberti aimed not to involve our senses but to appeal to the mischievous child within us. The elaborate verbal jokes which composed some of Quevedo's ballads, like the tasteless 'Boda de negros', are matched by a novel *romance* like 'Don Homero y Doña Ermelinda', in which Alberti strained the process of *novelización* to record the quaint dialogue of a pelican and Don Homero continually punctuated by the noises of a newly mechanized civilization:

Doña Ermelinda, pelícano
de verde, por el paseo
—coches, taxis, bicicletas—
del brazo de Don Homero.

. . . .

Urgentes, echan las sombras
cien cubos de polvo negro
sobre la tarde, y estallan
—Junto a mí, no tengas miedo
de los taxis y tranvías...—
los verdes globos eléctricos.† (pp. 232–3)

In 'Don Homero y Doña Ermelinda' Alberti was clearly having fun with the ballad, which he dismantled and reconstructed with skill, humour and originality. With his staccato interplay of stage directions and snippets of conversation he reflected something of

* Now dressed as a shopkeeper of a grocer's shop (the chickpea dances in my coffin, the lentil in my pocket; in a row one hundred hired cars; in a taxi, the Archbishop; speechless on its velocipede, the Spanish Academy), I am wept by the tramdrivers—bells in the stillness of the evening—, the sellers of stoves and the watchmen of the cold.

† Doña Ermelinda, a pelican dressed in green, walks the promenade—cars, taxis, bicycles—on the arm of Don Homero.

Urgently, the shadows throw one hundred buckets of black dust over the evening, and—At my side, don't be afraid of the taxis and trams...—the green electric globes explode.

71

the chaos of city life and simultaneously proved like Aleixandre and Guillén the flexibility of an old form.

The other ballads of *Cal y canto* are marked not simply by their broken pattern and strange fantasy but by a powerful charge of eloquence which blunts our senses, abducts our reason and rushes us over the trivial subject. Unlike the poems of *Romancero gitano* with their *agresión lírica*, Alberti's ballads vibrate with an *agresión retórica* signalled by the sparks flashing in 'Metamorfosis y ascensión' and 'El caballero sonámbulo' (pp. 220, 232). The power accumulating in the seemingly endless and indiscriminate enumeration with which Alberti began '¡ Eh, los toros!' stuns us and carries us helplessly along on a surge of words:

> Toros rempujan, sin mando,
> vientos de piedra, que muerden
> muros y sombras de muros,
> siglos de perfil y frente,
> ojos de niños y hombres,
> llantos, pechos de mujeres,
> reposo de los difuntos,
> sangre parada, corriente.*   (pp. 219–20)

What Alberti did in *Cal y canto*, which is a work of verbal daring, was to convert the *romance* into a vehicle for acrobatic linguistic games in which he sported his absorption of Góngora's manner and his ability to reproduce it. The conviction expressed by a poetic follower of Góngora, Pedro Espinosa, that 'only one person in the world writes like Góngora'[1] was echoed centuries later by Domenchina, who may have been led to diagnose in Alberti '*gongorismo* without Góngora or hare pie without hare'[2] by the dense texture of a ballad like 'Fuego', where Alberti described in his deliberate but rhythmically tense list of clauses the destructive heat and unpredictable movements of a fire:

> Gubias de metal hirviendo,
> rojos formones y clavos,

---

* Uncontrolled, bulls push winds of stone, which bite walls and shadows of walls, centuries of profile and brow, eyes of children and men, tears, women's breasts, repose of the dead, still blood, current.

contra los yunques partidos
de las piedras, martillando.

Astillas clavan las nubes,
de acero, en los campanarios,
tumbadas torres y agujas,
antorchas ya los espacios.* (p. 219)

Alberti's passion for Góngora made him into one of his most
active and ardent partisans. While other poets bobbed a dutiful
curtsy to a passing fashion, he worshipped wholeheartedly a style
of poetry which, as he recalled later, left a particularly deep scar on
himself and on Gerardo Diego, who echoed the sonority of Góngora's 'Fábula de Polifemo y Galatea' in the playfully inflated stanzas
of his 'Fábula de Equis y Zeda'.[1] Góngora's imprint is immediately visible in the type of words Alberti chose in *Cal y canto*; in the
first place he introduced into his poems what Antonio Machado
censured as 'the dry and arid Gongorine tropology':[2] musical
instruments like the zither and the flute, and precious stones and
minerals like crystal, ivory, marble, jasper and ruby. In the second
place he used words as recherché as *álgido, arbóreo, célico, flébil* and
eurítmico, and others as common in Góngora's poetry as *albo,
áureo, cano, cándido, céfiro, lino* and *raudo*. It was a lavish use of such
words and elements organized into careful contortions that made
his 'Soledad tercera' so close in spirit and texture to its models and
justified Alberti's aim of making each poem of *Cal y canto* 'a
difficult course of obstacles':[3]

Al pie, dócil ya y muda,
del ileso extranjero,
la tierna y no mortífera metralla
de la silvestre, ruda,
mal fingida batalla,
el descendido guardabosque fiero,
sus diez uñas calando bayonetas,
hiere, abriendo en la umbría miradores,
las de vidrio cornetas

---

* Gouges of boiling metal, red chisels and nails, hammering against the split
anvils of the stones.
Splinters nail the clouds, which are of steel, in the belfries, fallen towers and
spires, all space is now flaming torches.

73

de la gloria y clamores
del clarín de la luna y ruiseñores.*   (pp. 223–4)

Although Alberti's reminiscences of his childhood in Puerto de Santa María were full of nostalgic allusions to the sea, his vision of the sea owed as much to the poetry of Góngora and Espinosa as to direct experience and artistically treated recollection. The underwater world Alberti imagined with great zest in *Marinero en tierra* and *Cal y canto* is thronged with sirens, dolphins, naiads, tritons and hamadryads, who inhabit a 'corte / espumosa del agua' †(p. 23) as opulent as the submarine gardens Espinosa described in *La fábula de Genil*:

> Hay blancos lirios, verdes mirabeles
> Y azules guarnecidos alhelíes,
> Y allá las clavellinas y claveles
> Parecen sementera de rubíes.‡¹

Marinero en tierra and *Cal y canto* are linked not simply by these submarine worlds and creatures, for the cultured phrases and elegantly sculptured images of *Cal y canto* were foreshadowed in the stylized lines and images of Alberti's first work. The sonnets of *Marinero en tierra*, one of which he wrote in alexandrines, clearly anticipated the rhetorical fireworks contained in the sonnets, tercets and ballads of *Cal y canto*; and a line like 'un plinto verde de algas marinas' §(p. 23) was as symptomatic of his infection by Góngora's poetry as his beautifully stylized description of blood in 'Joselito en su gloria' of *El alba del alhelí*, which with its rubies and crimsons owed a great deal to Góngora and has much in common with the elegant images Lorca coined in *Romancero gitano*:

> Mírame así, chorreado
> de un borbotón de rubíes

---

* The tender and non-lethal grapeshot, now docile and dumb, of the rustic, rude, ill-feigned battle, now at the foot of the unharmed foreigner, the fierce gamekeeper, who has now descended, his ten nails fixing bayonets, wounds, as he opens galleries in the shadows, the glass cornets of glory and clamours of the clarion of the moon and nightingales.

† foaming court of the water.

‡ There are white lilies, green sunflowers and blue adorned wallflowers, and there the pinks and carnations look like a seed-bed of rubies.

§ a green plinth of marine seaweed.

que ciñe de carmesíes
rosas mi talle quebrado.* (p. 176)

The first lines of *Cal y canto*, opened by the *no si* formula of
which Góngora was so fond, project us firmly into a world of
verbal artifice so far removed from normal experience and banal
expression that the reader must with care follow Alberti's search
for 'linguistic beauty' through the intricate tracery of splintered
syntax and elegant diction.[1] It was this passion for linguistic
beauty that made him describe a bullring in 'Corrida de toros'
as a 'volandera / grana zumbando'† (p. 208) and a woman's
breasts in 'Amaranta' as

Pórticos de limones, desviados
por el canal que asciende a tu garganta.‡ (p. 200)

In appealing to the eyes and ears in the first image and to the eyes,
taste and touch in the second, Alberti revealed himself like Góngora and Lorca as a 'master of the five senses'; moreover, like
Góngora and Lorca, he went hunting for verbal beauty 'dis-
guised', to use Lorca's happy word (p. 77), for in *Cal y canto* he
was as emotionally detached from the people he presented in his
poems as Góngora was from his pilgrim and Lorca was from
Preciosa. Enclosed within his skills, he set out to transform the
commonplace, visualizing the goalkeeper Platko as a 'llave áurea
caída ante el pórtico áureo!'§ (p. 239)

The reader undeterred by the dense verbal texture and the syntactic booby-traps of *Cal y canto* can win for himself entry into a
world of stylized elegance where Alberti's elaborate recasting of
the commonplace reveals richness of vocabulary, vitality of imagination and great resources of linguistic skill which would have
undoubtedly aroused Quevedo's hostility, for the poems of this
work are clotted with the type of word he condemned in his tart
'Receta para hacer Soledades en un día':

* Look at me thus, drained by a bubbling of rubies which girds my broken form
  with crimson roses.
† a fluttering, buzzing cochineal.
‡ Porticos of lemons, divided by the canal which rises to your throat.
§ golden key fallen before the golden gate.

> Quien quisiere ser culto en sólo un día,
> la jeri (aprenderá) gonza siguiente:
> *fulgores, arrogar, joven, presiente,*
> *candor, construye, métrica armonía*. . .*[1]

Quevedo would have had far less to censure in the other poets of Alberti's generation, who merely flirted with a fashion which took Alberti by storm. Although none could shield himself as firmly as Cernuda against what Antonio Machado deprecated as 'our superficial baroque',[2] the rash of recherché words and fractured periods which pocked the poetry written around 1927 was an accidental by-product sometimes as spectacular as two lines of Villalón's *La toriada*:

> Turiferario hocico, blanco humo
> exhalan sus ollares respirando. . .†[3]

Words that came as readily to Góngora's pen as *aljófar, concha, grama, nácar* and *romo* are as conspicuous in Aleixandre's *Ámbito* as the phrase 'canora clausura' in a poem of Guillén called 'La sala pequeña', which was the early version of 'El cisne'.[4] When in the same poem Guillén described the swan as 'El cisne cano en la canora onda',‡ he used in *cano* and *canoro* two adjectives favoured by Góngora as he adapted Góngora's definition of the swan as 'el blanco Cisne / envuelta en dulce armonía'.§[5]

Despite Guillén's doctoral thesis on Góngora's poetry and Salinas's admiring description of it as 'poetry of exaltation and adventure',[6] they had so little in common with Góngora that they—and Cernuda, Prados and Altolaguirre—could have chorused with Quevedo: 'Yo no escribo con plumaje, / sino con pluma.'‖[7] Altolaguirre's grave poetry is nearer in spirit to the sober *Coplas* of Jorge Manrique, whose famous lines likening life to a river and death to the sea fascinated him so much that he adapted them in *Poesía* (p. 73), *La lenta libertad* (p. 114) and *Soledades juntas*, where the reminiscence borders on direct transcription:

---

* He who would like to be a *culto* poet in just one day, must the following jargon learn. . .
† Censer-bearing snout, its nostrils expel white smoke as it breathes.
‡ The white swan on the canorous waves.
§ the white swan enveloped in sweet harmony.
‖ I do not write with plumage, but with a quill.

Nuestras vidas son los ríos
que van a dar al espejo
sin porvenir de la muerte.*   (p. 95)

Equally conscious and undisguisable was Guillén's use of two
sonnets of Quevedo in his sonnet 'Muerte a lo lejos', which
appeared in the 1936 edition of *Cántico*. What 'Miré los muros de
la patria mía' and 'Todo tras sí lo lleva el año breve' offered him
was Quevedo's dignified and resigned awareness of his own mortality and of the irrepressible passage of time; that Guillén's sturdy
conclusion—'El muro cano / Va a imponerme su ley, no su acci-
dente'†—echoed Quevedo's 'mas si es ley y no pena, ¿qué me
aflijo?'‡[1] has been freely admitted by Guillén, who revealed that
the 'muro cano' of his poem is 'the white wall of the cemetery of
Valladolid' and acknowledged that 'This line and others of Quevedo like it clearly influence my attitude and my writing.'[2]

When Salinas reminded us in a sonnet of *Presagios* that the
firework is as short-lived as human life (p. 30), he echoed Quevedo's cautions about death and imitated his use of the rocket as a
symbol of the brevity of life and of the overpowering ambition
that made Don Álvaro de Luna into a 'cohete en el mundo'.[3] In
a fine sonnet Quevedo warned man not to be gulled by the flamboyant rocket as it soars prettily through the sky, for it is composed
only of smoke:

No digas, cuando vieres alto el vuelo
del cohete, en la pólvora animado,
que va derecho al cielo encaminado,
pues no siempre quien sube llega al cielo.
. . . .
Mira que hay fuego artificial farsante,
que es humo y representa las estrellas.§[4]

* Our lives are the rivers which will flow into the futureless mirror of death.
† The white wall is going to impose its law on me and not its whim.
‡ but if it is a law and not a penalty, why do I grieve?
§ Do not say, when you see the lofty flight of the rocket, animated by gunpowder,
   that it is going straight to heaven, for he who climbs does not always reach
   heaven.
   Take note that there is a spurious firework, which is smoke and pretends to be
   the stars.

Salinas's exhortation to man to prepare for his 'divino salto' and not be blinded by the rocket's colourful flight repeats Quevedo's solemn warning against the superficial and deceptive attractions of something that can last only a very short time:

> Deja ya de mirar la arquitectura
> que va trazando el fuego de artificio
> en los cielos de agosto. Lleva el vicio
> en sí de toda humana criatura:
> vicio de no durar. Que sólo dura
> por un instante el fúlgido edificio
> para dejarnos ver el beneficio
> sagrado de una luz en noche oscura.
> Ven... Hay que ir a buscar lo más durable.
> Esta noche de estío por ti enciende
> sus innúmeras luces en lo alto;
> cállate bien y deja que ella hable.
> Y del vano cohete sólo aprende
> a ir preparando tu divino salto.* (p. 30)

Although Salinas's 'fuego de artificio', 'fúlgido edificio', 'innúmeras luces en lo alto' and 'vano cohete' are reminiscent of Quevedo's 'Festivo rayo', 'en alto radiante', 'centellas', 'fuego artificial farsante' and 'estrellas', these two sonnets offer only an incidental parallel compared with the strong bridge of imagery linking Quevedo to Alberti and Cernuda. The melancholy and sepulchral Quevedo, whom we glimpsed in the 'muro cano' of Guillén's sonnet, cast a shadow over some of the poems of Cernuda, who was as dismayed by what he called in *Perfil del aire* 'el tiempo tirano' as Quevedo was by the 'tiempo ligero'.†[1] Cernuda's statement in *Los placeres prohibidos* that 'Si muero sin conocerte, no muero, porque no he vivido'‡ (p. 73) reproduced a

---

* Stop looking at the architecture which the firework is tracing in the August sky. It contains within it the vice of all human creatures: the vice of not lasting. For the shining edifice lasts only for a moment to let us see the sacred benefit of a light in darkness.
  Come...You must seek what is most lasting. For you this summer night ignites its countless lights in the heavens above; still your tongue and let the night speak. And from the vain rocket learn only how to prepare your divine leap.   † tyrant time; nimble time.
‡ If I die without knowing you, I do not die, because I have not lived.

conceit favoured by St John of the Cross and other mystic poets at the same time that it perpetuated Quevedo's view of life as a 'morir vivo' and 'un es cansado'.*[1] His realization in *Primeras poesías* that 'Postrada y fiel huye la edad mudable' †(p. 21) was as chilling as Quevedo's constant reminders that death is drawing nearer every moment:

> ¡ Cómo de entre mis manos te resbalas !
> ¡ Oh, cómo te deslizas, edad mía !
> ¡Qué mudos pasos traes, oh muerte fría,
> pues con callado pie todo lo igualas !‡[2]

Quevedo's references to cold death, cold marble, cold time and cold snow[3] make it clear that as a symptom of cheerless life and frigid death cold horrified him as much as it did Cernuda, who defined snow in *Ocnos* as 'that sarcastic image of nothingness'.[4] So saddened was he by dead roses, whose brief beauty he lamented in *Perfil del aire* as wistfully as those Golden Age poets who often mourned its withering,[5] that in *Ocnos* he regarded the rose as a plaything with which time taunts and teases man: 'O time, cruel time, which destroyed the sweet rose of yesterday to tempt us with the fresh rose of today !'[6]

When Alberti called a poem of *Sobre los ángeles* 'El cuerpo deshabitado' and entitled his *auto El hombre deshabitado*, he chose in 'uninhabited' a key word in Quevedo's bleak description of the relationship between man's body and soul. When Quevedo described the body or soul as a building, he himself was exploiting the religious poems of the sixteenth and seventeenth centuries, particularly those of Alonso de Ledesma, whose exploration of the motif provided Quevedo with a range of ready-made variants. Nouns like *alcázar, aposento, casa, huésped* and *posada*, complemented by such verbs as *aposentar, deshabitar, despoblar* and *hospedar*, thus gave Quevedo a visual base for his indictment of the void within himself and within mankind:

* living death; a weary 'is'.
† Changeable age flees prostrate and faithful.
‡ How you slip from between my hands ! Oh, how you slide away, my days ! What silent steps you use, o cold death, since you level everything with silent tread !

Siento haber de dejar deshabitado
cuerpo que amante espíritu ha ceñido;
desierto un corazón siempre encendido,
donde todo el Amor reinó hospedado.*[1]

Quevedo's diagnosis of his malady was succinct: 'Desierto estoy de mí.'[2] He was devoid of his inner self; a soulless shell, he stood as the seventeenth-century ancestor of Alberti's *hombre deshabitado*. These simple images were symptoms of a spiritual malaise which three centuries later was to disturb Alberti, who himself saw in such images the perfect vehicle to describe his own sense of loss, of emptiness and inner ruin. Not surprisingly, the majority of these images are to be found in the troubled pages of *Sobre los ángeles*. In the poem immediately following the introductory 'Paraíso perdido'—entitled significantly 'Desahucio'—Alberti described the soul as vacant:

Sola,
sin muebles y sin alcobas,
deshabitada.†   (p. 249)

'El cuerpo deshabitado' in particular shows that Alberti applied the images of the uninhabited house to the body because he was painfully aware of the disparity between outward appearances and the inner self. Just as Quevedo exposed the corpulent giant in one of his sonnets as a pile of rags,[3] so did Alberti condemn humanity in *El hombre deshabitado* as 'walking corpses..., empty dwellings, painted on the outside to conceal the neglect and darkness in which they live on the inside'.[4] His presentation of himself in *Sobre los ángeles* as a limp and empty figure, a 'negro saco' (p. 250), 'un traje / deshabitado, hueco' (p. 252) and a 'funda vacía' ‡(p. 254), is a despairing self-analysis at that critical time of his life when he saw the past as irretrievably lost and the future as grimly empty.

Across the gap of three centuries, spanned by the community of feeling between Quevedo and Alberti, we find a bridge of style as

---

* I lament having to leave uninhabited a body which a loving spirit has girt on; deserted an always ardent heart, where love lodged and reigned.
† Alone, without furniture or bedrooms, uninhabited.
‡ a black sack; a hollow, uninhabited suit; an empty sheath.

well: the imagery both poets used to express their horror at the void within all men. The original images which abound in Alberti's poetry prove that he did not turn to Quevedo because he lacked imagination, but because he found that Quevedo had expressed his feelings in a strikingly visual group of images. The exploration conducted by Alberti, Aleixandre, Cernuda, Lorca, Guillén, Prados and Salinas into Spain's poetic past was selective, individual and sporadic. Their interest in Spanish poetry was an open-minded, questing curiosity and a part of their formation; they looked back because they wanted to, not because they had to; they sang the scales invented by their poetic predecessors because they wished to train their voices in a tradition to which they were proud to belong. Even when Alberti and Lorca seemed to rely most heavily on tradition, a close reading of their poetry shows that they put into it more of themselves than they took from the past; no amount of earnest copying could have let them write *Romancero gitano*, *La amante* or *Cal y canto*, which are the works of original poets who chose what they wanted with confidence, assimilated it with ease and used it with skill. Neither Alberti, Lorca nor any of the other major poets of this generation borrowed so heavily from Spanish tradition that he lost his identity or integrity as a writer.

2

THE GAME OF POETRY

'What is the meaning of all this clownery?' Mrs. Viveash
inquired.
  'What indeed?'

Aldous Huxley, *Antic Hay* (1923)

When Alberti presented St Raphael in *Cal y canto* as a chauffeur
driving people to and from the lively Hotel de Dios, he remodelled a sacred figure with the frivolity and lightheartedness which
led one of Evelyn Waugh's Bright Young Things, Nina, to ask in
Vile Bodies: 'Darling, am I going to be seduced?' In the 1920s her
seducer's reply: 'It's great fun, ...I promise you', was on the lips
of many people who in their pursuit of mirth worshipped the
great buffoons Charlie Chaplin, Buster Keaton and Harold Lloyd.
And it was the uninhibited cult of gaiety that made the flappers
crack one another's shins as they threw themselves into what
Antonio Espina called in his novel *Luna de copas* (1929) 'the audacious pirouettes of the Charleston',[1] whose infectious and international frenzy prompted Giménez Caballero to state in *Julepe de
menta* (1929) that 'The Charleston has metal clamps.'[2]

Giménez Caballero diagnosed accurately the high spirits of the
young writers producing their first works in the 1920s when he
listed eight things championed by the 'new literature', five of
which are as follows:

                    PRO — Cinema (1)
                       — sport   (2)
                       — circus (3)
                       — gaiety (4)
                       — games   (5).[3]

When he framed his definition Giménez Caballero might have had
in mind the smart young man with cane, grey hat and yellow
gloves who in Espina's *Pájaro pinto* (1927) 'busies himself in sport
and cultivates frivolity';[4] he might also have been thinking of the

82

young writers whose capers in honour of Góngora and whose frolics in the pages of *Lola* provoked Cernuda's haughty censure of 'that fondness for irresponsible games which characterized the acts and the poems of some young poets between 1920 and 1930'.[1]

While *Lola* offered an outlet for poetic games like the 'Declinación de Chabás' and the 'Tontología' of unsuccessful poems,[2] the Residencia de Estudiantes provided a centre for the ebullience fermented in particular by Buñuel, Dalí, Lorca and Alberti, who in later years reminisced about 'the ferocious pranks of Buñuel', the gaiety of Lorca and the meetings held generally in the latter's room to compose *anaglifos*: tiny nonsense verses consisting of three nouns, the second of which had to be 'la gallina' and the third of which had to have no connection with the first, as in:

> El té,
> el té,
> la gallina
> y el Teotocópuli.[3]

The 'revolutionary spirit' which, according to Moreno Villa,[4] inspired the invention of the *anaglifo*—and which also procreated the youthfully harmless disdain summarized in the freely used adjective *putrefacto*—had already been at work outside Spain in art and in literature. It had already led Marcel Duchamp to submit as a sculpture one of his 'ready-mades', a urinal, for exhibition in the Salon des Indépendants in New York; and it had already generated the incoherent and disconnected verses of such Dada poets as Tristan Tzara, who, postulating in Spain 'the leap of images' and preaching that 'Art needs an operation,'[5] spawned with tireless vigour what Edmund Wilson has defined as 'systematic comic nonsense':[6]

> l'ange a des hanches blanches (parapluie virilité)
> neige lèche le chemin et le lys vérifié vierge...*[7]

Tzara's advocacy of dynamism in poetry anticipated the restless vitality of the 1920s, when life appeared to be abruptly accelerated and countries seemed to be suddenly nearer. The car, the aero-

---

* the angel has white haunches (umbrella virility) snow licks the road and the lily verified virgin.

plane, the telephone, the radio and the cinema are now such a normal part of our existence that it is difficult to imagine the wonder and excitement they aroused half a century ago. In *Luna de copas* Espina sensed the quickening of life when he wrote that 'Things dance to the combined music of the jazz-band and the spluttering motor...'[1] Ramón Gómez de la Serna's belief that 'In the jazz-band is the fun of modern life, its absurdity, its incoherence'[2] was shared by Moreno Villa, who, captivated by jazz in North America, pledged in *Jacinta la pelirroja* (1929) to dance with Jacinta 'el ritmo roto y negro / del jazz'.[*3] And Cernuda, who described his life at the University of Toulouse as 'Twilight, mist, sherry and jazz', translated a title he saw in a catalogue of jazz records, 'I want to be alone in the South', into the title of one of the poems in *Un río, un amor*, 'Quisiera estar solo en el sur'.[4]

Cernuda himself indicated that two poems of *Un río, un amor* revealed his enthusiasm for the cinema. The first talking picture that he saw in Paris, *White Shadows of the South Seas*, was the starting-point of 'Sombras blancas'; and he embedded a line he saw on a cinema poster in Toulouse into the first verse of 'Nevada':

> En el Estado de Nevada
> Los caminos de hierro tienen nombres de pájaro...[†5]

(p. 44)

Such details hint at the magnetism of the cinema, whose hypnotic powers in the 1920s were summarized by Giménez Caballero's description of it as a 'vampire with eyes. A brainsucker';[6] when the young hero of Espina's story 'Pájaro pinto' went to visit his relatives, he learned that everyone was at the cinema.[7] Moreno Villa's indifference to what he called in *Jacinta la pelirroja* 'kilómetros, millas de aburrimiento'[‡8] was isolated amid the clamorous enthusiasm immediately apparent in such titles as Salinas's 'Far West' and 'Cinematógrafo' of *Seguro azar* and in the poems of Alberti's *Yo era un tonto y lo que he visto me ha hecho dos tontos*, where he paid slapstick tribute to comics like Harold Lloyd, Keaton and Chaplin, who, idolized in Spain as 'Charlot', won a

---

* the black and broken rhythm of jazz.
† In the State of Nevada the iron tracks have names of birds.
‡ kilometres, miles of boredom.

vocal and devoted following. What these comics took to the screen and what their admirers took in turn to literature was speed, fantasy and capricious, disjointed actions. Like a child listening to fairy-tales, the spectator was invited to suspend reason as he witnessed the evergreen struggle between good and evil delivered in a profusion of comic, pathetic or fantastic situations like the one imagined by Torre, who, parodying the adventure serial, presented in a poem called 'El 7° episodio' the good Mary and William in peril of drowning while

> Bajo un puente el odioso Tom
> prende la mecha explosiva.*[1]

The dynamic images which attracted writers to the cinema also led them to admire new modes of transmission and transport. When Torre wrote in *Hélices* (1918–22) that

> (Los mejores poetas
> madrigalizan a tus pies
> oh Tour Eiffel...),†[2]

he signalled immodestly the enormous popularity enjoyed in the 1920s by the Eiffel Tower, which, as Huidobro stated in *Tour Eiffel* (1917),

> Atrae las palabras
> Como un rosal a las abejas.‡[3]

In the eyes of many poets the Eiffel Tower signposted a new age of adventure, mechanical progress and rapid communication which made it seem to a bewildered Alberti in 'Carta abierta' of *Cal y canto* that

> Nueva York está en Cádiz o en el Puerto.
> Sevilla está en París, Islandia o Persia.§ (p. 241)

The transatlantic flights of Alcock and Brown in June 1919 and Lindbergh in May 1927 heralded a life that with the aeroplane would be faster, more frantic and more international. When in Espina's *Pájaro pinto* Xelfa asked his fiancée Andrea 'What sport do

---

* Beneath a bridge the hateful Tom lights the touchpaper.
† The best poets compose madrigals at your feet, o Eiffel Tower.
‡ Attracts words as a rose-bush attracts bees.
§ New York is in Cadiz or in Puerto de Santa María. Seville is in Paris, Iceland or Persia.

you like best now?', she replied 'Aviation'[1] with the enthusiasm
which had led Marinetti to advocate in his futurist manifestos 'the
idea of mechanical beauty', to preach 'love of the machine' and to
record mechanical energy in free verse that was 'an uninterrupted
gallop of images and sounds'.[2] Marinetti's determination to worship velocity, to keep his pulse racing, to rush frantically from
image to image for the joy of going fast, is seen in a poem called
appropriately 'España veloz. Poema en palabra libre (Fragmento)', where he pants before he has even begun to run:

> A escape a escape tiznarse la cara de bermejo verde
> rosa para fascinar al enemigo...*[3]

Speed and machines did not lack their devotees in Spain. In *El
esfuerzo* (1917) Mauricio Bacarisse, 'drunk with dynamism' like
Marinetti, heard music in the hum of dynamos:

> Igual que flautas las máquinas silban. Como contrabajos
> zumban roncos dínamos un sinfónico scherzo.†[4]

And when in *El paraíso desdeñado* (1928) he sang to 'los bru-
ñidos émbolos / en la gimnasia sueca de las máquinas',‡[5] he exalted
something essential to the motors which excited Marinetti: the
hyperactive, energetic piston whose precise and monotonous
movements—rhapsodized in the 1920s with the zeal other poets
have used to praise the dawn or a woman's hair—were neatly
described by Guillén in 'Las máquinas':

> Fragor. Y se derrumba en un escándalo
> De máquinas, sin transición monótonas.
> Se deslizan los émbolos. Son suaves
> Y resbalan. Exactos, casi estúpidos,
> Los émbolos se obstinan.§[6]

---

* At full speed at full speed smear one's face with crimson green pink in order to
deceive the enemy.

† Like flutes the machines whistle. Like the double-bass hoarse dynamos hum a
symphonic scherzo.

‡ the burnished pistons in the Swedish drill of the machines.

§ Clamour. And it collapses in a scandal of machines, suddenly monotonous. The
pistons glide. They are gentle and slip. Exact, almost stupid, the pistons persist.

Torre's tribute to the piston as a '¡ Lírico surtidor incendiario !'[*1] in a poem called simply 'Poema ultraísta. Émbolo' not only pointed to the machine as the theme and muse of *ultraísmo*, but showed how impudent Torre was to censure futurism for 'Taking the elements of the new beauty as beauty itself.'[2] In Torre *ultraísmo* had its most dedicated theorist, prolific practitioner and conscientious chronicler. Just as Marinetti's career of images and sounds recorded his love of mechanical vigour, so did the 'double, triple and multiple images' which Torre postulated[3] make most of the poems of his movement into disconcerting swirls of images which E. López Parra described as

> Espirales de imágenes
> en el vórtice polifacético.[†4]

When Torre claimed that in the new vitality of *ultraísmo* 'the external world prevails, seen with the lenses of the inner world',[5] he tried to give the movement an importance not justified by its poems, which with their acrobatic images and ornate and technical words are repetitive proof that he and his companions, according to Pedro Raida's 'Confesión',

> embriagaban la inspiración
> con automóviles, aeroplanos, turbinas, dínamos
> y el express.[‡6]

Ultraísmo's eager championing of the machine and of mechanical vigour was a stillborn enthusiasm and a sterile creed requiring its devotees to celebrate the same things and repeat the same words, which hardened into a rhetoric so predictable that it is difficult to distinguish one *ultraísta* poet from another. Torre's prophecy that

> Sobre el tablero poliédrico
> de nuestro arte novimorfo
> todo se va a destorsionar[§7]

---

* Incendiary lyrical fount !
† Spirals of images in the polyhedral vortex.
‡ intoxicated the inspiration with cars, aeroplanes, turbines, dynamos and the express train.
§ On the polyhedral table of our new-shaped art everything is going to contort.

was a hollow boast, for he dislocated nothing more than his own writings. The writhing patterns of words with which, suppressing punctuation, he tried to create 'a plastic relief, a visible architecture'[1]—a poetic equivalent of the shapes and structures found in cubist paintings—were a desperate mechanical device which could not conceal the emptiness of a doctrine that presumed to claim that 'Literature no longer exists. *Ultraísmo* has killed it.'[2] The indigestible words Torre used freely in his poetry and prose—like *arácheo, dendriforme, diplopía, giróvago, lactescente, simisoide* and *velivolante*—congealed into a rhetorical pose which alone justified his belief that 'the only logic possible, the most sincere cerebral logic is the logic of the absurd'.[3]

When the *ultraístas* accepted as an authentic, *bona fide* creation the parody which Dámaso Alonso submitted to them under the pseudonym of 'Ángel Cándiz',[4] they exposed the absurd crudeness and limitations of their stylistic canons; when one of *Lola's* satirists caricatured 'Guillaume de Tour' as

> Ultraporvenirista,
> zodiacal, novimorfo, fotogénico,
> cuatridimensionista,
> autóctono, roentgénico...,[*5]

his mischievous description characterized Torre's diction as effectively as Quevedo's grotesque vocabulary debunked Góngora:

> De lo ambágico y póntico troquiscas
> fuliginosos vórtices y varios...[†6]

It is unlikely that Quevedo would have been more tolerant towards a type of poetry monotonously repetitive in theme and language, and lacking a poet who, sinking all of himself into his poems, could have given shape and coherence to jerky, bombastic and superficial pieces.

With its motto of 'words in liberty',[7] *ultraísmo* subscribed to the cult of the dislocated and fragmentary which influenced many poems and prose works of the 1920s. That many prose pieces were

---

* Ultra-futurist, zodiacal, new-shaped, photogenic, four-dimensionist, autochthonous, Roentgen-like.

† From the circuitous and Pontic you render in trochees divers fuliginous vortices.

dated by their spasmodic, twitching rhythm was recognized by Moreno Villa, who acknowledged that 'our shortened forms are poematic and have a nervous tic which becomes the postmark with the date and place of despatch'.[1] But what was a nervous tremor in some writers was a forced, simulated shudder in others who promoted disorder and incoherence into a literary canon. Numb to the sad fact that he was uninteresting, Giménez Caballero, who tried to shock his readers with the self-debasing title *Yo, inspector de alcantarillas* (1928), consciously pursued the anarchy which resulted from his determination to 'Disembowel myself. Shuffle my cards.'[2] And Espina's suggestion in *Luna de copas* that the novelist, in order to write 'the disjointed, monstrous novel', should 'close his eyes and pick up at random ingredients from all compartments, mixing them and throwing them in handfuls over the chapters'[3] was echoed by Hinojosa, who explained in *La flor de California* (1928) that 'I carefully collect on a white thread all my ideas and when I have a good string of them I swing them in space and when the thread breaks they fall on my head as snowflakes.'[4]

Like Hinojosa, Dámaso Alonso aimed in a prose piece called 'Cédula de eternidad' to record the 'Broken breathing of my thought'; but the hiccoughs which prevented his narrator from pronouncing the name Sabino Miramón made the sequences of Alonso's thoughts disintegrate into a stutter and splutter of sounds and words that defy rational explanation and fully justify his resolve that 'I shall think up absurd and amusing things':

I want to live glu-glu they are extinguished they are extinguished because we do not tolerate fraudulent coalitions against the prices of the united manufacturers if the cellular protoplasm is traumatically uprooted...[5]

When Alonso wrote in another prose extravaganza, 'Acuario en virgo', that 'the two sea serpents...modulate, undulate, pullulate, ululate, entrance...',[6] it is clear that in order to pursue the aims of 'much amusement' and 'ab-surd' which he established in 'Cédula de eternidad',[7] he set out to lull and gull his reader with a flux of words and a display of cleverness that have much in common with the verbal ingenuity of Joyce, who devised in *Ulysses* games as playful as: 'Tipping her tepping her tapping her topping her. Tup.'[1]

Dámaso Alonso seemed keen to prove along with many writers of his day that words in quantity could with little effort create nonsense as empty as Espina's poem 'Tarde de Madrid':

> Hace un frío frío
> De frío muy frío
> Y un azul de tul
> Muy tul. Tul azul... [*2]

Ortega's starchy comment in *La deshumanización del arte* that 'It is easy to say or paint something that completely lacks sense...: all you have to do is string words together without links, or draw lines at random'[3] may have been prompted by the boring eccentricity of Espina's doggerel chant and by the senseless verbiage which Giménez Caballero advocated in *Yo, inspector de alcantarillas*, where, implementing his creed of 'words without substance', he exposed his sterility of mind, his restless pen and his childish ambition to be novel. What purported to be a striking new technique was no more than a verbal diarrhoea as uncontrollable as:

> my sex is in the orange but I do not I do not
> eat it I am not but my sex is in the orange my
> sex is I do not eat it my sex not I orange
> is I do not eat it my sex.[4]

When Bergamín wrote in *Enemigo que huye* (1925-6) that

> La luna se redondea,
> pavipavapavonea;
> y continúa rodando,
> rodeando,
> redundaredondeando,[†5]

he showed how right he was to warn himself in *La cabeza a pájaros* (1925-30) that 'If I begin to play with words, words will

---

[*] It is cold cold with a very cold cold and with a blue of very tulle tulle. Blue tulle...

[†] The moon goes round, swig-sweg-swaggers, goes on rolling, circling and roundly going round.

end up by playing with me.'[1] The title of one of his articles, 'Aforística persistente',[2] accurately diagnosed and labelled his chronic failing: he was so entranced with his own ingenuity, so keen on coining epigrams, so enthralled with the glitter of words that he marshalled them in patterns more impressive to the eye than to the understanding. Hamlet's statement in *Enemigo que huye* that 'Silence is polar; and a polar silence freezes me: a glacial silence; Arctic glacial silence and Antarctic glacial silence'[3] is nothing more than a verbal drill which categorized Bergamín as the 'literary virtuoso' censured by Jarnés for 'trying to make of prose a chain of facile fineries'.[4]

The novelty and abrasive waggishness of Bergamín's play *Tres escenas en ángulo recto* (1924) is evidence for those critics who have criticised the art and literature of the 1920s as juvenile, flippant, shallow and scatterbrained. Cernuda reminded himself years later that 'In the days of your youth some used to affirm. . .that art was a game. You will not say that they were right. . .'[5] The title of Ernst's painting *In Praise of Folly* represented an attitude inimical to Ortega y Gasset, whose reproachful observations that art and literature revealed a 'flight from the person' into 'the sea of sport'[6] were justified by such demonstrations of exuberance as the 'Manifiesto antiartístico' in which Dalí, Sebastián Gasch and Luis Montanyà maintained that 'new factors of intense joy and joviality claim the attention of the youth of today'.[7] In *Luna de copas* Espina, who sensed and recorded in his essay on *Lo cómico contemporáneo* (1928) the playfulness of his age, intruded into his story to mime an apt diagnosis of the mental attitudes of many writers in the 1920s: 'The novelist. . .makes a significant gesture behind his character. He lifts a finger to his temple and moves it with a drilling motion. . .'[8]

That 'art is purely a "distraction"' was maintained by Max Jacob in *Le coup de dés*, where he not only cultivated with a title like 'Poema sin forma, de consistencia floja' the disjointedness endemic to much literature in the 1920s, but strained to coin images as novel and elaborate as 'Niebla, estrella de la araña'* and 'Un incendio es una rosa sobre la cola desplegada de un pavo

---

* Mist, star of the spider.

real.'*¹ When Gómez de la Serna described the letter 'k' as 'a biting, searing letter with two krokodile jaws' and the earth cut open as 'a plum-cake of bones', he relied like Jacob on ingenuity to realize the ambition he expressed in his *Greguerías* to 'freely amuse life'.² His conviction that he could amuse by writing about anything explains why he advocated absurdity, *el disparate*, as 'the most sincere form of literature'³ and why he pursued triviality in his *Greguerías*, where subjects as commonplace as tripe, a tooth-pick, an inkwell and a dead cat in a street were treated with a flippancy and facetiousness at times as silly as 'Opera tenors seem something more than opera tenors, but are nothing more than opera tenors.'⁴ A mildly naughty exclamation like 'Oh, what wrinkles a corset makes in the flesh!' and such limp statements as 'A lamp that flickers is winking at us' and 'Smiles go out like lights'⁵ were symptoms of an imaginative anaemia which jeopardized his constant and determined attempts to be novel and striking.

Although he censured ingenuity in the poetry of Salinas, Cernuda, generally sparse in his praise, admired it in Gómez de la Serna, whom he championed as 'the most important historical antecedent for certain forms of "the new".'⁶ To prove Gómez de la Serna's influence, Cernuda adduced six images of Alberti, Altolaguirre, Diego, Lorca, Guillén and Salinas which he suggested would not have been possible without the experiments of the *greguerías*; but Guillén could have imagined the radiator as a 'ruiseñor del invierno' and Salinas the rose as 'la prometida del viento'† if Gómez de la Serna had never written a line. Cernuda seemed not to realize that Gómez de la Serna was no solitary pioneer of the new and audacious, but one of the many writers who strove for a new mode of writing at once playful, fantastic and consciously disorganized. Cernuda also forgot that the feverish passion for images infected more writers than Gómez de la Serna and stimulated the authentic imaginative vitality of Alberti, Aleixandre, Lorca and Salinas in particular. Waggishly but aptly Espina mused in *Luna de copas* that

* A fire is a rose on the unfurled tail of a peacock.
† nightingale of the winter; the fiancée of the wind.

The geniuses who knew how to create their metaphors made a fortune.
The millionaires, the prostitutes and the writers of the period 1918–1928 know this better than anyone.[1]

Antonio Machado's warning that 'The most absurd fetishism into which a poet can fall is the cult of metaphors' fell on deaf ears,[2] for, as Guillén has recalled, in the 1920s 'The cultivation of the image became a kind of superstitious cult...'[3] The dogged pursuit of the image to the exclusion of feeling which fired *ultraísmo* and futurism also animated *creacionismo*, which, introduced into Spain by the Chilean Vicente Huidobro and nurtured by Gerardo Diego, set out to transform poetry into an autonomous organism that would complement rather than represent creation. It was no chance that Diego called his first *creacionista* work *Imagen* (1922); but the title of his second volume, *Manual de espumas* (1923), diagnosed with accidental irony the frothy texture of a type of poetry soon doomed to burst and disappear in its search for the vague ideal of 'lo otro' stated in *Imagen*:

> Repudiar lo trillado
> para ganar lo otro.*[4]

Diego conceived *lo otro* as a self-supporting world of images and melodies. But the 'free melody of harmonies'[5] into which he wanted his words to fall was an ideal he did not achieve in those lines that were paralysed by a liberal use of *esdrújulas* into a chant as tedious as:

> Mis visiones de noctámbulo
> acrobatizo sonámbulo
> en equilibrio funámbulo
> una a una.†[6]

Diego's advocacy and pursuit of the 'Free image' with a 'plastic surface'[7] made *Imagen* into an anthology of insights and mental gymnastics in which he did nothing more than exercise and parade his fantasy. Although one can find amid the many eccentric or banal images such novel visions as:

* To repudiate the hackneyed in order to attain the other.
† One by one balancing like a funambulist I do somnambulant acrobatics with my nocturnal visions.

> Yo he visto una mujer
> modelando su hijo
> con una máquina de coser,*

and:

> Habrá un silencio verde
> todo hecho de guitarras destrenzadas,†[1]

it is difficult not to long for these disconnected and autonomous snippets to be buttressed by theme, disciplined by a critical mind, and linked and animated by emotion.

Imagen is a series of images so formless and at times pedestrian that they fail to justify Diego's proud boast that *creacionismo* was the 'doorway or threshold of a whole new Art'.[2] Like the *ultraísta* poems and the 'free prose' of Dámaso Alonso, Espina, Giménez Caballero and Gómez de la Serna,[3] *creacionismo* subscribed to the cult of the fragmentary and disorganized which led Huidobro to disperse phrases over his page with a nervousness apparent in 'Luna o reloj' of *Poemas árticos* (1917–18):

> Las tardes prisioneras
> En los rincones fríos
> Y las canciones cónicas de los jardines
> Golondrinas sin alas
> Entre la niebla sólida
> Angustia en mi garganta...‡[4]

Despite his occasional references to his anguish, Huidobro followed the tendency common in the 1920s of concealing himself in fiction, fantasy and image, which was, according to an anonymous reviewer of *Imagen*, 'a cerebral stimulant which translated little or nothing into emotion'.[5] Diego's prophecy in *Imagen* that

> Sembrando mis imágenes
> me hallaréis olvidado entre la nieve§[6]

is an epitaph both on his own efforts and on those writers of the 1920s who tried to rest their works on little more than a rash of

* I have seen a woman modelling her son with a sewing-machine.
† There will be a green silence made out of unplaited guitars.
‡ The captive evenings In the cold corners And the conical songs of the gardens. Larks without wings Amid the solid mist Anguish in my throat.
§ Sowing my images you will find me forgotten amid the snow.

images. It is possible to admire in Chabás's *Espejos* the attractive humour and fantasy of

> El pobre farol lleva
> vendada la cabeza,*1

but such a moment of pleasure is swamped by dissatisfaction at Chabás's failure to mould a series of successfully turned single images into a coherent whole. And although Pedro Garfias wrote in *El ala del sur* (1926) images as striking as

> El alba cruza cantando
> hosannas por los sembrados
>
> La brisa se desmelena
> jugando sobre la yerba,†2

he could have echoed the question Diego asked himself in a poem ironically called 'El espejo': '¿Cuál es mi yo verdadero?'‡3 The *yo verdadero* of Garfias, Diego, Huidobro and Torre in particular did not penetrate a screen of images. When Larrea stated in a poem aptly called 'Evasión' that 'Aún tengo que huir de mí mismo',§4 he sheltered inside a maze of images and eccentric statements as ebullient as the Charleston, which he celebrated in a poem appropriately called 'Locura del Charlestón':

Ella come las víctimas de un durmiente solitario
al andar desprende una estatua a cada paso
pero cuando su piel no es más que una nueva forma de obediencia
la pelusa que mi alma despide hacia su ombligo
sale en tribus de nieve o de huesos sacudidos por la danza
sale de los pequeños túneles de mis piernas fatigosas‖5

Not even Cernuda and Altolaguirre could remain immune to the fever of image-making. Absent from *Primeras poesías* but pre-

---

* The poor lamp has its head bandaged.
† Singing, the dawn traverses the corn-fields with hosannas. The breeze ruffles its hair as it plays on the grass.
‡ Which is my real self?   § I still have to flee from myself.
‖ It eats the victims of a solitary sleeper as it walks it unfastens a statue at each step but when its skin is nothing more than a new form of obedience the down which my soul sends towards its navel emerges in tribes of snow or of bones shaken by the dance it emerges from the small tunnels of my troublesome legs.

sent in *Perfil del aire* are a number of those 'gratuitous and sensational metaphors' which Cernuda censured in later years as a characteristic of the early writings of his generation.[1] His choice of a train as a symbol of fleeting hopes and illusions tempted him to coin a contrived series of metaphors in which the station is a 'nest of transit', his dreams are 'lyrical luggage' and his heart, in an uncomfortable and grating echo of 'restaurant car', is a 'resonant car':

> ¡ Cuán tierna la estación,
> sólo nido de tránsito,
> abre un vuelo de trenes
> hacia el aire lejano !
>
> Ya la mano conduce
> al vagón resonante,
> la ternura, los sueños:
> su lírico equipaje.[*2]

Cernuda's omission of these lines from *Primeras poesías* is inconsistent with the claim he made many years later that *Perfil del aire* 'is the work of one who knows both what he wants and what he does not want to say'.[3] These lines, together with such strained metaphors as 'Facturados...sueños' and 'sombra aduendada',[†4] sit as uneasily within the corpus of Cernuda's poetry as the playful and contrived images which obtrude from Altolaguirre's *Las islas invitadas* as proof that not even a basically sad and sober poet could remain detached from a fashion and resist the temptation to explore and display his ingenuity. Although Altolaguirre visualized in a novel way something as exploited as the dawn, he failed to recognize that his picture of sunbeams as washing hung out by a woman is a flippant extravaganza unredeemed by its pompous phrasing and inflated tone:

> Cuando se oculte entre las yerbas altas,
> las blancas ropas que tendió en sus rayos

---

* How tender is the station, only a nest of transit, as it releases a flight of trains towards the distant air !
    Already the hand leads to the resonant coach tenderness, dreams: its lyrical luggage.

† Registered dreams; elfish shadow.

la guapa lavandera de la aurora,
en vidrios paralelos
deshiladas caerán.*   (p. 17)

And when he imagined that 'jugamos al billar con nuestras voces't
(p. 18) and that

La noche—negro médico—
le toma al pulso al río
y despide a la tarde,‡   (p. 17)

he experimented with his erratic fantasy as he joined skittishly but
briefly in the cult of the image, which attracted followers more
single-minded and enthusiastic than he.

What made Alberti, Altolaguirre, Cernuda, Lorca, Guillén,
Prados and Salinas survive and transcend the amusing, fascinating
but transient experiments and fashions of the 1920s was their
capacity to develop and mature as they learned from their mis-
takes. What distinguished Guillén from Diego or Torre was his
ability to recognize the immaturity of his early writings and so
correct the excesses of his style. When in 1923 he wrote in a prose
piece called 'Cinco florinatas' that bubbles of laughter—'those
little spheres of hilarity'—'sail in search of the God of the aero-
stats' and urged: 'Lead them, Lord, to your aerodrome',[1] he was
exploiting the newly popular motif of aviation with the frivolity
which enlivened his early poems and prose pieces, where he
worked out of his system the juvenile posturing and extravagant
phrasing so inconsistent with the candour and technical rigour of
Cántico.

That Guillén enjoyed toying with words in his early writings is
apparent from his playfully pointless question that 'If a human
form stands in the wind, does it not immediately stand against
the wind?'[2] And, choosing words with mischievous care, he inflated an event as commonplace as the opening of an umbrella
into a minor drama and a mock-serious geometrical problem:

* When she hides among the tall grasses, the white garments which the pretty
  laundress of the dawn stretched out on beams will fall unravelled in parallel
  panes.
† we play billiards with our voices.
‡ The night—black doctor—takes the river's pulse and sends the evening away.

The metamorphosis of each one of its slopes into the courteous cathetus of the liquid right-angle—the other cathetus. Because there is a triangle. Suddenly the fantastic hypotenuses have stretched out. O marvel, synthesis of the Firmament, Pain and Human Will—O umbrella![1]

Guillén's early poems also reveal an equally obtrusive mental tension, for the trivial topics and similes he sometimes used in his efforts to be novel and imaginative debase rather than enhance what he set out to present. His description of time as an 'hucha / de ahorros de dulzura'*[2] is, although unusual, as forced as his likening of sunbeams to shining coins:

> Las onzas del sol,
> discretas, furtivas,
> lucen su esplendor
> como calderilla.†[3]

In the first edition of *Cántico* Guillén's strikingly taut description of a woman's breasts as 'blancas algazaras' (p. 40) and of illuminated signs in a street as 'Silabario de vértigo'‡ (p. 35) contrasts with the contrived and flabby images of his early poems, whose immaturity he has acknowledged by leaving them to languish in the pages of the journals in which they appeared. Although he included in *Cántico* lines from his early writings, he had the acumen to discern and disdain gauchely pretentious phrases and preposterous images. One of the stanzas of 'Oda inicial', which he published in 1923, reads:

> A la vacua deidad clemencia imploran
> Otros también artífices
> En sus casi obeliscos.§[4]

Guillén transposed this stanza into 'Pino', but only after recognizing the rarity of 'vacua', simplifying the first line and transforming the clumsy third line into a smooth and simple phrase:

---

* a money-box of savings of sweetness.
† The sun's coins, discreet, furtive, sport their splendour like coppers.
‡ white revels; spelling-book of vertigo.
§ Others who are also artisans in their quasi-obelisks beg the vacuous deity for clemency.

> A la común divinidad imploran
> Otros también artífices,
> Juntos en el espacio.* (p. 30)

Another poem, 'Rigor', published in 1922, contained the following stanza:

> Libro de bachiller:
> página tantas: vértice.
> ¡ Sutil, sutil Euclides !†[1]

When he incorporated this stanza into 'Ciudad de los estíos' in the first and second editions of *Cántico*, he remedied the artificiality of the third line and highlighted 'vértice' with conspicuous inverted commas which signal the topic on the page:

> Libro de bachiller,
> Página tantas. 'Vértice':
> Fatalidad sutil.‡ (p. 33)

But Guillén became so weary with the book and its topic that he banished them from his 1950 edition of *Cántico*, changed the first line-and-a-half into a neat and simple sentence and, releasing 'vértice' from its contrived inverted commas, made it stand in its own right as a sign of the geometrical precision he so much admires:

> Con toda sencillez
> Es sabio Agosto. Vértice,
> Fatalidad sutil.§[2]

Guillén's sharp eye for the trivial theme and the awkwardly manufactured phrase led him to exclude from *Cántico* many early poems whose fatuousness and pomposity were symptoms of the youthful experimentation and skittishness which he purged from his system. When he made Don Juan ask if his mistress wore silk stockings, he behaved with a frivolity apparent in another early poem whose playful title—'Antilógica'—was akin to Diego's 'Antipoema' in *Imagen*.[3] 'Antilógica' suffered like much of Guillén's—and Lorca's—early writings from the resonant but

---

* Others who are also artisans together in space entreat the common divinity.
† Text book: page so-and-so: vertex. Subtle, subtle Euclid!
‡ Text book. Page so-and-so. 'Vertex': Subtle inevitability.
§ With all simplicity August is wise. Vertex, subtle inevitability.

hollow pomposity which weighed down the following passage, deadened even further by the inelegant simile in the last line:

> ¡ Oh fácil numismática amorosa,
> propicia al numen simplificador!
> El brazo de ella y mi brazo se anudan
> como en un silogismo las premisas.*

With his exclamation 'Salve, retórica', uttered in 1923,[1] Guillén saluted the rhetorical extravaganzas which also disfigured Lorca's *Libro de poemas*, whose florid diction and forced images were the tentative efforts of a poet who had not yet learned his craft or found his voice. Like Guillén, who peppered his early writings with such words as *arcanizar*, *esfericidad*, *hipotético* and *luctuoso*, Lorca used words which he would never repeat. To write in *Libro de poemas* of an 'arqueológica / pupila' (p. 143) and 'mi sangre / filarmónica't (p. 165), and to use elsewhere verbs like *japonizar* (p. 339) and *salomonizar* (p. 265) was to strain after rhetorical resonance as hard as Darío, who may well have given Lorca a taste for the proper names out of which he fashioned stilted images, as well as for the adjective *lírico* and *divino* which recur in *Libro de poemas* and *Impresiones y paisajes* (1918).[2] His descriptions of a woman in *Libro de poemas* as a 'Danaide del placer' (p. 138) and of a guitar in *Poema del cante jondo* as 'un Polifemo de oro't (p. 253) rely as much on our knowledge of mythology as on our powers of imagination.

Lorca's description of a poplar in *Libro de poemas* as 'el Pitágoras / de la casta llanura'§ (p. 185) points to the fondness he shared with Guillén for geometric terms and symmetrical patterns, which stimulated images like 'La elipse de un grito'‖ in *Poema del cante jondo* (p. 226) and led him to imagine in 'Tarde' of *Canciones* that

> En el río
> un árbol seco,

---

* O facile amorous numismatics, propitious to the simplifying divinity! Her arm and my arm are joined like the premises of a syllogism.
† archeological pupil; my philharmonic blood.
‡ Danaid of pleasure; Polyphemus of gold.
§ the Pythagoras of the chaste plain.
‖ The ellipse of a shout.

ha florecido en círculos
concéntricos.*   (p. 307)

In 'La monja gitana' of *Romancero gitano* light plays 'el ajedrez /
alto de la celosía't (p. 362) with a light-heartedness which prompted
Lorca to suggest in 'Suicidio' of *Canciones* that 'el joven rígido,
geométrico'‡ killed himself '(*Quizás...por no saberte la Geometría*)'§ (p. 334).

With his description of Amparo in *Poema del cante jondo* as
'(Ecuador entre el jazmín / y el nardo)'‖ (p. 246), Lorca was
trying hard to celebrate and paint in words the colour of the
woman's skin. Studded with images, his early works provide
ample evidence of a vigorous fantasy not yet properly lubricated
or fully controlled. In *Libro de poemas* his colloquial, sing-song
evocation of the moon's 'cara bonachona / de jamona'¶ (p. 153)
shows that in his keenness to exploit his strongly visual imagination he subjected it to stresses which revealed his immaturity. It
was by mining his rich vein of fantasy with indiscriminate energy
that Lorca suggested in *Libro de poemas* that 'una alucinación /
me ordeña las palabras'** (p. 124), imagined a presentiment as a
'Nariz del corazón'†† (p. 141), thought of frogs as 'muecines de la
sombra'‡‡ (p. 184) and visualized a prickly-pear tree in *Poema del
cante jondo* as a 'Múltiple pelotari'§§ (p. 255), reminiscent of
Guillén's description of God as the 'Primer Pelotari'.‖‖[1]

Lorca's writings offer abundant proof of the range and vitality
of his imagination; what his *narraciones* relate is understandable
only if one suspends reason and enters a world of fantasy in which
with mock solemnity he communicated nonsense masquerading as
careful argument, as when he advised in 'Degollación de los Ino-
centes' that 'One must have two hundred children and deliver
them up for beheading. Only in this way would the autonomy of

---

* In the river a dry tree has flourished in concentric circles.
† the lofty chess of the lattice.   ‡ the rigid, geometric youth.
§ Perhaps because you did not know Geometry.
‖ Equator between the jasmine and the spikenard.
¶ good-natured face of a buxom woman.
** a hallucination milks me of words.   †† Nose of the heart.
‡‡ muezzins of the shadows.   §§ Multiple pelota-player.
‖‖ First Pelota-player.

the wild lily be possible' (p. 21). His stories are a display of inventiveness and flippant humour where eccentric figures like Monsieur Meermans, who in 'Historia de este gallo' (1928) enjoys eating 'big plates of raw cocks'-combs with a fork studded with emeralds' (p. 13), live amid a mass of quaint details which Lorca sometimes herded into lists as amusing and incongruous as the 'phial, an Agnus Dei, a shrivelled potato and a celluloid doll' which Joyce imagined falling out of Ellen Bloom's 'striped blay petticoat' in *Ulysses*.[1] To specify in 'Degollación del Bautista' that 'Salome had more than seven sets of false teeth and a phial of poison' (p. 19) was to present a surprisingly novel vision of an old character.

Lorca's apparently earnest lament in *El paseo de Buster Keaton* (1928) that the inhabitants of Philadelphia 'will never be able to understand what very subtle poetic difference exists between a cup of hot tea and another cup of cold tea' (p. 805) is a clear sign of his desire to mystify and amuse; the humour of his tales and experimental plays is at once extravagant and delightfully deadpan. In *Así que pasen cinco años* (1931) the Youth's description of Chartreuse as 'a great night of green moon inside a castle where there is a youth with golden seaweed' (p. 1052) is an elaborate piece of nonsense as preposterous as the strange characters and impossible stage directions of some of his plays. In *La zapatera prodigiosa* (1930) the Author makes it clear that Lorca was urging the public to jettison its prejudices and not be alarmed if in the world of fantasy which they have dared to enter 'a tree...becomes a ball of smoke' or 'three fishes...become three million fishes' (p. 821). Lorca's instruction in the 'Escena del teniente coronel de la Guardia Civil' that 'The tobacco and white coffee soul of the Lieutenant Colonel of the Civil Guard goes out through the window' (p. 260) indicated no action known to man or nature: it was a token of a volatile fantasy and a romping sense of humour to be savoured but not taken too seriously.

Lorca's fusion of humour and fantasy is one of the attractions of his *Romancero gitano*. The unlikely combination of seraphim and gipsies playing accordions in 'Muerto de amor' strikes a playful note which the murders and deaths related in his ballads do little to dispel. His tongue was firmly in his cheek when he put tobacco vendors into 'San Rafael (Córdoba)' and grouped the famous Pedro Domecq with three sultans from Persia in 'Romance de la Guardia Civil española', where he dressed the Virgin

> con un traje de alcaldesa
> de papel de chocolate.* (p. 382)

Before *Poeta en Nueva York* Lorca enjoyed himself in poetry. His sunny and magnetic personality, which led Guillén to reminisce that when Lorca was with him 'Federico shone like the sun',[1] was reflected in the gay and festive *Canciones*, where in order to amuse the children he made the 'Tío-vivo' revolve, the 'Arlequín' prance and accompanied his 'Ribereñas' with peals of 'balalín' and 'balalán' (p. 315). The dialogue which takes place between him and the children in 'Balada de la placeta' of *Libro de poemas* was paralleled in reality by the bond of affection linking him to Guillén's son and daughter; 'Teresina and Claudie send you their love,' wrote Guillén on 1 September 1926; 'Love to Teresina and Claudie,' replied Lorca on 7 September.[2]

Indulging their love of make-believe, Lorca invented for children fairy-tales with titles as simple and alluring as 'Fábula', 'Mi niña se fue a la mar', 'Dos marinos en la orilla' and 'Canción de las siete doncellas', in which he acknowledged the capriciousness of infants' tales when he asked:

> (¿Por qué no han sido nueve?
> ¿Por qué no han sido veinte?)† (p. 287)

With his group of 'Canciones para niños' he built for children a private world of pretence, entry to which is given only to those who can recapture the gaiety and candour of childhood games. In 'El lagarto está llorando...', which he dedicated delightfully 'To Mademoiselle Teresita Guillén playing a piano of six notes', he invites us to sympathize with two lizards who, dressed in white aprons, mourn the loss of their wedding ring while overhead the sun shines in its satin waistcoat:

---

* with a mayoress's dress made out of a chocolate wrapper.
† Why have they not been nine? Why have they not been twenty?

El lagarto está llorando.
La lagarta está llorando.

El lagarto y la lagarta
con delantaritos blancos.

Han perdido sin querer
su anillo de desposados.

¡ Ay, su anillito de plomo,
ay, su anillito plomado !

. . . .

El sol, capitán redondo,
lleva un chaleco de raso.

. . . .

¡ Ay cómo lloran y lloran
¡ ay ! ¡ ay ! cómo están llorando.*   (p. 301)

And in 'Friso' he presented in only four lines a moment of romance in which

Las niñas de la brisa
van con sus largas colas,†

and

Los mancebos del aire
saltan sobre la luna.‡   (p. 293)

The playfulness which incited Lorca in *Canciones* to replace Eros's bow and arrow with a walking-stick (p. 326) inspired Alberti to give the same figure a toga, monocle and birreta in 'Venus en ascensor' of *Cal y canto*, where he placed on seven heavens connected by a lift seven mythological figures remodelled with the grotesque inventiveness that provided Narcissus with green garters and rubber breasts (p. 229). Chanting in *Marinero en tierra* infant songs like 'De 2 a 3', Alberti invented for children fantasies as delightful as 'Amor de miramelindo', 'La niña que se

* The male lizard is crying. The female lizard is crying.
  The two lizards in their little white aprons.
  Without wanting to they have lost their wedding ring.
  Alas, their little lead ring, alas, their little leaden ring.
  The sun, round captain, wears a satin waistcoat.
  Oh how they weep and weep, oh, oh, how they are weeping !
† The girls of the breeze go with their long trains.
‡ The youths of the air jump over the moon.

va al mar'—akin to Lorca's 'Mi niña se fue a la mar'—and 'Nana de la cabra', which like many children's tales was based on strange, mock-serious reasoning:

> La cabra te va a traer
> un cabritillo de nieve
> para que juegues con él.
> Si te chupas el dedito,
> no te traerá la cabra
> su cabritillo.* (p. 38)

Out of events as quaint as the conversation of two hens in 'La oca y el gorrión' of *El alba del alhelí*, Alberti created a mythical world peopled by characters as fantastic as Cal-y-nieve, Descalza-de-los-caminos and Agua-dulce, who are found in *El alba del alhelí*, and Rosa-fría and Blanca-nieve, who figure in *Marinero en tierra* and reappear in the children's tales which Alberti's wife, María Teresa León, published in 1934 under the title of *Rosa-fría, patinadora de la luna*.[1]

The 'niño más chiquitito / dando vueltas por la era'† in one poem of *La amante* (p. 98) and the dog wagging its tail in another (p. 93) show an energetic delight in life generated by the gaiety Bergamín evoked in his tribute to Alberti 'El alegre'.[2] Nothing marred the brisk and buoyant lyrical journey recorded in *La amante*, where Alberti found much pleasure in things as trivial as encountering a solemn carter (p. 95) or watching ducks float on the water (p. 112). Without rancour he took leave of his 'Niña del pecho de España' and she bade farewell to her 'buen amante andaluz'‡ (p. 118), who erupted in *El alba del alhelí* into an ebullience celebrated in the first poem by song, tambourines and an intoxicated sense of direction:

> ¡Muchachas, las panderetas!
> De abajo yo, por las cuestas,
> cantando, hacia el barrio alto.§ (p. 131)

---

* The goat is going to bring you a kid of snow for you to play with.
  If you suck your finger, the goat will not bring you its kid.
† the tiniest little child running round the threshing floor.
‡ Girl from the heart of Spain; good Andalusian lover.
§ Girls, the tambourines! Down the slopes I sing as I go towards the high district.

Although Alberti inflated 'Joselito en su gloria' and 'Seguidillas a una extranjera' into resonant and mock-serious poems, his humour was gay and mischievous in 'El Niño de la Palma' and 'A Jean Cassou' where, jauntily rhyming 'marabú' with 'Cassou', he wanted his friend the French critic Jean Cassou to savour with him the mixture of accents and the extrovert tourists' activities:

> Andaluces y franceses
> se dan la mano en Sevilla,
> mientras en la manzanilla
> yerven las *ges* y la *eses*.
> Para a los tontos ingleses
> ver bailar el marabú:
> arranca, viento andaluz,
> de París, a Jean Cassou.*   (p. 151)

Turning his irony and verbal jokes against himself, Alberti composed in 'El tonto de Rafael' a caricature which with its savage insults and its self-deprecating refrain of '¡El tonto de Rafael!' anticipated the painful self-exposure of *Sobre los ángeles*:

> ¿Quién aquél?
> ¡El tonto de Rafael!
>
> Tan campante, sin carrera,
> no imperial, sí tomatero,
> grillo tomatero, pero
> sin tomate en la grillera.†   (p. 180)

That Alberti discovered like Quevedo the delights of distortion is apparent in *Cal y canto*, where he cultivated the absurd and the grotesque with a tenseness which replaced the ease and affability of *Marinero en tierra* and *La amante*. To imagine himself in 'Mi entierro' as a dead carp in a coffin hauled to Paradise by four boiled geese was to let his imagination play a macabre joke. But

---

* Andalusians and French shake hands in Seville, whilst the 'ochs' and the 'isses' bubble in the *manzanilla*. To see the English fools dance the marabou [an Andalusian dance popular in the nineteenth century]: snatch, o Andalusian wind, from Paris Jean Cassou.

† Who is that? That fool Raphael!
So buoyant, without a career, not sceptred, but a tomato-seller, a tomato-selling cricket, but without a tomato in the cricket-cage.

the jerky tempo and splintered structure of 'Don Homero y Doña Ermelinda'—which I discussed in chapter 1—disintegrated even further into the boisterous pranks and verbal clowning of *Yo era un tonto y lo que he visto me ha hecho dos tontos*, which was both a tribute to the great cinema comics whom he exalted as 'real angels of flesh and blood'[1] and a sign of his diminishing geniality and growing eagerness to outrage. The emotional and physical stresses which exploded in *Sobre los ángeles* put on Alberti's sense of humour a hard edge which increased his isolation, exacerbated his bitterness and sharpened his desire to 'take revenge on everyone and place real bombs', like the lecture he gave on 10 November 1929 on the preposterous subject 'Palomita y galápago (¡ No más artríticos!)' to the Lyceum Femenino, which, he has reminded us, was situated appropriately near to the Circo de Price.[2]

With a dove in one hand and a tortoise in the other, Alberti arrived for his lecture 'dressed as a clown—enormous, shapeless, frock-coat; baggy trousers; wide, fly-away collar, and a tiny bowler hat perched on the top of my head'.[3] To judge from the number of women who catcalled or walked out, he certainly succeeded in provoking his audience; in her frankly hostile report 'Señora de X' concluded with blind contempt that Alberti 'did not have even one moment of originality. He was like a bull-ring Chaplin.' The poetess Ernestina de Champourcin, on the other hand, recognized that Alberti's aim to 'study the fright produced in the mysterious soul of woman by the pedagogic threat of releasing a rat recently caught by me in a sewer or latrine' was nothing more than a deliberately abrasive 'explosion of humour'.[4]

In *Yo era un tonto*... Alberti employed the shock-tactics he adopted in his increasingly pungent assault on people's sensibilities. Buffooning in verse like the comics on the screen, he devised with jerky, disjointed actions, gratuitous vitality, mock gravity and imaginative vigour a verbal slapstick as absurd as 'Larry Semon explica a Stan Laurel y Oliver Hardy el telegrama que Harry Langdon dirigió a Ben Turpin', where he communicated nonsense with telegraphic concision:

Angelito constipado cielo.
Pienso alas moscas horrorizado
y en dolor tiernas orejitas alondras campos.* (p. 328)

It was the speed and freshness of the cinema that fascinated and
thrilled Alberti. When he wrote in 'Cita triste de Charlot' that

A las tres en punto morirá un transeúnte.
Tú, luna, no te asustes,
tú, luna de los taxis retrasados,
luna de hollín de los bomberos.

La ciudad está ardiendo por el cielo,
un traje igual al mío se hastía por el campo,† (p. 319)

he was moved by what he called in a splendid line of 'Harold
Lloyd, estudiante' 'este puro amor mío tan delicadamente idiota'‡
(p. 321) to duplicate in print the capricious fantasy of images
which flit across the screen so rapidly and unpredictably that in
'Carta abierta' he imagined that 'Ana Bolena, / no sé por qué, de
azul, va por la playa'§ (p. 241).

On the cinema screen life, already accelerated by cars, trains and
aeroplanes, seems to move with a speed which Alberti has admitted trying to emulate in the rapid series of images with which
he constructed the poems of *Cal y canto*. Although such images of
Marinero en tierra as 'los radiogramas de tu estrella Polar' (p. 23)
and 'aviones del sueño'‖ (p. 24) suggest that Alberti was attracted
by the new modes of transport and communication, he was no
robot recorder of the machine age. When he sang in 'Dialoguillo
de otoño':

¡ Oh qué tarde
para irse en avión,
en volandas,
por el aire !¶ (p. 44)

* Little angel-with a cold-heaven. I think wings flies scandalized and in pain
tender little ears larks fields.
† At three o'clock sharp a passer-by will die. You, moon, do not take fright,
you, moon of the delayed taxis, moon of the firemen's soot.
   The city is burning across the sky, a suit like mine gets weary in the country.
‡ this pure love of mine so delicately idiotic.
§ Anne Boleyn, I don't know why, dressed in blue, goes across the beach.
‖ the radiographs of your Polar star; aeroplanes of sleep.
¶ Oh what an evening to go off in an aeroplane, flying through the air !

the aeroplane melts unobtrusively into the lyrical exclamation,
which is as touchingly simple as 'El aviador', where the girl,
whose lament to her mother echoes the plaints of many *cantigas de
amigo*, mourns the death of the young airman, the 'knight of the
air', drowned before promotion to captain:

> Madre, ha muerto el caballero
> del aire, que fue mi amor.
>
> Y en el mar dicen que ha muerto
> de teniente aviador.
>
> ¡ En el mar !
>
> ¡Qué joven, madre, sin ser
> todavía capitán !*   (p. 36)

But the easy absorption of telephones and torpedo-boats into
the poems of *Marinero en tierra* (pp. 52, 58) gave way to an enthusiastic and clamorous tribute in *Cal y canto*, where Alberti
pulsated with 'la sincopada sangre, ya intranquila' (p. 210) and
celebrated 'la fuga del tren y los tranvías'† (p. 242). That he was
familiar with *ultraísmo*'s veneration of the machine is clear from
his memoirs, where he has confessed that, while he was recovering
from tuberculosis, he would await 'with real interest and impatience' each number of the magazine *Ultra* and actually submitted a poem to it.[1] But *Cal y canto* proves that his passion for
machines did not banish his sense of humour, stunt his growing
maturity, blunt his verbal and technical skills or clash with his
intimate knowledge and love of Spain's poetic traditions. Although in 'Carta abierta' he celebrated like Torre 'la nueva vida'
(p. 243), he exercised a control over his theme, form and enthusiasm which justifies his affirmation that *Pasión y forma*—his
original title for *Cal y canto*—'is not a vanguard work'.[2] The
'malaise' which he acknowledged to be a point of contact between his poetry and *ultraísmo*[3] did not lead to a deranged and

---

* Mother, the knight of the air, who was my love, has died.
  And they say that he has died as a lieutenant aviator in the sea.
  In the sea!
  How young, mother, when he is not yet a captain!
† the syncopated, restless blood; the flight of the train and the trams.

breathless dynamism; his individuality, imagination and eloquence
as a poet did not allow him to be trapped within the 'network of
cables and planes' which choked the *ultraístas*:

> Yo nací—¡ respetadme !—con el cine.
> Bajo una red de cables y de aviones.
> Cuando abolidas fueron las carrozas
> de los reyes y al auto subió el Papa.
>
> Vi los telefonemas que llovían,
> plumas de ángel azul, desde los cielos.
> Las orquestas seráficas del aire
> guardó el auricular en mis oídos.*   (p. 242)

Swelling the already loud chorus of tributes, Alberti exalted the
Eiffel Tower in 'Nadadora', where he relayed a string of quaintly
concise statements and exclamations with telegraphic urgency:

> La Torre Eiffel tira un cielo
> de anuncios y telegramas.
> ¡ Huye, mar !
> ¡ Viva mi nombre en todos los sombreros
> del bulevard !
> ¡ Y mi fotografía en bicicleta !
> ¡ Ah !
> ¡ Y mis derechos a una isla en el Sena !
>
> ¡ Corre, playa !
> ¿Qué pensará el Rey de Inglaterra?†   (p. 237)

His ears filled with 'La música del riel' (p. 207), Alberti celebrated the 'Rieles de yodo y plata'‡ (p. 204) on which trains
whisk people so fast that the passengers on the Andalusian Express
can see nothing more than a blur of scenery:

---

* I was born—respect me !—with the cinema. Beneath a network of cables and
aeroplanes. When the coaches of kings were abolished and the Pope stepped
into the motor car.
   I saw the dispatches raining from the skies like the feathers of a blue angel.
The telephone receiver kept in my ears the seraphic orchestras of the air.
† The Eiffel Tower propels a sky of announcements and telegrams. Flee, sea !
Long live my name on all the hats of the boulevard ! And my photograph on a
bicycle ! Ah ! And my rights to an island in the Seine !
   Run, shore ! What will the King of England think?
‡ The music of the rail; Rails of iodine and silver.

> —¡ Adiós, adiós, adiós ! En los viajes,
> beba usted sólo, con la vista, el viento
> de los precipitados paisajes.*   (p. 213)

Trains and planes and cars quickly bring more people into contact; but they part so quickly that they make no mark. Miss X, with her fashionably cropped blonde hair, moves within her cocoon of anonymity from one air-conditioned paradise to another and is quickly forgotten:

> ¡ Ah, Miss X, Miss X, qué fastidio !
> Bostezo.
>   Adiós...
>   —Goodbye...   (p. 236)
> ....
> *Ya nadie piensa en ti, Miss X niña.†*   (p. 237)

The sad barman mechanically serving drinks reflected the boredom of the new breed of cosmopolitans who made more time to be bored as they exhausted the places marked, according to Salinas in *Seguro azar*, with a 'doble asterisco en el Baedeker' (p. 78), or flitted from country to country, hotel to hotel, or beach to beach. The car provided by the hotel in 'Guía estival del Paraíso' goes significantly 'al mar y los andenes' (p. 212): to sea-side revelry, celebrated in the swimming costumes worn by Diaghilev's dancers in *The Blue Train*, first performed in 1924, and then to the station platform and another journey.

But the speed and energy with which modern life vibrates exploded in *Sobre los ángeles* and *Sermones y moradas* into a destruction marked by the derailed trains found in the second *ángel bueno* poem (p. 261). Alberti now recoiled from the city, which was no longer for him the symbol and centre of mechanical progress but a place of horror and indifference; like Salinas in *Todo más claro* (1949), he suddenly found himself an outsider who in *El hombre deshabitado* made Sight point in disgust to 'the city whose blood rushes towards death, without turning its head, amid the smoke of

---

* Goodbye, goodbye, goodbye. On journeys just drink in with your eyes the wind of the rushing landscapes.
† Oh, Miss X, Miss X, what boredom ! Yawn. Goodbye... Au revoir.
  Now no-one thinks of you any more, Miss X child.

the trains and the factories'.[1] Salinas was filled with an equally strong revulsion when in 'Hombre de la orilla' he railed in lines that recall Lorca's lament in *Poeta en Nueva York* that 'Cantaba la lombriz el terror de la rueda'* (p. 420) against

> Ruedas, sólo ruedas, ruedas.
> Confuso caudal frenético...† (p. 352)

But although Salinas no longer enjoyed speed as he once did, he was still attracted in 'Hombre de la orilla' by the illuminated signs which, composing what he called 'the rhetoric of the advertisement',[2] exercised a strong fascination on him. In a delightfully mock-heroic fantasy of *Seguro azar*, 'Placer, a las once', he visualized illuminated letters as soldiers enlisted by 'El arcángel del domingo'‡ and swollen by his volunteer troops of 'maquinaria americana, / ágiles volatineros'§ to campaign with squadrons of volts which flash like lances against the foe: mystery:

> Del hombro cuelga la aljaba
> toda llena de alfabetos:
> las letras que clavará
> —¡qué propaganda del gozo!—
> luminosas en el cielo.
>
> ....
>
> Escuadrones de cien voltios
> alancean los reflejos.‖ (p. 65)

The 'máquinas maravillosas' which in 'Cinematógrafo' of *Seguro azar* put speech to film (p. 69) captivated Salinas so consistently that his description in 1933 of 'the industrial objects manufactured by man' as 'the expression of an involuntary beauty' was echoed by his statement in an essay published after his death that 'The great modern city is an incomparable compendium of poetic feasts for the eyes.'[3] Machines and gadgets—the 'useless and

---

* The tape-worm sang of the terror of the wheel.
† Wheels, only wheels, wheels. A confused and frenzied flood.
‡ The archangel of Sunday.
§ American machinery, agile acrobats.
‖ From his shoulders hangs the quiver full of alphabets: the luminous letters he will nail—what advertisement of joy!—in the sky.
  Squadrons of one hundred volts spear the reflections.

11   Lorca, Salinas and Alberti in 1927

costly toys' of twentieth-century civilization—transformed his poetic universe into what one of his favourite English poets, Francis Thompson, called a 'box of toys':[1] a world of adventure fashioned with much humour and imagination and peopled by graceful new beings procreated in Salinas's mind. Just as the radiator is magically and mock-heroically transformed in 'Radiador y fogata' of *Fábula y signo* into a

> Nueva
> criatura, deliciosa
> hija del agua, sirena
> callada de los inviernos,* (p. 106)

so does the electric light bulb change into a princess in '35 bujías' of *Seguro azar*, where Salinas, reversing Gómez de la Serna's simile that 'That woman was in the light of day like an electric bulb lit in full sunlight',[2] locks her in a crystal castle and surrounds her with an imposingly epic guard of

> —cien mil lanzas—los rayos
> —cien mil rayos—del sol.† (p. 71)

The excitement Salinas found in things that generally thrill and amuse children was due to his ingenuous ability to marvel and admire, which Guillén has called 'that faculty of the child-poet'.[3] Salinas's passage through life was one of constant elation and continually generated wonder; his love of speed and movement explains why in 'Font-Romeu, noche de baile' of *Fábula y signo* the gaily dancing 'sílfides de aluminio y celuloide' have 'anuncios / de automóviles nuevos en la frente'‡ (p. 106). At the beginning of 'Navacerrada, abril' 'Los dos solos' summarizes the intimate companionship not of a man and woman but of a man and his car; savouring for a moment the landscape which the two have conquered, Salinas has only to press the starter to surge into yet another exhilarating adventure in which man and machine are as close and harmonious as man and wife:

---

* New creature, delicious daughter of the water, silent siren of the winters.
† one hundred thousand lances—the rays—one hundred thousand rays—of the sun.
‡ sylphs of aluminium and celluloide; advertisements of new cars on their brows.

> Alma mía en la tuya
> mecánica; mi fuerza,
> bien medida la tuya,
> justa: doce caballos.* (p. 57)

The R.A.C. sign which in 'Aviso' of *Seguro azar* suddenly warns him to brake hard did not blunt the excitement he felt on the open road or in a busy street, where, as Alberti has recorded, 'In his Fiat A–4.014, Pedro Salinas, every morning, eagerly seeks death, accompanied by insults, threats, angry glares of police and pedestrians.'[1] One of the things Salinas particularly remembered about his visit to Paul Valéry was the drive through Paris,[2] as entrancing and thrilling as the car ride through Seville which he described in a striking passage of *Víspera del gozo*. His statement that 'The street, motionless, but with the movement of the car possessed of a dizzy, theatrical activity, began to display forms, lines, motley and changing spaces'[3] captured the dizzy, kaleidoscopic confusion of a rapid journey as dramatically as Alberti's compact lines in the second section of 'Romeo y Julieta' of *Cal y canto*:

> *Las aceras*
> *saltando atrás, en fila, comprimiendo,*
>
> *tumulto y colorín, multiplicadas,*
> *árboles, transeúntes, vidrieras,*
> *en una doble fuga de fachadas.*† (p. 215)

In a car Salinas entrusted himself to the *azar*, the chance, on which he based his poetic creed. Rebelling against a sterile humdrum existence he censured as 'Years and years of habit',[4] he sought like Gómez de la Serna new insights into commonplace objects and routine events. His descriptions of sand in *Presagios* as a 'novia versátil y clara' (p. 25) and of a leaf in *Seguro azar* as the 'Rubia, desheredada, morganática / esposa del gorrión'‡ (p. 57) show that he was matching his forays into his fantasy with adven-

---

* My soul in your mechanical soul; my energy in your precise and well-measured energy: twelve horse-power.

† Multiplied, the pavements go leaping back, in a line, compressing—all tumult and bright colours—trees, pedestrians, panes of glass in a double flight of façades.

‡ bright, versatile sweetheart; Blonde, disinherited, morganatic wife of the sparrow.

tures of language. Determined to observe his principle that 'The poet has as his object the creation of a new reality within the old reality',[1] Salinas inflated things with a grandiloquence that at times ennobles and enhances his subject and at others appears gratingly contrived. In *La voz a ti debida* his striking visions of his *amada* as an 'amazona en la centella' (p. 144) and of yeses as 'relámpagos / de plumas de cigüeña'* (p. 149) were the products of a rich and agile imagination which twisted itself into uncomfortable and inelegant shapes when he wrote in *Seguro azar* that 'Ventanas dobles... / ...guillotinan tentaciones'† (p. 84) and that

> Escribe blanca espuma
> en el cantil su acróstico.‡   (p. 61)

Salinas's precious description of cars in *El desnudo impecable* as 'crystal-covered refuges of rapid effusions, on wheels'[2] is a rhetorical extravaganza paralleled in his poetry by phrases as inflated as 'encanto esdrújulo' (p. 109) and 'Cifras elíseas, letras / vestidas de paraíso'§ (p. 123). With language Salinas indulged in 'the most prudent and delicious flirting', to use a phrase from *Víspera del gozo*,[3] for what rescued his diction from hollow bombast was the deft lifeline of humour and lightheartedness. That he loved toying with words is clear from the many paradoxes and conceits in his work, some of which I mentioned in chapter 1; statements like 'te vas, pero te acercas' of *Razón de amor* (p. 249) and '¡Cuánto tiempo te he mirado / sin mirarte a ti...'‖ of *Presagios* (p. 20) were symptoms of Salinas's attitude to his *amada* and displays of the ingenuity which he prized in poetry after 'authenticity' and 'beauty'.[4] His conceits and paradoxes were the product of humour and mental agility, as Alonso Quesada neatly pointed out:

> Salinas, desde el fondo de su ingenio
> hace un guiño silencioso con el ánimo.¶[5]

---

* rider mounted on the star; lightning flashes of storks' feathers.
† Double windows guillotine temptations.
‡ White spray writes its acrostic on the cliff.
§ proparoxytone delight; Elysian numbers, letters decked in paradise.
‖ you go, but you draw near; How long have I looked at you, without looking at you!
¶ Salinas, from the depths of his ingenuity, winks silently with his mind.

Behind the visiting card that in his play *El director* introduced 'Miss Cleopatra de Lenclos. Speciality: urgent seductions'[1] was the wink of a man classified by Guillén as a 'Master of Delights' enjoying toys, gadgets, desserts, museums and shop windows.[2] The 'Pasajero en museo' who appeared in *Todo más claro* was still looking around him as avidly and attentively as the 'Pasajero apresurado' who in *Seguro azar* glimpsed in a shop window a calf sheathed in a silk stocking (pp. 365–70, 52–3). That Salinas called one of his early and uncollected poems 'Voz de jugar' is significant and not surprising,[3] for there is in his poetry a levity and a festive spirit which animated the foxtrots danced in 'Font-Romeu, noche de baile' and 'The great game of crepuscular roulette' played in *Víspera del gozo*.[4] The agile lights flashing in 'Placer, a las once' signal an acrobatic gaiety also radiated by the woman in 'El teléfono' of *Fábula y signo* (pp. 118–19), who, balancing pole in hand on the telegraph wire, proves Giménez Caballero's contention that the 'new literature' is 'Procircus'.

These gay movements of mind and lithe tricks of language enabled Salinas in *Presagios* to imagine the poplar and the water in which it is reflected as lovers who gaze at each other all day long but who quarrel angrily when the autumn winds disturb their peace (pp. 37–8). By presenting the agitated branches and ruffled water as a lovers' tiff, Salinas was not only visualizing water and a tree in a playfully new way but imparting a false sense of drama to what is nothing more than a minor natural event. The headline of 'Está / más hermosa cada día' proclaimed by the newspapers 'en ediciones / especiales'* in 'La otra' of *Fábula y signo* (p. 96) is a piece of humour as playful as Joyce's invention in *Ulysses* of the 'Stop press edition. Result of the rocking-horse races. Sea serpent in the royal canal. Safe arrival of Antichrist.'[5] And although Salinas censured telegrams as 'offences...against the nobility of language in the name of economy of time',[6] he saw in their concision possibilities of humour, which in 'Los adioses' of *Fábula y signo* he exploited more guardedly than Alberti:

* She is more beautiful each day; in special editions.

> Poner telegramas:
> 'Imposible viaje. Surgió adiós imprevisto.'*   (p. 122)

The feigned gravity of such quaint telegrams masks a humour apparent in *Presagios* in his poem to the ship 'Manuela Pla' and to her owner Doña Manuela, whose devout love of God he punctured with his impish reference to her love of a four per cent return on her investments (pp. 36–7). His seemingly earnest recital in *La voz a ti debida* of what he would relinquish if his *amada* were to call to him contains such incongruous details that he amuses rather than convinces the reader of his readiness to make a great sacrifice:

> Lo dejaría todo,
> todo lo tiraría:
> los precios, los catálogos,
> el azul del océano en los mapas,
> los días y sus noches,
> los telegramas viejos
> y un amor.†   (pp. 134–5)

Salinas's poetry suggests that, although the infant must grow into an adult, he need not leave behind the child's gift of wonder and innocence; he can still eagerly await his dessert, try out a toy or play with a child. There is something warm and revealing in Aleixandre's description of Salinas writing poetry and playing with his grandchildren at the same time;[1] the homely vision of stars in *Presagios* as 'niñas bien bañadas'‡ (p. 24) shows that Salinas infused into his poetry an affection for children which allowed him to see the world through the eyes of the baby girl who in *Presagios* chirps 'Tatá, dadá' to her father, mother, food, the mountain and the sea not because, as one critic has claimed, Salinas was influenced by Dada,[2] but because the world appears to her as a jumble of shapes (pp. 17–18).

Freud suggested that 'every child at play behaves like an imaginative writer, in that he creates a world of his own'.[3] Had Freud

---

* Send telegrams: 'Journey impossible. Unforeseen goodbye cropped up.'
† I would leave it all, I would throw it all away: prices, catalogues, the blue of the ocean on maps, the days and their nights, old telegrams and a love.
‡ well bathed little girls.

read an anthology of Spanish poetry and prose of the 1920s, he might have concluded that many imaginative writers behave like children at play. Some, infected by what Espina acutely diagnosed as

> Este afán nuevo, fiebre moderna
> De explorar fuera lo que no hay dentro...,*[1]

strained to conceal their lack of self-control, distinctive personality and vigorously individual imagination in a series of extravagant poses and still-born verbal arabesques. Others, gifted with authentic eloquence and fantasy, responded temporarily without losing their identities or freezing into an artificial pose to the fashions of a decade still remembered with nostalgia across the débris of two world wars and the Depression. *Sobre los ángeles, Poeta en Nueva York* and the growing political turbulence of the 1930s marked the end in Spain of the light-hearted games and audacious experiments of the 1920s. I hope these pages have shown that they were fun while they lasted.

* This new longing, this modern fever of exploring without what does not exist within.

IN PRAISE OF CREATION

Of Life immense in passion, pulse, and power
Cheerful, for freest action form'd under the laws divine...

Walt Whitman, *Leaves of Grass*

The publication of Guillén's *Cántico* in 1928 coincided with the emotional and spiritual crises which Alberti and Lorca were to transpose into the anguished poetry of *Sobre los ángeles* and *Poeta en Nueva York*; while the stresses of despair intensified their disillusion with life and with people, Guillén solidified into a creed the exuberance which all three had recorded in the writings I looked at in the preceding chapter. In the year when Alberti lamented his disintegration in poems that, despite the impotence he mourned, testified to a vital imagination, Guillén sang full-throatedly his virile enjoyment of the normal world around him, which in his eyes has a wholeness and a simple grace matched by the limpid elegance of his poetic tributes to it. Although some lines of his early, uncollected pieces reappeared in *Cántico*, Guillén had disciplined his style, sharpened his censor's pen and expunged his immature but poetically useful experiments in his single-minded pursuit of the 'Demoniac perfection'[1] which made *Cántico* into a mature, ecstatic yet studiously measured exaltation of what he neatly called in his crisp commentary on *Cántico*, *El argumento de la obra*, 'the extraordinary phenomenon of normality'.[2]

In *Cántico* Guillén was immune from the tensions and torments which disturbed Alberti, Cernuda and Lorca; his eyes were questing and clear; his reason was unclouded; his voice was firm; his pleasures were simple. But although his voice was distinctively and vigorously personal and his emotional stance unmistakable, he has gone through life with a ghost at his shoulder and a cross on his back: the ghost is Paul Valéry; the cross is the witless charge of coldness. Those critics who have accused him of being a 'cerebral' poet, as if it were wrong of a poet to have and use a brain, have not seen that he set out to demonstrate in his poetry the compatibility of emotional ebullience and intellectual discipline; the union of 'Thought and feeling' he advanced in 1961 as a feature of *Cántico* is the same equation he established forty years earlier when in his essay on Anatole France he wrote of 'Technical efficiency: human efficiency.'[1]

Guillén's enthusiasm for Valéry, which he has made no attempt to conceal, has exposed him to the assaults of critics like A. Monterde, whose statement that 'Valéry is the master *par excellence* of Guillén'[2] signals the readiness he shares with others to interpret interest as influence. When Guillén confessed that he 'read and re-read' *Charmes*,[3] he was merely confirming a curiosity obvious in his translation of Valéry's 'Les grenades' in 1927 and 'Le cimetière marin' in 1929.[4] But his firm reasons for translating them prove that his was not an idle choice nor an indiscriminate interest, for they contained ideas and feelings which he had already expressed in his work. He was attracted to 'Le cimetière marin' because 'The poem is...a hymn to life, to the triumph of the momentary'.[5] He translated 'Les grenades' because his enthusiasm for the pomegranate's 'secret architecture' conformed to his passion for precision and symmetry, just as his eager delight in the physical world in all its essential beauty and simplicity led him to adjust the line 'La vie est vaste, étant ivre d'absence' to 'Ebria de esencia al fin, la vida es vasta.'* And the discovery in Guillén's rendering of 'Le cimetière marin' of words so dear to him as *cima, techo* (stanza 3), *luz* (stanza 7) and *el don de vida* (stanza 15) is to sense the overlap of *Cántico* onto Valéry rather than the intrusion of Valéry into Guillén. The careful structure of their poems and the flimsy similarity between such titles of *Cántico* and *Charmes* as 'Interior', 'Intérieur', 'El durmiente' and 'La dormeuse', in no way conceal the fundamental differences of aim and attitude dividing the two poets; while Valéry could not understand why people 'do not try to go as deeply as possible into themselves',[6] Guillén's refusal to look inside himself plotted a

---

* Life is vast, being drunk with absence; Drunk with essence at the end, life is vast.

trajectory away from introspection towards what he called in 'Noche de luna' an '¡Ascensión a lo blanco!'* (p. 34).

Guillén's disarming remark in 'Cima de la delicia' that '¡Ya sólo sé cantar!'† (p. 21) invites us to listen to the melodious, enthusiastic but controlled hymn to life in no way chilled or paralysed by his use of words like *geometría, recta, equilibrio* and *sumando*, which signal a mathematical precision some critics cannot reconcile with genuine emotion. So intent was he to demonstrate the existence in Spain of 'pure poetry' that Monterde, clearly deluded by Guillén's exact scales of form and language, has affirmed that the poetry of *Cántico* is 'poetry for the intelligence, never for the heart'.[1] When Guillén decided to write 'complex poetry', he also opted in a revealing phrase that emphasizes the normality of his experiences for 'the poem with poetry and other human things'.[2] Lorca had no difficulty in recognizing the warmth of 'human things' in his friend's poetry; because he sensed the emotional charge behind carefully constructed poems and precisely chosen words, he protested indignantly about 'that excessive cerebralism they accuse you of', described Guillén's *romances* as 'exact and beautiful' and compared Guillén's poetry with the music of Bach, where, he said, emotion is 'wrapped up in perfect mathematics'.[3] Lorca realized that poetry can appeal at the same time to the heart and the head, which in Guillén co-operate to make of his poems the 'exactas delicias' he admires in life (p. 33). In *Cántico* Guillén used his vast expertise as a poet to voice those feelings he experienced as a normal man.

That Guillén wrote the poems of *Cántico* by applying his technical skills to his intensely human experiences is shown by his advocacy in two precise lines of 'El otoño: isla' of

> Estilo en la dicha,
> Sapiencia en el pasmo...‡ (p. 50)

His conjunction of technique and emotion, of mental discipline and emotional fervour, explains why in his poems he demands

---

* Ascent to the white spaces.
† Now all I know is how to sing!
‡ Style in joy, wisdom in rapture.

our attention with exclamation marks as often as he offers us precise alternatives with colons, why he expressed his delight with *prodigio, delicia* and *plenitud* as often as he did so with *exacto, recta, línea* and *terso*. His description of the city in 'Ciudad de los estíos' as 'Loca de geometría'* (p. 33) is not an absurd paradox but a succinctly enthusiastic tribute to the exactitude he admired so passionately. The angel which in 'La florida' 'poda / Sin cesar la frondosidad!'† (p. 83) constantly pruned Guillén's language, thoughts and feelings and kept the world as sparse and stark as the tree in 'Rama del otoño', the branches of which are stripped by the autumn wind. What Guillén achieved by his mental discipline the wind achieved by its gusts: a 'Mundo terso, mente monda'‡ (p. 49), a union, harmonious in sound and spirit, of the skeletal, unadorned world and the poet's bare, uncluttered mind, whose simple thoughts and impressions he summarized economically in a series of pithy alliterative phrases as euphoniously charged with sense as 'Raptos de bruscas rachas' (p. 42), 'choques en chispas' (p. 94), '¡ Frescor hacia forma !' (p. 25) and 'rigor de rayas'§ (p. 28).

This *rigor de rayas* was no painful discipline, for it imposed on his pen and on his eyes the pleasant duty of seeing and recording the world as a compact whole. The symmetrical permutations of the straight line created a balance, revered with a capital letter in 'El prólogo', which Guillén found perfectly displayed in the city, which is not, like Salinas's vision of New York, a 'city of implacable geometry', but 'the exaltation of human energy'.[1] The city which Guillén hymned in the fluid, lively heptasyllables of 'Ciudad de los estíos' is in the fourth stanza 'elemental' and in the last line 'esencial' because it reveals itself as openly before his eyes as the sunbeams to which it clings to form a neat mesh of warmth and geometric harmony. In this city animated by the summer sun, light and line co-operate to chart a simple map which Guillén avidly studies with growing wonder, conveyed in his excited alliterations and repetition of 'corre', that his eyes can with so little effort travel up and down so many straight channels:

* Mad with geometry. † ceaselessly prunes the foliage.
‡ Lustrous world, clean mind.
§ Abductions of violent gusts; collisions in sparks; Freshness towards form !; rigour of lines.

III Guillén, *c.* 1965

Resbala en su riel
La recta: corre, corre,
Corre a su conclusión.

¡ Ay, la ciudad está
Loca de geometría,
Oh, muy elemental !
. . . .
Por una red de rumbos,
Clarísimos de tarde,
Van exactas delicias.

Y a los rayos del sol,
Evidentes, se ciñe
La ciudad esencial.*   (p. 33)

In 'Capital del invierno' the 'essential city' of summer with its
interplay of street and sun has given way to the 'extreme city' of
winter, where people can hug the tranquil warmth of the '¡ Chime-
neas de calma!'† (p. 81), while outside the world is stripped to
elemental nakedness at the command of the god who disposes that
what grows in the spring and summer must die in the autumn and
winter. Just as the wind in 'Rama del otoño' cleaned the branches
of dead leaves and exposed the sturdy framework of the 'nuevas
nervaduras'‡ (p. 49), so does the cold of winter return the world
to its basic simplicity, allowing the treeless avenues to reveal once
more in all its starkness the frame of the new life that will be
reawakened in the spring:

Vuelven las avenidas a su esquema.
Vivaces nervaduras
De lo interior asumen las figuras
De una ciudad extrema.
. . . .
El dios más inminente necesita
Simple otra vez el mundo.

* The straight line slides on its track: it runs, runs, runs to its conclusion.
  Oh, the city, most elemental, is mad with geometry !
  Exact delights travel through a network of paths, brilliant in the afternoon light.
  And the essential city clings to the sharply visible sunbeams.
† Fireplaces of peace !   ‡ new veins.

> Lo elemental afronta a lo profundo.
> El Invierno los cita.* (p. 81)

That Guillén enjoyed finding in the world around him a simplified, symmetrical design and a panoramic richness normally visible from a tall building or an aeroplane is apparent from a letter he wrote to Lorca in December 1926, where he said that 'The balconies open onto the whole city, and onto the mountains. And what better position for living than that of a panorama!'[1] The vantage point which he adopted in 'Panorama' enabled him to look down on the pedestrians who, as tiny as ants, move purposefully within the network of streets which in Guillén's eyes compose 'La claridad del sistema'† (p. 66), something he elevated to an ideal and a creed. What he admired in 'Desnudo' was not the nakedness of the body, whose sex he does not disclose till the last stanza, but the vigour and crispness with which its sharp lines and distinct contours combat confusion. Less important than the sex of the nude, sterilized like a painting or sculpture by his clinical references to 'Desnudo', 'forma', 'carne' and 'cuerpo femenino', is its precise shape and volume, whose stillness he conveyed in the measured interplay of hendecasyllables and heptasyllables:

> Claridad aguzada entre perfiles,
> De tan puros tranquilos,
> Que cortan y aniquilan con sus filos
> Las confusiones viles.‡ (p. 79)

Guillén's search for cleanly defined outlines was jeopardized only by accidents or atmospheric conditions alien to the ordered, sunny world of *Cántico*. The yells and shrieks uttered by space in 'La tormenta' forecast its 'límites perdidos' (p. 18), the disruption of its symmetry; the tree which in 'Rama del otoño' and 'Capital del invierno' juts out starkly melts into the grey confusion which in 'Niebla' clouds and dislocates everything:

---

* The avenues return to their plan. Lively veins from within assume the forms of an extreme city.
  The most imminent god needs the world to be simple again. The elemental confronts the profound. The Winter convenes them.
† The clarity of the system.
‡ Profiles, still and so pure, that sharpen the clarity and cut and destroy with their keen edges all base confusion.

¡ Oh masa de figuras sin memoria,
Oh torpe caos !: todo se es remoto.
Lo gris relaja el árbol, ya inexacto.*　　　(p. 41)

And the sudden gyrations which whirl Guillén in 'Tránsito' in-
duce in him a vertigo which, as destructive as the storm and the
mist, sinks all clean lines into the horror of a 'nulo perfil';
frightened by this haphazard blur, he uttered in short, stabbing
lines a desperate, anguished question and a frenzied exclamation:

¿ Tan fácil un fin
De veras final?
¡ Oh nulo perfil,
Croquis del azar !

¡ Horror !†　　　(p. 27)

Guillén's horror at the brief victory of chance and chaos deepens
his delight in a world simply deployed and clearly signposted. The
birds and trees which abound in *Cántico* point upwards to the
unlimited expanse of the heavens, perpetually present in *cenit,
cima, altura, altitud* and *elevación*, and dominated by the sun, which,
'rectilíneo' at noon (p. 88), represents the peak of creation. The
streets of the city and the horizon in the distance follow crisp
straight lines which join with the circle in 'Meseta' to compose
the graceful harmony of 'Horizontes en círculo'‡ (p. 91) situating
Guillén at the centre of an enfolding circle of the universe. The
ecstatic battle-cry with which he ended 'Playa'—'¡ Acorde, cierre,
círculo !'§ (p. 88)—hymned his delight in the circle, whose mystery aroused in him not scientific curiosity but an excited wonder
that made him utter in 'Perfección del círculo' a breathless litany
in which his thoughts and lips are dominated by a few words and
cognate sounds:

Misterio perfecto,
Perfección del círculo,

---

* O mass of figures without memory, o clumsy chaos ! Everything is remote
from everything else. The grey relaxes the tree, now blurred.
† Can a truly final finale be so easy? O null outline, o sketch of chance ! O horror !
‡ Horizons in a circle.　　　　　§ Close in on me, harmony, circle !

> Círculo del circo
> Secreto del cielo.* (p. 13)

As his mind circled giddily within the circus of creation, his lips droned a tribute to something he could not see but felt he could hear; his statement in 1962 that the verb *zumbar* made him think of 'a circle that produces a kind of buzzing'[1] explains his description of the 'celeste Círculo' in 'Gran silencio' as 'invisible y zumbón'† (p. 40).

The droning Guillén heard all around him sang reassuringly of the perpetual harmony of creation, just as the hoops of the children in 'Festividad' create ripples as endless as the waves which reproduce in miniature the circular perfection of the world:

> Y los aros de los niños
> Fatalmente multiplican
> Ondas de gracia sobrante,
> Para dioses todavía.‡ (p. 93)

The children playing with their hoops and the girl who in 'El manantial' emerges from the water revealing

> Blancuras en curva
> Triunfalmente una...§ (p. 25)

not only act with the 'Instinct, elemental impulse' which Guillén exalted in *Cántico*,[2] but demonstrate with their toys and their form the unity of the universe; the girl displaying her 'triumphally single curve' is at one with the sea, whose 'Incorruptibles curvas' (p. 28) Guillén celebrated in many poems.

The unity which Guillén described in 'Presagios' as 'La unidad invasora y absoluta'‖ (p. 36) guarantees both the intactness of the sea and the joining of breeze with breeze in a chain of natural activity:

> ¡ Trabazón de brisas
> Entre cielo y álamo !¶ (p. 51)

Guillén based his mathematical calculations on such a sure principle that there was no room for error; unlike Alberti, who sig-

---

* Perfect mystery, the perfection of the circle, the circle of the secret circus of heaven.   † celestial Circle; invisible and jocose.
‡ And the hoops of the children inevitably multiply waves of surplus beauty which gods can still use.   § Whiteness in a triumphally single curve.
‖ Invading, absolute unity.   ¶ Union of breezes between sky and poplar !

nalled his perplexity and malaise by making in *Sobre los ángeles* such haphazard calculations as '4 y 4 son 18' (p. 283), Guillén used a perpetually optimistic plus sign to add no matter how many elements into a round figure. The leaves he added up in 'Bosque y bosque' are noughts, which, he quickly pointed out, are not ciphers of the void which frightened Alberti and Cernuda but rings of infinite possibilities with which he will forge on high another forest as dense and tightly woven as the trees on earth:

> Los sumandos frondosos de la tarde,
> ¡ Prolija claridad: uno más uno !,
> Son en la suma de la noche ceros.
> No los ceros solemnes de la nada:
> Anillos para manos de poetas
> Que alzarán un gran bosque sobre el bosque... * (p. 39)

Because of his faith that 'Everything joins with everything in perpetual creation',[1] Guillén paid tribute in 'La florida' to the bonds that tie the world into an interlaced but vibrating web:

> (Alrededor, ¡ haz de vivaces
> Vínculos !, vibran los enlaces
> En las nervaduras del orbe,
> Tan envolventes. ¡ Cuántos nudos
> Activos, aún más agudos
> Dentro de quien tanto se absorbe !)† (p. 83)

This stanza is as compact and interlocking as the universe which, pulsating with the movements expressed in 'vibran', 'vivaces', 'vibran' and 'Activos', is rounded and contained by the 'Vínculos', 'enlaces' and 'nudos' as completely and lovingly as the embraces which in the ecstatically staccato climax of 'Los amantes' melt the two lovers into a rapture where the two bodies matter less than the powerful love which joined them:

* The leafy summands of the evening—painstaking clarity, one plus one !—are noughts in the sum of the night. Not the solemn noughts of nothingness, but rings for the hands of poets who will raise a great forest over the forest.
† All around—a bundle of live links !—the bonds, so enfolding, vibrate in the veins of the globe. What a wealth of active knots, even tighter within him who submits so readily !

> Sólo, Amor, tú mismo,
> Tumba. Nada, nadie,
> Tumba. Nada, nadie.
> Pero...—¿Tú conmigo?*　　　　　　　　　　(p. 23)

Cántico is a work of love: love of living, love of loving, love of 'essential company'.[1] This love is a firm base on which Guillén built his hymn, which grew through the years into an ever more solid and unified tribute. His admiration of the 'rigid construction' of Baudelaire's *Les fleurs du mal* and Whitman's *Leaves of Grass*,[2] his comments that in Góngora 'every verse, every phrase, every stanza is an architectonic composition' and that St John of the Cross's 'poem is erected like the most subtle work of architecture',[3] justify and illustrate the importance he attached to the architectural precision with which he tried to make of *Cántico* not 'a series of texts mixed capriciously' but 'an organic unity, like a building'.[4] Whether *Cántico* contained in its successive editions 75, 125, 270 or 334 poems, Guillén organized with care his solid faith in life, in nature and in the foolproof cycle that guaranteed his recovery at dawn of everything he lost at night:

> Todo lo que perdí
> Volverá con las aves.
>
> Sí, con las avecillas
> Que en coro de alborada
> Pían y pían, pían
> Sin designio de gracia.†　　　　　　　　　(p. 11)

This dawn chorus celebrates with the arrival of yet another day Guillén's love of light which, demonstrated by the recurrence of *claridad, luz, sol, arrebol* and *tornasol*, was so strong that he could never echo Salinas's complaint in *La voz a ti debida* about 'el gran error del día' (p. 163). As he explained in *El argumento de la obra*, the light which illuminates the world every morning 'is reborn in the eyes and consciousness of a man stirred by a deep feeling of

---

* Only you yourself, Love, like a tomb. Nothing, no-one, a tomb. Nothing, no-one, but...You with me?

† Everything I lost will return with the birds.
　　Yes, with the little birds which in a dawn chorus chirp and chirp, chirp with no plan of beauty.

wonder'.[1] His inexhaustible reserves of wonder transformed into prodigies those simple things of life that most people take for granted. Guillén's enthusiastic but reverential delight in the world as it is contrasts with Valéry's eagerness to extract from life fuel for intellectual exercise. While Guillén was happy to accept reality as it is, Valéry aimed to mould it to his own liking, as he stated in 'Aurore' of *Charmes*:

> Tout m'est pulpe, tout amande.
> Tout calice me demande
> Que j'attende pour son fruit.[*2]

So happy was Guillén with reality as he perceived it through his senses that he scorned the 'empty babble' of the surrealists on the one hand[3] and could see no reason on the other, as he stated in a letter to Lorca written in October 1926, for the *creacionistas*' desire to replace creation with an artificial world of images and melodies: 'Marvellous creation! And not *creacionismo*! (Why, for heaven's sake? What for?)'[4] Like Góngora, whom he classified as 'an enthusiast of the material world' whose 'whole soul is concentrated in his five senses', Guillén undertook in life and recorded in *Cántico* an eager but controlled adventure of the senses, which enabled him, to quote his words on Gabriel Miró, to take 'possession of this immediate world'.[5]

This immediate world is full of simple phenomena which, like 'La noche, la calle, los astros' of one title and 'El campo, la ciudad, el cielo' of another, delighted him, corroborated his existence and gave him a point of reference in the universe. When he wrote in 'Presagios' that 'nuestras almas invisibles / Conquistan su presencia entre las cosas'[†] (p. 36), he postulated as a canon the longing he expressed in 'Hacia el sueño, hasta el sueño' not to exist merely in the spirit but to live with the body: '¡No ser, estar: estar profundamente!'[‡] (p. 53). His determination to use and enjoy the powers given him by his senses made him admire, like a child playing on a beach, the 'Adorables arenas' (p. 34) and 'Conchas

---

* Everything is pulp, everything is almond to me. Every calyx invites me to await its fruit.
† Our invisible souls conquer their presence amid things.
‡ Not to exist, but to be physically alive, to be profoundly and physically alive.

del Paraíso'* (p. 89) because their texture and shape appeal to his hands and eyes rather than to his imagination; if sand is adorable because it is as it is, he had no need to transform it like Salinas into a coquettish sweetheart blown about by the wind. Nor does the naked woman lying prostrate in 'Desnudo' have to do anything other than fulfil her destiny of 'absoluto Presente' and represent for Guillén the fullness of matter; whether tall or short, fat or thin, ugly or beautiful, she is present in this room as a living example of physical volume, clear to the eye and firm to the hand. Guillén, seeking no sensual thrill, is seeing and admiring in this timeless episode a form that is totally committed here and now to the physical world:

> Desnuda está la carne. Su evidencia
>   Se resuelve en reposo.
> Monotonía justa: prodigioso
>   Colmo de la presencia.
>
> ¡ Plenitud inmediata, sin ambiente,
>   Del cuerpo femenino !
> Ningún primor: ni voz ni flor. ¿ Destino?
>   ¡ Oh absoluto Presente !†   (p. 79)

The stillness of 'Desnudo', where the poet and the woman are both suspended in time, prompted Guillén to write that 'Cántico tries to attend to this immediate present when nothing happens.'[1] 'Beato sillón' is a hymn to inactivity in which he reveres the chair because it allows him to be still, close his eyes—something he rarely does willingly—and yet still know that the world is perfectly made. In this interlude of repose, where Guillén expressed his confidence and well-being in simple, tranquil, self-satisfied statements, the universe is lifted onto a peaceful high-tide with no swell or backwash, a peak moment whose perfection is not menaced:

---

* Adorable grains of sand; shells of Paradise.
† The flesh is bare. The proof that it is there resolves itself into repose. Precise monotony: the prodigious ripeness of existence.
  Immediate fullness, without atmosphere, of the female body ! No touch of beauty: no voice or flower. Its destiny? O absolute Present !

No pasa
Nada. Los ojos no ven:
Saben. El mundo está bien
Hecho: el instante lo exalta
A marea, de tan alta,
De tan alta, sin vaivén.* (p. 68)

Animated by the crisp '¡Fuerza de Festividad!'† he experienced in 'La florida' (p. 94), Guillén clung tenaciously to the present. But his determination to enjoy to the full the 'Redondo Ahora'‡ (p. 72), which inspired the abundant present tenses in *Cántico*, did not blind him to its brevity. Guillén refused to be inhibited by his awareness of the 'velocísimo Ahora'§ (p. 69) or by the presence beneath the flesh of the patient skull. Although he realized that one day he will be dead, in *Cántico* he is alive and able to fill his lungs with the air which transformed the rhythm of *Cántico* into a pulsating 'rhythm of breathing'.[1] When the wind blows in 'Meseta', the whole universe seems to vibrate as vigorously as Guillén, who, as he told Lorca in a letter of February 1927, is 'penetrated more and more acutely by what I call atmospheric happiness: it comes to us in the air, and in the light of the air'.[2] Invigorated by this atmospheric joy, he transferred to the horse his own '¡Prisa de vivir más!'‖ (p. 17); in 'El otoño: isla' he calls in short lines quick with impatience for his horse to be saddled because he is confident that the road ahead of him presents no obstacles:

—¡Pronto, pronto, ensilla
Mi mejor caballo!
¡El camino es ancho
Para mi porfía!¶ (p. 51)

In 'Festividad' the horses themselves, whose gallop reverberates in the simple repetition, are the targets rather than the pursuers of joy:

Caballos corren, caballos
Perseguidos por las dichas.** (p. 93)

---

* Nothing happens. The eyes do not see: they know. The world is well made: the moment exalts it to a high tide, so high, so high, with no ebb and flow.
† Force of Festivity! ‡ Round Now.
§ rapid Now. ‖ Haste to live more!
¶ Hurry, hurry, saddle my best horse! The road is wide for my stubborn pursuit!
** Horses run, horses pursued by happiness.

Even the statue of the horsemen in 'Estatua ecuestre', although necessarily immobile, aims 'A la maravilla fiel'* (p. 65) as hopefully as the eager lovers who in 'Festividad' seek some miracle:

> Los enamorados buscan,
> Buscan una maravilla.† (p. 93)

Guillén's search for marvels was satisfied every time he looked around him. His frequent use of *evidencia, claridad, mirada, transparente, panorama* and *visible* suggests that the wonders of creation are openly displayed to those who care to look at them. With the last line of 'Interior'—'—Mira. ¿ Ves?...Basta' (p. 59)—Guillén expounded in three simple words his faith that the act of using one's eyes is enough to corroborate the perfection of the world. As if proving the principle he established in a prose piece called 'Aire-aura', published in 1923, that 'Sight exercises the essential power',[1] he began 'La rosa' by saying 'Yo vi la rosa' (p. 73) and started 'El manantial' with the order 'Mirad bien' (p. 25). And a line of 'Niño', 'Total en la mirada' (p. 20), reappeared slightly modified at the end of 'Los aires', whose original version lacked a line as symptomatic of Guillén's sunny creed as 'De los siempre amadores':

> Sí, visible, total
> ¡ Ah ! para la mirada
> De los siempre amadores.‡2 (p. 90)

Unlike Salinas, who preferred according to a title of *Seguro azar* to 'Mirar lo invisible', Guillén enjoyed all that was evident to his own eyes. The window in 'Presencia del aire' is not a barrier to, but a conductor of, creation:

> Este cristal, a fuer
> De fiel, me trasparenta
> La vida cual si fuera
> Su ideal a la vez.§ (p. 19)

Through windows that, he insisted, 'never belong to ivory towers',[3] he saw a world so delightfully stable and unchanging

---

* At the faithful marvel.   † The lovers seek, seek a marvel.
‡ Yes, visible, complete for the eyes of the permanent lovers.
§ This pane of glass, because it is faithful, transmits life transparently to me as if it were at the same time its ideal.

that he used the word 'familiar' not as a sign of weariness but as a term of praise and an expression of relief. The *red de rumbos* Guillén followed led him always to the world he knew; even the night, according to 'La noche, la calle, los astros', is a 'seguro laberinto' (p. 41) too firm and predictable to allow private musing. Only rarely, as in 'Noche del gran estío', does night threaten to bring the chaos whose presence was more obtrusive and whose challenge was more insistent in the 1950 edition of *Cántico*, where poems like 'Estación del Norte', 'Las cuatro calles' and 'Cara a cara' anticipated the disorder which was to erupt in *Clamor*. More often night offered him the security of a 'Robustez envolvente'* (p. 53), which kept out the nightmares and bogey-men tormenting Alberti in *Sobre los ángeles*; in the soothing, stately, balanced hendecasyllables of 'De noche' he assures himself that night will bring him enchantment and not horror or mystery:

> He ahí lo más hondo de la noche.
> No te turbes, que dentro de lo oscuro
> Te rendirás a sus potencias breves
> Bajo un sigilo sin horror ni enigma,
> Hostil al coco, dócil al encanto.† (p. 39)

Even when he could not sleep there was always something to see. The streets he admired by day for their straightness and symmetry now attract him because they shine in an operatic performance:

> ¡Óperas, sí, divinas,
> Que se abren por las noches
> En las estrellas vivas!‡ (p. 55)

Although Guillén's unfailing sense of wonder transformed the routine into the marvellous, ordinary streets at night into 'divine operas', there is nothing grandiloquent about the words he used, which, like Berceo's '"prosaic" language that is not at all prosaic',[1] express his thoughts and emotions with a precision matched by his carefully constructed poems. Loving the straight, un-

---

* enveloping vigour.
† Here is the deepest part of night. Do not be alarmed, for sunk in the darkness you will surrender to its brief powers beneath a secret calm without horror or mystery, hostile to the bogey-man, docile to enchantment.
‡ Yes, divine operas which open at nights in the live stars!

cluttered line as much as the autumn, Guillén saw in the denuded trees and plants an ideal representation of the sparse frame of his own poetry, whose fibres are never concealed beneath ornate words and elaborate images, as he suggested in 'El otoño: isla':

> ¡ Amor a la línea !
> La vid se desnuda
> De una vestidura
> Demasiado rica.* (p. 50)

When Domenchina blindly censured Guillén for using 'fetish' words,[1] he clearly failed to understand that Guillén repeated *perfecto*, *cima*, *total*, *real*, *gracia*, *prodigio*, *evidente* not because he knew no other words but because they expressed with simple eloquence his thoughts and emotions. 'Violently opposed', like San Juan, 'to visions of any kind',[2] he was so delighted with things as they are that he saw no reason to convert them into what they are not. In *Cántico*, to quote his comments on Berceo, 'Direct mention of things is prevalent, with no need for adornment or transformation, because reality felt in this way is itself marvellous... Rugged reality...'[3]

Cernuda recognized that Guillén did not exalt 'Rugged reality' with hollow bombast; in 1926 he paid an eloquently simple tribute to him as 'The Singer' in four lines that seem to refer to 'Beato sillón':

> Del cristal, a un lado, el cielo,
> Al otro, la estancia. ¿Quién
> sueña, en el sillón, su vuelo?
> El Cantor: Jorge Guillén.†[4]

In an essay he wrote in 1948 called 'El crítico, el amigo y el poeta' Cernuda wrote of Guillén in a different tone. While Guillén has remained majestically aloof from the guerrilla warfare which sometimes scars the world of writers, Cernuda felt bound to challenge the critical commonplace that *Perfil del aire* revealed the influence of Guillén. The temperamental difference between the two poets was enormous; Guillén, so far as I know, has not deigned to

---

* Love of the line! The vine is stripped of an over-rich covering.
† On one side of the window, the sky. On the other, the room. Who dreams of his flight in the chair? The Singer: Jorge Guillén.

demolish the myth of his debt to Valéry; Cernuda, on the other hand, touchily went to some pains to establish his independence of Guillén, pointing out that the *Revista de Occidente* published nine poems by him in 1925 and twelve by Guillén in 1924 and 1925, and that *Perfil del aire* appeared in 1927 and *Cántico* in 1928. However, his claim that 'in those years Guillén was a poet who had published almost as little as Cernuda'[1] is disproved by the many poems and prose pieces which Guillén published in *España* and *La Pluma* and which Cernuda chose not to mention. Although Cernuda stressed that Guillén's poetic output before 1920 was too meagre to influence him, it was clearly enough to make a deep impression on him; in 1926 he would not have written the little verse tribute to a poet whose work he did not know, nor would he have dedicated the last poem of *Perfil del aire* to a writer whose poetry he did not admire. When he transformed *Perfil del aire* into *Primeras poesías*, he eliminated not only the immature and contrived phrases and images I mentioned in chapter 2 but also this dedication to Guillén. Although he tried hard to appear objective and impartial in his painstaking reconstruction in 1948 of the genesis of *Perfil del aire*, Cernuda failed to mention these small but significant tributes he paid to Guillén in 1926 and 1927.

Acknowledging some similarities between *Perfil del aire* and *Cántico*, Cernuda attributed them to a common source: Mallarmé. Claiming that Mallarmé influenced Guillén indirectly through Valéry, Cernuda adduced in self-defence some of the lines and motifs of Mallarmé which he said he transposed into his own poetry: the blank sheet of paper, the lamp, the empty room. Nevertheless, the 'desnudas estancias / grises, blancas' which appear in *Perfil del aire* have more in common with the 'cándida estancia' which is found in a poem Guillén published in 1923 than with Mallarmé's 'salle d'ébène' and 'salon vide'.*[2] And the way in which Cernuda and Guillén treated the theme of seclusion at night is more striking than the verbal parallels between Cernuda and Mallarmé. In two lines of 'Noche encendida' which were originally published in 1923,[3] Guillén condensed succinctly the motifs of the lamp, the closed door and the enclosing world:

* bare grey, white rooms; white room; ebony room; empty room.

> ¿ La claridad de la lámpara es breve?
> Cerré las puertas: el mundo me ciñe.*   (p. 42)

Cernuda's confession of debt to Mallarmé's 'la clarté déserte de ma lampe'†¹ could not bypass the affinity between these lines of Guillén and others of *Perfil del aire* in which Cernuda used the three motifs grouped by Guillén:

> ¿ De qué nos sirvió el verano,
> oh ruiseñor en la nieve,
> si sólo un orbe tan breve
> ciñe al soñador en vano?‡

> Surge viva la lámpara
> en la noche desierta
> defendiendo el recinto
> con sus fuerzas ligeras.§

> ¿ He cerrado la puerta?‖²

Although the eager can find a series of similarities between *Perfil del aire* and the antecedents of *Cántico*, two verbal parallels suffice to eliminate Mallarmé as a common source: Cernuda's phrase 'todo espacio desierto'¶³ is akin to Guillén's description of light in 'La luz sobre el monte' as

> densa
> Del espacio sólo espacio,
> Desierto, raso!**   (p. 67)

And Cernuda's treatment of the window-blind is remarkably similar to Guillén's in 'Tornasol'; when Cernuda wrote that

> La ventana
> traza su verde persiana
> en la enramada a la aurora,††⁴

---

* Is the lamp's brightness short-lived? I closed the doors: the world encircles me.
† the deserted brightness of my lamp.
‡ What use was the summer to us, o nightingale in the snow, if only a fleeting globe encircles the dreamer in vain?
§ The lamp erupts in the deserted night defending its precinct with its weak strength.   ‖ Have I closed the door?
¶ all deserted space.   ** dense [light] of space which is only space, deserted, clear.
†† At dawn the window sketches its green blind in the bower.

he used the three elements found in Guillén's lines: greenness, foliage and light:

> Tras de las persianas
> Verdes, el verdor
> De aquella enramada
> Toda tornasol... *
> (p. 15)

Occasionally in *Perfil del aire* Cernuda forgot his misery and fear of *la nada* in order to affirm the fact of being alive; in these brief moments only the peevish and aggressive independence of '¡ Dejadme estar !' reminds us that it is Cernuda and not Guillén who is singing to life:

> Sobre la tierra estoy;
> ¡ Dejadme estar ! Sonrío
> a todo el orbe: extraño
> no le soy, porque vivo.†¹

So immersed is Cernuda in his privacy and sadness that only briefly could a reader feel that he has strayed into the world of *Cántico*. The profound differences of mood and attitude dividing these two poets far outweigh the incidental similarities of phrasing between their poems. The elation of Guillén and the melancholy of Cernuda, in no way bridged by mere verbal parallels, justify Cernuda's insistence that they were 'opposite poets'.²

The similarities of word and topic between *Cántico* and *Ámbito* could never let Aleixandre claim that he and Guillén were contrasting poets. With exclamations like '¡ Vivo, vivo !' (p. 114) and '¡ Te adoro, / luz del día !'‡ (p. 126) he shouted his delight in life, whose solidity, balance and precision he celebrated with words and phrases as familiar to readers of Guillén as 'Una curva graciosa / y dulce' (p. 76); 'aire sólido' (p. 95); 'volumen y forma' (p. 96); 'exacto, verdadero' (p. 107); and

> Evidente, exacta.
> Equilibrio firme
> de presencia.§
> (p. 120)

---

* Behind the green blinds, the green of that bower all light...
† I am on earth; let me be ! I smile at the whole world: I am not a stranger to it, because I am alive.
‡ I live, I live ! I adore you, light of day !
§ A sweet and gracious curve; solid air; volume and form; exact, true; Evident, exact. Firm equilibrium of presence.

Other verbal parallels help to justify Chabás's detection in *Ámbito* of 'the temperamentally elaborated influence of Guillén and Salinas'.[1] Aleixandre echoed Guillén's pleasure in the compactness of the world when in 'Luz' he celebrated the light which frames and encases creation:

> Llegas tú, y el marco acaba,
> cierra, y queda firme el día.* (p. 109)

And the 'Robustez envolvente, noche sólida'† which Guillén admired in 'Hacia el sueño, hasta el sueño' (p. 53) is closely paralleled by Aleixandre's reactions to night in 'Íntegra':

> Siento en mi cuerpo, ceñido,
> un tacto duro: la noche.
> Me envuelve justo en su tino.‡ (p. 113)

But it was in their attitudes to night that the two poets diverged: whereas Guillén saw it as an interlude, a hiatus in which he remained suspended till day gave him back the world he loved, Aleixandre found in the night a new energy which animated his body and ignited his passion:

> ¿ Mi alma sola? Aquí estoy,
> cuerpo, pasión. ¡ Vivo, vivo !
> ¿ Me sientes? La noche.§ (pp. 113–14)

Cántico described a sunlit world; *Ámbito*, despite the tributes to '¡ Mañana dulce... !'‖ (p. 126), is an ecstatic song to the darkness with which Aleixandre came to identify himself so completely that in the last poem, 'Noche final', which closes the frame opened by 'Noche inicial', he said simply: 'La noche en mí. Yo la noche'¶ (p. 144). In *Ámbito* night is an actor as well as a backcloth; it has shape and blood, like a living creature, and senses so stimu-

---

* You come, and the frame ends, closes up, and the day is firm.
† Enfolding robustness, solid night.
‡ I feel a hard pressure encircling my body: night. It enfolds me with its unerring aim.
§ Is my soul alone? Here I am, body, passion. I live, I live ! Do you hear me? Night.
‖ Sweet morning!   ¶ Night in me. I [am] the night.

lated that in 'Agosto' it offers itself to the poet with all the licentiousness of a whore:

> te vendes, ¡ te das !, en sueltos
> ademanes sin frontera
> para los ojos abiertos.*　　　　　　　　　　(p. 83)

With a frank and earthy sensuality Aleixandre visualized a woman's body as the warm soil of southern Spain; the landscape she presented to his fevered mind was shaped like a cross, her legs and arms splayed open inviting and provoking him at the same time:

> Tu cuerpo al fondo tierra me parece:
> un paisaje de sur abierto en aspa.†　　　　　(p. 91)

He seemed so blinkered and hypnotized by woman that he summarized his limited vista in the simple and sensual equation: 'carne: horizonte'‡ (p. 91). Unlike Guillén, whose eyes swept creation, Aleixandre did not want to look further than the woman's body; this was all that his eyes saw and his hands explored. When he plunged his arms into the night in 'Materia', he wanted to find food for his fingers in female flesh:

> He buceado en la noche,
> hundido mis brazos
> —materia de la noche—,
> y te he tropezado entre mis dedos,
> concreta.§　　　　　　　　　　　　　　(p. 137)

Aleixandre's feverishly probing hand, which he presented in 'Posesión' as 'mi mano caliente'‖ (p. 144), demonstrated his reliance on the sense of touch, which for him was 'more decisive' than sight, to use Guillén's phrase. Simply to see and look did not satisfy him: he had to hold, bite, feel, caress, fondle; when he surveyed the naked body in 'Amante', he enjoyed it for the

---

* you sell yourself, you give yourself!, in loose gestures presenting no barrier to open eyes.
† In the background your body looks like land to me: a southern landscape opened in a cross.　　　　　　　　　　‡ flesh: horizon.
§ I have dived into the night, sunk my arms—matter of the night—and I have come across you among my fingers, concrete.
‖ my hot hand.

pleasure it gave to his senses and not, like Guillén's tranquil contemplation of the nude, for what it represented. Guillén's equation of 'Desnudez, hoyuelos'* in 'Cuna, rosas, balcón' (p. 16) was a rapid summary of the first thing he saw on the naked body; in 'Amante' Aleixandre, lingering over the mentionable and over the normally unmentionable, saw the 'real meaning' of this woman composed not of her spiritual gifts but of her physical assets: his standards are simply *cuerpo, pasión*:

> Tu sentido verdadero
> me lo ha dado ya el resto,
> el bonito secreto,
> el graciosillo hoyuelo,
> la linda comisura
> y el mañanero
> desperezo.†　　　　　　　　(pp. 78–9)

The erotic stimulus which Aleixandre received from the night and from a woman's naked body generated a feverishness reflected in his vision of the world as constantly moving. Just as his own 'hot hand' sought and explored a form, so in 'Mar y aurora' do the tongues of light lick and spread over the world like slowly growing tentacles:

> Las largas lenguas palpan
> las pesadas aguas, la tensa
> lámina de metal...
>
> ....
>
> 　Todo el ámbito se recorre, se llena
> de crecientes tentáculos...‡　　　　　(p. 99)

There is nothing controlled or measured in Aleixandre's poetic universe; casting himself according to a prose piece published in 1928 as a 'horseman on a most lusty horse',[1] he accelerated into a blind stampede Guillén's pursuit on horseback of the marvels of life:

---

* Nakedness, dimples.
† Your real meaning has been given to me by the rest: the pretty secret, the gracious dimple, the fetching corners of your mouth, and the morning stretch.
‡ The long tongues touch the heavy waters, the tense sheet of metal...
　The whole ambit is covered, is filled by growing tentacles.

Derrota diáfana
de las sombras: tumulto equino ciego.

¡Qué llanuras! Galopes de lo oscuro,
desbridados.* (p. 135)

In *Ámbito* Aleixandre's imagination began a frenzied gallop which transformed the world into a place of violence in which, as in 'Riña', the moonbeams stab the night:

¡Cuchillos blancos! ¡Qué armas
de listo filo brillante
entierran sus lenguas vivas
en la torpe sombra mate!† (p. 71)

Aleixandre's excited depiction of a turbulent world created an uneasy truce between form and content; as I suggested in chapter 1, his ejaculations, parentheses, jerky phrases and contorted periods strain moulds as regular as the *romance* and heptasyllabic quatrains which Guillén respected with elegant ease. Nor did Aleixandre's feverish imagination let him present creation as simply and directly as Guillén. The opening of 'Las seis'—'Seriá como si...' (p. 130)—suggests that to name things did not satisfy him. What marked *Ámbito* as an immature work was Aleixandre's failure to control his image-making, which in *Pasión de la tierra* was to become hysterical and anarchic. He strained too hard to create images, some of which were so clumsily manufactured that, like his description of daybreak in 'Mar y aurora', they obstruct rather than aid the poem:

Afilados asoman por oriente
sonrosados atrevimientos del día.‡ (p. 99)

Lines as precious as these take us away from the universe which Aleixandre loved so much. There is no doubting his vigour and enthusiasm, even though his perpetual orgasms are tiresomely re-

---

* Diaphanous defeat of the shadows: blind equine tumult.
  What plains! Wild gallops out of the dark.
† White knives! What weapons with a shining edge all ready bury their live tongues in the sluggish, lustreless shadow!
‡ Rosy darings of the day appear sharpened in the east.

petitive; what Aleixandre failed to see when he wrote *Ámbito* was that the uncommon cultured words he used with relish hinder rather than help; he had no love of bare lines or hostility to lush foliage to make him prune from his poems obtrusively rare words like *gajo*, *prieto*, *livor* and *hialino*. Nor was he perceptive enought to recognize the artificiality of phrases as reminiscent of Góngora and Espinosa as 'el manto líquido', 'culto / bebedor de las ondas' (p. 100), 'álgidos despidos' and 'mullida grama'* (p. 102).

Words and phrases such as these were generated by unpredictable bursts of energy which were to convulse Aleixandre's subsequent works and which made *Ámbito* into a tense chant to creation pink with female flesh and succulent with the juices he sucked in 'Posesión'. Although in 'La salida' Guillén celebrated

> el tino
> Gozoso de los músculos
> Súbitos del instinto,† (p. 87)

he never allowed his instinct or his senses to accelerate into a feverish pose or distort his vision of the universe as a compact and marvellously normal sphere encircling a man humbly grateful to be inside it. In *Cántico*, as Guillén himself has pointed out, there is 'No fusion, no magic', only 'the enrichment of him who lives by exalting his life'.[1] What *Cántico* offers is poise, control, harmony and a classic simplicity of form, feeling and diction. It is no accident that in describing Guillén's poetry as precise, intact, sparse, incisive and balanced, one is using some of the words Guillén himself favoured as he tried constantly to achieve the aim expressed in the final dedication to the 1950 edition of *Cántico*: 'to consummate the fullness of being in the faithful fullness of words'. The timeless dignity and measured eloquence of his tribute to the gift of life make *Cántico* transcend the age in which it was written.

---

* the liquid mantle; cultured drinker of the waves; algid farewells; springy sward.
† the joyful accuracy of the sudden muscles of instinct.

4

THE CLOSED DOOR

Ya cerradas son las puertas
De mi vida,
Y la llave es ya perdida.*   Juan del Encina

Proust's belief that 'to be completely within the truth of spiritual life an artist should be alone'[1] was shared and upheld by Altolaguirre, Cernuda, Prados and Salinas, who focused on a narrow area of private thoughts, feelings and experiences insulated from the outside world. That solitude is the pivot of the poet's life and activity was maintained by several Spanish writers in the 1920s and 1930s: Bergamín's theory that 'The poet comes and goes from solitude to solitude' was echoed by Arturo Serrano Plaja, who stated in an essay on 'Arte de soledad y silencio' that 'the greatest sobriety in the poet is solitude, and also his greatest sacrifice'.[2] But Bergamín and Serrano Plaja were advocating nothing new; that 'The poet is the antithesis of society', as Enrique Azcoaga claimed in an essay aptly called 'Sentido antisocial del poeta',[3] had already been affirmed in different ways by, for example, Mallarmé and Gide in France, and Bécquer, Antonio Machado and Juan Ramón Jiménez in Spain. Like his character Manrique in 'El rayo de luna', Bécquer 'loved solitude'.[4] Machado often presented himself in his poetry as a solitary figure, 'a solas con mi sombra y con mi pena'.†[5] And Jiménez's tenacious defence of his belief that 'The real dance is the dance of a person alone with his or her soul'[6] ensured his aloofness, self-sufficiency and poetic virginity, which he strove constantly to keep intact, as he emphasized in *Olvidanzas* (1906–7):

Nada me ha quitado nadie, nada; nada
le he dado yo a nadie, le daré yo a nadie,
si tengo mi cuerpo y mi alma.‡[7]

* The doors of my life are now closed, and the key is now lost.
† alone with my shadow and with my sorrow.
‡ No-one has taken anything from me, anything; I have given nobody and shall give nobody nothing, as long as I have my body and my soul.

143

Machado's suggestion that Jiménez's influence on the younger poets was 'healthy and fertile'[1] supported Jiménez's smug claim in *Dios deseado y deseante* (1949) that 'Yo nada tengo que purgar',* which boasted of an impeccable poetic hygiene explicit in his contemptuous censure of the body in *Pureza* (1912) as 'ese montón de podredumbre'.†[2] Jiménez's rejection of the world, which he summarized in *El silencio de oro* (1911–13) in the brusque exclamation: '¡Nada del mundo de todos!'‡[3] clearly appealed to Altolaguirre, whose dedication of *Ejemplo* to Jiménez was a mark of gratitude amplified in his admission that 'My poetry reveals as the main influence that of Juan Ramón Jiménez...'[4]

Stating with simple candour that 'Poetry is in my soul and my soul is in poetry',[5] Altolaguirre gave himself as single-mindedly as Jiménez to poetry, which he regarded as an escape from humdrum routine into a private, timeless sphere; his belief that poetry 'frees us from the circumstantial, from the transitory' (p. 11) echoed Jiménez's hope in *Piedra y cielo* (1917–18) that his poems would be 'todo verdad presente, sin historia'.§[6] Convinced that 'the poet never has anything new to say' (p. 11), Altolaguirre confined his role to that of an 'Editor de cristales / de mí mismo'‖ (p. 130). His determination, also expressed in *Nuevos poemas de las islas invitadas*, to be a 'Narciso siempre' (p. 133) restricted the thematic range of his poetry, which with its lacklustre diction and economically recurrent symbols and images is so limpid, deliberate and undemanding that it seems to have observed Jiménez's dictum that 'Repetition with exactitude is more valuable than variety with demerit.'[7]

The doors, circles, walls, rooms, houses and islands recurring in Altolaguirre's poems form a visually simple framework for his solitude; his shout of '¡Cerrad todas las puertas!'¶ in *Poesía* (p. 78) was the cry of a poet who recalled in 1932 that 'I was always shut away indoors.'[8] Because he imagined life in *Ejemplo* as a succession of 'Círculos de soledad'** (p. 30), he presented himself

---

* I have nothing to purge.   † that heap of decay.
‡ I want nothing to do with the world of everyone else!
§ all present truth, without history.
‖ Publisher of reflections of myself.
¶ Close all the doors!   ** Circles of solitude.

in the same work hammering pathetically against the walls that encase him:

> atravesaba las estancias,
> golpeando las paredes sordas.* (p. 40)

His simple description of himself in *Ejemplo* as an 'estancia silenciosa' (p. 41) and of woman in *Soledades juntas* as an 'isla de carne't (p. 99) which he besieged shows that the title of the book is no capricious paradox but a neat diagnosis of a relationship in which each partner is isolated, independent and impenetrable; he is enclosed within his room; in *Poesía* she, aloof and hidden as he stands forlornly outside her body, repulses his attempts to penetrate her secrets:

> tú, pálida, escondida,
> yo como ante una puerta
> ante tu pecho frío.‡ (p. 49)

When in 'Calle' of *Las islas invitadas* he dispensed with the cautious crutch of *como* and drew a picture rather than composed similes of separation, he coined a number of images that succeed one another stiffly; his fantasy was not sufficiently trained or supple to convince the reader of the visual coherence of houses, pages, sewing and binding:

> Tu casa frente a mi casa.
> Tu balcón frente del mío.
> Entre tu casa y mi casa
> una página del frío.
> Mi mirada cose al viento
> estancado de la calle.
> Tu aliento empaña el cristal
> cuadrado de tu ventana.
> Entre tu aliento y mis ojos
> encuadernamos la página
> amarilla y fría del viento.§ (p. 22)

---

* I crossed the rooms, beating on the deaf walls.
† silent room; island of flesh.
‡ you, pale and hidden; I stand before your cold breast as if before a door.
§ Your house is opposite my house. Your balcony is opposite my balcony. Between your house and my house there is a page of cold. My eyes sew the wind stagnant in the street. Your breath mists the square glass of your window. Between your breath and my eyes we bind the yellow, cold page of the wind.

The house, which illustrates Altolaguirre's conviction that 'todo / se queda siempre dentro'* (pp. 49–50), locks him in an inscrutable privacy which in *Ejemplo* he postulated as his ideal; the key he turned in this short narrative of inaction guaranteed his paralysis in a limbo devoid of sensation:

> Cerré con llave el rostro,
> cofre de lo indecible,
> permaneciendo inmóvil,
> indiferente al aire.
> Y quedé reclinado,
> hermético, interior,
> de tactos, luz y música,
> olvidado y ausente.† (p. 35)

When he moves, he drifts as solitary as Antonio Machado, who frequently presented himself in his poems as a 'viajero / a lo largo del sendero';‡1 accompanied only by his reluctant shadow, he haunts the shores as compulsively as his mind hovers around thoughts of sadness, creating with pairs of words the sense of robot motion and inescapable sadness:

> Arrastrando por la arena,
> como cola de mi luto,
> a mi sombra prisionera,
> triste y solitario voy
> y vengo por las riberas,
> recordando y olvidando
> la causa de mi tristeza.§ (p. 24)

The sadness induced and intensified by solitude attracted rather than depressed Altolaguirre, who prefaced his *Antología de la poesía romántica española* with the words: 'And the moon? And the flowers? I should like to think of them. The world is so sad!'2

---

* everything remains always within.
† With a key I locked my face, the coffer of the ineffable, remaining motionless and indifferent to the air. And I stayed reclined, hermetic, absorbed in myself, oblivious of and absent from touch, light and music.
‡ traveller along the path.
§ Dragging my captive shadow like the train of my mourning along the sand, sad and lonely I come and go along the shores, remembering and forgetting the cause of my sadness.

Although he tartly described the egoist in *Poesía* as 'dueño de sí, dueño de nada'* (p. 53), he lamented the loss of solitude as poignantly as if he were mourning a person. With its solemn rhythm and obsessive repetition of 'sin', 'solo' and 'soledad', 'Sin ella' of *Poesía* is a tribute to his own company and a criticism of everyone else's; fearing contamination by what he called in *Soledades juntas* 'Un mundo de seres malos'† (p. 98), he bewailed the invasion of his privacy by people who made him long for the perfect solitude impossible in their company:

> Mi soledad ausente.
> ¡Qué soledad sin soledad !
> Sentirme solo al lado
> de tanta compañía,
> solo, sin soledad...‡ (p. 72)

By remaining alone and detached from life, Altolaguirre maintained intact what Bergamín has called 'that kind of angelic innocence'.[1] Although his poem on 'Un reloj' and his reference to 'el abismo de la nada'§ in *Nuevos poemas de las islas invitadas* (pp. 127, 125) reveal his awareness of time and of the finality of death, he did not succumb to the despair which overwhelmed Alberti, Cernuda and Lorca, but disengaged himself from routine existence to seek freedom in a virginal world unspoilt by decay and darkness. Adopting the motto of 'Vivo para olvidar'‖ (p. 127), he explained in some deliberate and prosaic lines of the same work that his blunted senses could not respond to the stimuli of the world outside him:

> Estoy tan insensible,
> que el mundo inexistente
> es como un doble sueño
> que no me sobresalta.¶ (p. 127)

It was by steadfastly avoiding the kisses and caresses he vetoed in *Ejemplo* (p. 31) that Altolaguirre could regard his poetry as a

---

* master of himself, master of nothing.   † A world of evil beings.
‡ My absent solitude. What solitude without solitude ! To feel myself beside so much company, alone, without solitude.
§ the abyss of nothingness.   ‖ I live to forget.
¶ I am so insensitive that the non-existent world is like a double dream which does not startle me.

'younger sister'[1] of that of Salinas, whose disdain of 'los sentidos de siempre'* (p. 164) was echoed by the hostility to sensations which Altolaguirre specified in *Poesía*:

> Hay que no sentir la forma,
> ni los roces, ni los fríos,
> ni las caricias, ni el fuego.† (p. 52)

Verbs as weakening or destructive as *desangrar, desclavar, desconchar, descoser, desencadenar, desenvainar, deshabitar, deshacer, despeinar, despoblar* and *destrenzar* are recurrent symptoms of the ideal he shared with Bécquer, Juan Ramón Jiménez and Salinas of advancing 'Más allá de la forma'‡, as he stated explicitly in *Poesía* (p. 65). Fusing his senses like Salinas to create new sensations that removed him still further from reality into an area of private experience, he resurrected the traditional *ojos del alma* to look at life with what he called in *Poesía* his 'anhelantes ojos de mi alma'§ (p. 79). When Salinas told his *amada* in *Fábula y signo* that 'Te deshojaste toda lentamente' (p. 103) and in *La voz a ti debida* that 'me doy contigo, adentro'‖ (p. 164), he was celebrating his discovery of a woman freed from her public identity, which Altolaguirre also wanted to bypass, aiming in *Poesía* to ignore and penetrate 'tus bellos / límites exteriores' (p. 69), thereby 'deshojándote...de tu presente'¶ (p. 64). Salinas's conviction in *La voz a ti debida* that 'No eres / lo que yo siento de ti'** (p. 134) was echoed by Altolaguirre's insistence in *Poesía* that only after repudiating his senses could he identify and possess the woman:

> Ahora sé que eres tú.
> Ahora, cuando no te siento,
> cuando mis sentidos no te limitan.
> Ahora es cuando te tengo.†† (p. 78)

---

* everyday senses.
† One must not feel physical form, or contacts, or cold, or caresses, or fire.
‡ Beyond form.   § eager eyes of my soul.
‖ You slowly stripped yourself bare; I find you deep within you.
¶ your beautiful outer limits; stripping you of your present.
** You are not what my senses tell me you are.
†† Now I know that it is you. Now, when I do not hear you, when my senses do not confine you. It is now that I possess you.

IV   Prados in 1936

v   Altolaguirre in 1930

With his determined flight from sensations and physical contact, signalled by his repetition of *fuga, huir* and *desnudo*, Altolaguirre won for himself a freedom which he represented in a group of natural terms as familiar as the doors, walls and houses he used to describe his containment. The fields, plains, paths, clouds, air and beaches recurring in his poems were convenient but exhausted ciphers which not only make us feel like Gide's Narcissus that 'it is always the same thing',[1] but failed to lift his verse off the level of sober statement where explanation eclipsed illustration. When he expressed his enjoyment of the bare fields in *Ejemplo*, he did not compensate for the clumsiness of the verb *expansionarse* with his novel description of man's will as 'elástica' (p. 32); and the anaphora introducing the visually unadventurous images communicated no excitement to the liberty he narrated in a *romance* of *La lenta libertad*:

> Mi vida riega los campos,
> mi vida vuela celeste,
> mi vida se queda blanca
> sobre las cumbres, perenne.*   (p. 114)

Altolaguirre's statement in *Poesía* that 'Siento las cosas / y comprendo sus íntimas verdades'† (p. 73) indicated his nearness to and understanding of nature. Prados, who in some respects paralleled and complemented him, deepened this closeness into a constant and enthusiastic communion. It was the water, the earth and the sky in all their elemental vastness that thrilled and entranced Prados, not the sea of Málaga, where he was born, nor the mountains near it, where he recuperated from a childhood illness. Prados did not set himself to paint nature but to ponder and absorb its mysteries, to sink into what Carlos Blanco Aguinaga has aptly called his 'pure repetitive contemplation'.[2] What Prados admired in his communion with nature is its harmony and wholeness; it is as compact and enclosed as the sky which in *El misterio del agua* is the pivot of his nervous, breathless gyrations:

> Cielo y cielo que mana
> del cielo, hacia la fuente

---

* My life waters the fields, my life flies celestial, my life remains white and eternal on the peaks.

† I feel things and understand their intimate truths.

> del cielo, sobre el cielo
> del cielo que sostiene...* (p. 35)

And in 'Bosque de la noche' of the same work he enmeshes the reader by organizing his thoughts into the neat formation of parallel lines and by shuffling as if by sleight of hand the five words that dominate the poem: *mirada, viento, alma, agua* and *rama*:

> Se alzó,—manzana de ébano—,
> la mirada en el viento
> y se quedó en el alma
> meciéndose en su rama.
>
> Se alzó—manzana de ébano—
> el alma sobre el viento
> y quedó la mirada
> meciéndose en el agua...† (p. 58)

Nature did not always appear to Prados simply as a harmoniously interlocking unit, but as an eddy flooding the separate compartments of reality. The melting of day into night and of night into day is a constant example of the fluidity of Prados's universe, where the fusion of his thoughts and sensations with the physical world guaranteed that in *Tiempo*

> El mar entra por la noche
> y la noche por el sueño...‡ (p. 11)

and that

> (Resbala el barco en el alma
> y el pensamiento en el agua...)§ (p. 20)

The title *El misterio del agua* shows that the water not only excited Prados as it flowed, in two pulsating lines,

> delirante y desnuda,
> sin cuerpo, palpitante,‖ (p. 42)

---

* Sky and sky which flows from the sky, towards the source of the sky, above the sky of the sky it supports.
† The eyes arose in the wind like an ebony apple and stayed in the soul rocking on its branch.
    The soul arose over the wind like an ebony apple and the glance stayed rocking on the water.
‡ The sea enters by way of the night and the night by way of dream.
§ The boat glides on the soul and the mind on the water.
‖ delirious and bare, bodyless and palpitating.

but that it fascinated him as much as the 'mágico espejo' found in
the same work (p. 42) and as the night which in *Cuerpo perseguido*
is 'redonda de misterio'* (p. 77). The belief he expressed in
Tiempo that

(Queda en el alma el temblor
de la sombra y el misterio)†   (p. 22)

explains why his 'magic mirror' never reflected things as they
are; like Salinas, who in 'El zumo' of *Seguro azar* wanted to
penetrate the skin of the orange to discover its inner secret (p. 53),
Prados disregarded all physical boundaries to explore beyond and
within; that is why in *Memoria de poesía* the world makes with
itself a 'Cita hacia dentro' (p. 61).

Withdrawn into himself and detached from the world around
him, Prados inhabited a private sphere of mystery where he was
transported, as he imagined in *Cuerpo perseguido*, on the wings of
dream:

Libre del mundo, el sueño
me colgó por sus alas.‡   (p. 86)

Although in *Andando, andando por el mundo* and *Llanto en la sangre*
he opened his eyes to human suffering, in his preceding books—
Tiempo, El misterio del agua, Memoria de poesía and *Cuerpo perseguido*—he savoured what he called in his *Diario íntimo*, compiled
between 1919 and 1921, 'that solitude I like so much',[1] drugging
himself in an atmosphere as drowsy and enchanted as the Málaga
he evoked in *Tiempo*, where the languid air is a 'péndulo del
ensueño'§ (p. 18).

His retreat into the countryside in 1929 to meditate, his refusal
to appear in Gerardo Diego's anthology and his dislike of Madrid,
which he accused in his diary of causing his neurasthenia,[2] exemplify the stern claim he made in *Cuerpo perseguido* that 'Cerré mi
puerta al mundo'‖ (p. 70). The tree which in *Jardín cerrado* (1946)

* magic mirror; round with mystery.
† The tremors of shadow and mystery remain in the soul.
‡ Free of the world, the dream suspended me from its wings.
§ Pendulum of dream.
‖ I closed my door to the world.

appears 'mitad buscando al cielo y medio entre las sombras'*
(p. 199) represents, like Altolaguirre's elm (pp. 119–20) and Cernuda's magnolia,[1] the loneliness which convinced Prados that
'only "I" will be my only friend'[2] and stimulated his efforts to
forget his physical frame. His explicit statement in *Cuerpo perseguido* that 'ya no estoy sino cuando me olvido'† (p. 69) echoed
Altolaguirre's creed that 'Vivo para olvidar' (p. 127).

Prados's conviction that 'whilst we live, each minute of our
existence has half of our being rooted in death'[3] generated what
he called in *El misterio del agua* his '¡Eterna pasión del tiempo!'‡
(p. 54). The question he posed in the same work: '¿Corrige / el
tiempo?'§ (p. 37) was echoed more solemnly in *Cuerpo perseguido*,
where he wondered:

> ¿Cuándo empieza la muerte?
> ¿Dónde se acaba el tiempo?...‖ (p. 101)

The death which dreamed in his arms in *Cuerpo perseguido* (p. 87),
just as it menaced his lungs in 1920, lifted him out of life onto a
plane where he fused body and mind in a self-effacing communion
with someone whose flesh he shunned in reality. That Prados, like
Altolaguirre and Salinas, pursued the body with his mind and
not with his person explains the illusion he created of moving in
two directions at the same time; like Juan Ramón Jiménez, whose
pursuit of the butterfly in *Piedra y cielo* (1917–18) left in his hand
only 'la forma de su huída',¶[4] Prados deliberately sought the
intangible:

> y, huyendo de tu cuerpo,
> sueño que te persigo...** (p. 73)

Emulating the fluidity of his universe, he aimed to abstract himself
from the physical world and soar, according to the simple similes
of his 'Afirmación' in *Cuerpo perseguido*, as freely as a bird and as
gracefully as a ship:

---

* half seeking heaven and half amid the shadows.
† I only exist when I forget myself.   ‡ Eternal passion of time!
§ Does time correct?
‖ When does death begin? Where does time end?
¶ the form of its flight.
** and, fleeing from your body, I dream that I pursue you.

¡Qué sereno en el cielo
mi corazón sin labios
sueña libre, desnudo
como un barco flotando!...
Mientras que sobre el suelo
mi cuerpo deshojado...*   (pp. 110–11)

Prados's uninhibited use of *sin* and of verbs beginning with
des-, together with his fondness for the adjective *desnudo*, which is
as important to him as *nu*, *pur*, *vierge* and *blanc* were to Mallarmé,[1]
signal his yearning for a pure, fleshless freedom in which, according
to *El misterio del agua*, time is 'sin piel' (p. 36), water is 'sin cuerpo'
(p. 42) and the wind is 'sin sangre't (p. 40). When the day in
El misterio del agua

sin conciencia, en desmayo,
por boca de su herida
derrama a borbotones
su calor...,‡   (p. 49)

its haemorrhage, which Prados described with medical coldness,
so drains it of life that it remains as limp as the body, which in
two earnestly repetitive lines of the same work he reduced to a
skinless shell, a

cuerpo y cuerpo sin piel
de carne inexistente.§   (p. 35)

Prados's description of himself in *Cuerpo perseguido* as a headless
body flying beneath the moon (p. 105), which parallels Alto-
laguirre's appearance in *Ejemplo* as a 'Decapitado cuerpo de aire'||
(p. 42), explains why he asked in the same work a question which,
in its complete contrast with Darío's lusty and confident boast in
Prosas profanas that 'Hombre soy',[2] revealed his anguished and
obsessive preoccupation with himself: '¿Soy un hombre?'¶
(p. 88). Like Altolaguirre, who appointed himself as his own
editor de cristales, Prados set himself opposite the mirror, as he

---

* How serenely does my lipless heart dream in the heavens, floating as naked as a
    ship! Whilst on earth my leafless body...
† without flesh; without a body; without blood.
‡ unconscious, fainting, spills out its warmth through the mouth of its wound.
§ body and skinless body of non-existent flesh.
|| Decapitated body of air.   ¶ I am a man; Am I a man?

stated in *Cuerpo perseguido* (p. 77), and undertook in his diary a painful 'spiritual self-analysis', lamenting his 'uselessness' and nurturing his 'melancholy' with quotations from Nietzsche and Lamartine and thoughts of Verlaine and the Russian novels of which he was so fond.[1] Alberti's recollection that 'a dark storm' raged within Prados[2] is justified by the latter's insistence in his diary on his 'anguish and despair', 'nervous tension' and 'strange neurotic character'.[3]

Prados's writings make it clear that he needed and thrived on self-revelation, that he had to exhibit his feelings and parade his themes. Unable to control what he frankly called in his diary 'the volubility of my feelings',[4] he repeated himself in his poetry more effusively than in his prose, circling restlessly around words as central to him as *cuerpo*, *cielo*, *huída* and *fuga*. Trapped within a tight web of words and themes, Prados infused into his poems a nervous tension and restless energy which erupted in a rash of parentheses, exclamations, questions, deliberations introduced by such formulas of doubt as 'Yo no sé si es que...'* (p. 97), and truncated thoughts that trail inconclusively into dots. Although the striking images which he sometimes coined are so deeply embedded in his perpetually seething lines that his poetry appeals only fitfully to the imagination, its fluid and insistent concentration on one man's communion with himself and nature makes more demands on our attention that Altolaguirre's verse, whose precise but limp expositions were compiled and delivered by a staidly reposed mind.

Like Prados, Cernuda had his 'Feet on earth; but eyes on heaven',[5] for the umbrella title of *La realidad y el deseo* contains two poles destined never to meet. The 'rectángulo frío' and 'orbe tan breve'† which encased him in *Perfil del aire*[6] represent a reality so dismal and restrictive that it drove desire into the impotent longings of the mind. Suspended between the institutions of religion, marital love and family life, which he found unacceptable, and his dreams of eternal love and eternal beauty, which he found unattainable, Cernuda meditated throughout his life on 'the eter-

* I do not know if it is that...
† cold rectangle; very small world.

nal struggle between the real and the ideal, the struggle that is the essence of poetry'.[1]

Estranged from a world governed in his view by 'a daemonic power',[2] Cernuda compiled in both his poetry and prose a dossier of his hopes, fears, longings and disappointments with a candour that was not a pose but a point of honour. Although he was always the axis of his poems, his flexible and resourceful imagination gave varied and graphic poetic shape to his solitude, independence and malaise; although he offered no remedy, his censure of orthodox values, beliefs and institutions infused into his poems the moral fervour of denunciation absent from those of Altolaguirre, Prados and Salinas. The conflict he recorded between illusions that transcended reality and disillusion within it was complex and constantly shifting. His acute sensitivity to what he read and where he lived, which he charted candidly in his essay 'Historial de un libro',[3] brought new colourings and new dimensions to the same basic struggle; his reading of Hölderlin in 1936 reinforced the interest in Greek myths aroused in him by a book he found when a child;[4] his discovery of Mexico consummated his lifelong search for 'an Eden where my eyes may see the transparent sea and the radiant light of this world; where the bodies are young, dark and agile'.[5]

Promising to leave behind him 'the memory of an image contemplated in the mirror',[6] Cernuda posed in *Perfil del aire* as Narcissus, frozen in a trance at the water's edge:

> Junto a las aguas quietas,
> sueño y pienso que vivo.*[7]

His frank admission that 'To do nothing is activity enough for you'[8] explains his fondness for describing languor and the recurrence in his writings of such words as *yacer, quieto, indolente* and *indolencia*. The prose piece called 'El indolente' which Cernuda published in 1926, and which may have been destined for the book of that title which he told Higinio Capote he was planning to write, presented a listless figure studying in the mirror his 'fragile and divine existence'.[9] In *Perfil del aire* especially Cernuda

---

* At the side of the still waters I dream and think that I live.

was pinned to the '¡ Tierra indolente!' and forced by 'ingrávida somnolencia' to think of no-one and nothing but himself;[1] he was both the creator and victim of what he called in *Égloga, elegía, oda* an 'estéril indolencia'* (p. 32).

Emotionally drained as he stayed locked within the circle of solitary introspection which he drew around himself, Cernuda lamented in *Un río, un amor* his 'Monótona tristeza, emoción en ruinas'† (p. 43). But although he stated bleakly in the same work that

> ...mi vida es ahora un hombre melancólico
> Sin saber otra cosa que su llanto,‡   (p. 53)

sadness was something that he needed and abhorred, which he celebrated in his 'Himno a la tristeza' in *Invocaciones* and mourned as his 'habitual sadness' and 'rather Byronic sadness' in his letters to Higinio Capote.[2] Neatly summarizing his life in *Égloga, elegía, oda* as a blank and unrelieved 'Nula felicidad; monotonía'§ (p. 29), Cernuda was numbed by an ennui and lethargy clearly signalled by his frequent use of *hastío*. The 'insuperable boredom' he confessed to Capote in 1929[3] caused the shrug of indifference he made in the colloquially abrupt title 'Qué más da' of *Los placeres prohibidos*. The 'Fatiga de estar vivo, de estar muerto'‖ he deplored in *Un río, un amor* (p. 44) made him chant in 'Estoy cansado' of the same work a litany of tedium as incoherent and pointless as the squawk of the parrot, pretty in body but empty in mind:

> Estoy cansado de estar vivo,
> Aunque más cansado sería el estar muerto;
> Estoy cansado del estar cansado
> Entre plumas ligeras sagazmente,
> Plumas del loro aquel tan familiar o triste,
> El loro aquel del siempre estar cansado.¶   (p. 49)

---

* Indolent earth; weightless somnolence; sterile indolence.
† Monotonous sadness, emotion in ruins.
‡ my life is now a melancholy man who knows nothing more than his tears.
§ Null happiness; monotony.
‖ Weariness of being alive, of being dead.
¶ I am tired of being alive, although being dead would be more tiresome; I am tired of being tired wisely among light feathers, feathers of that so familiar or sad parrot, that parrot of always being tired.

While in 'Estar cansado' he deliberately stuttered and repeated himself, in a poem of *Invocaciones* which he sourly called 'La gloria del poeta' it was with an image as compact, graphic and chilling as 'momia de hastío sepulta en anónima yacija'* (p. 117) that he impressed on the reader his exhaustion and impotence. Sunk in a body as neglected and commonplace as an unmarked tomb, he saw himself swathed like a mummy in a living death in which, according to a cheerless epigram of *Un río, un amor*, 'vivir es estar a solas con la muerte't (p. 61). When he insisted in *Invocaciones* that

> Todo, todo,
> Amarillea y cae y huye con el aire que no vuelve,‡ (p. 119)

he recognized that time, which haunted him in his poetry and prose, ravages things before it condemns them callously to an oblivion so irrevocable that he stated with chill conviction in *Un río, un amor* that 'el olvido está dentro del olvido'§ (p. 59).

Although Cernuda professed contempt for 'the intrusion of the person into what the poet writes',[1] his writings and his mannerisms fostered rather than combatted the legend of the prickly, acidulous hermit which he deeply resented. The belief he expressed in *Invocaciones* that 'Viven y mueren a solas los poetas'‖ (p. 127), clearly signalled by titles as explicit as 'Quisiera estar solo en el sur', 'Destierro' and 'Dejadme solo' of *Un río, un amor* and 'Esperaba solo' of *Los placeres prohibidos*, led him to affirm his individuality with the tartness and petulance he displayed in his essay on Eluard, where he wrote that 'everyone can be a critic, although if it rains I do not see why I have to go out with an umbrella'.[2] The disdain inspiring his comment in 1926: 'Public? I do not know what is is', erupted in the 'Poética' he wrote for Diego's anthology into an exaggerated nihilism which made him detest reality as I detest everything that belongs to it: my
> friends, my family, my country:
> I know nothing, I want nothing, I expect nothing.[3]

---

* mummy of weariness buried in an anonymous tomb.
† to live is to be alone with death.
‡ Everything, everything yellows and falls and flees with the air which does not return.   § oblivion is within oblivion.   ‖ Poets live and die alone.

His hymn to solitude in *Ocnos*, where he chanted that 'Solitude is in everything for you, and everything for you is in solitude',[1] showed that loneliness was not a refuge which he had been forced to seek but a goal to which he constantly aspired. That he was dissatisfied with other people is suggested by his comment to Capote in 1928 that the company of Altolaguirre, Hinojosa and Prados 'is not enough for me'.[2] The vigorous independence which grew into a delicate and sharply defended untouchability transformed his enthusiastic tribute to Salinas in 1929 into a waspish attack in 1957 on the latter's 'external and fictitious modernity';[3] it also prompted his suppression in *Primeras poesías* of his dedication to Guillén of the last poem of *Perfil del aire*. His rebuttal of Guillén's influence on *Perfil del aire* was, as I suggested in the previous chapter, an elaborate exercise in critical camouflage, which failed to conceal either his debt to Guillén or his punctured pride.

Presenting himself in *Invocaciones* as a person who had come to terms with his own solitude and with the indifference of others,

> Conforme conmigo mismo y con la indiferencia de los otros,
> Solo yo con mi vida,
> Con mi parte en el mundo,* (p. 120)

Cernuda championed in his essays writers as distinct as Góngora and Dashiell Hammett, who he felt were as neglected and misunderstood as he. Scorning the solace of religion, marriage and family life, he put himself outside society and aligned himself in reality with the disdainful homosexuals appearing in *Ocnos*, who shared his conviction that 'he who is not with me, is against me'.[4] Like Bécquer, in whom he displayed a consistent and sympathetic interest,[5] he found in the privacy of his thoughts and poems a substitute existence, an escape from a world as chill and lifeless as the hollow grey man who in *Un río, un amor* stumbles blindly through the mist (p. 41) and as the spectre who in *Los placeres prohibidos* wanders numbly 'En medio de la multitud':

---

* In accord with myself and the indifference of others, I am alone with my life, with my part in the world.

Vacío, anduve sin rumbo por la ciudad. Gentes extrañas pasaban a mi lado sin verme. Un cuerpo se derritió con leve susurro al tropezarme. Anduve más y más.

No sentía mis pies. Quise cogerlos en mi mano, y no hallé mis manos; quise gritar, y no hallé mi voz. La niebla me envolvía.

Me pesaba la vida como un remordimiento; quise arrojarla de mí. Mas era imposible, porque estaba muerto y andaba entre los muertos.*

Cernuda's pained cry in *Invocaciones*:   (p. 70)

> Cómo llenarte, soledad,
> Sino contigo misma,†   (p. 108)

shows that he visualized life, to use Altolaguirre's expressive phrase, as a series of *círculos de soledad*, for he acknowledged that solitude has to be fed with solitude, that oblivion is contained within oblivion and that the freedom of love is a prison, which in *Donde habite el olvido* he likened sombrely to a series of tombstones:

> No hay besos, sino losas;
> No hay amor, sino losas
> Tantas veces medidas por el paso
> Febril del prisionero.‡   (p. 99)

The walled garden which in *Perfil del aire* offered him

> sus ramas y sus aguas
> de secreta delicia§¹

was a haven secure from reality's siege, a pure and timeless enclave governed by the *acorde*, the 'spiritual and physical harmony'² that ruled the pagan world, which he celebrated throughout his work and idealized in *Égloga, elegía, oda* as an

---

* Empty, I wandered aimlessly through the city. Strange people walked at my side without seeing me. As it brushed against me a body melted with a light sigh. I walked on and on.

  I could not feel my feet. I wanted to hold them and I did not find my hands; I wanted to shout, and I did not find my voice. The mist enfolded me.

  Life weighed on me like remorse; I wanted to cast it from me. But it was impossible, because I was dead and wandered amid the dead.

† How can I fill you, solitude, if not with you yourself.

‡ There are no kisses, only tombstones; there is no love, only tombstones so often measured by the feverish pacing of the prisoner.

§ its branches and its waters of secret delight.

> Idílico paraje
> De dulzor tan primero,
> Nativamente digno de los dioses.*   (p. 30)

Paradise for Cernuda was always somewhere remote in time and place; Daytona and Nevada in America, the southern seas evoked in 'Sombras blancas', the Eden of religious belief and the Sansueña of Spanish legend offered him escape routes as comforting as the poetry of Rilke and the works of Gide, which he admitted helped him to regard his homosexuality not as a moral and physical aberration but as a freely chosen destiny.[1]

When Cernuda repeated *huir* and *fuga* and echoed Mallarmé's 'Où fuir dans la révolte inutile et perverse?' by wondering in *Perfil del aire* '¿Dónde huir?',[†][2] he revealed his desire to run away from life; but his escape, like the mechanical wanderings of his phantom figures, was, he confessed in *Un río, un amor*, as futile as the wind on a stormy night, whose sharp but impotent gusts cannot penetrate the tightly closed windows:

> Como el viento a lo largo de la noche,
> Amor en pena o cuerpo solitario,
> Toca en vano a los vidrios,
> Sollozando abandona las esquinas...‡   (p. 45)

When *el indolente* in the prose piece of that title closed the door, 'leaving the winter outside',[3] he inflicted on himself what Cernuda diagnosed crisply in *Un río, un amor* as

> ...dolor con la puerta cerrada,
> Dolor frente a dolor...§   (p. 59)

The closed doors with which he illustrated his solitude explain why he singled out for comment in his essay on Juan Ramón Jiménez the line 'Otra vez la puerta cerrada';[||] but to censure Jiménez for 'egoistic subjectivism'[4] was to gloss over his own

---

* Idyllic place of such primeval sweetness, naturally worthy of the gods.
† Where can I fly in the useless, perverse rebellion?; Where can I flee?
‡ Like the wind throughout the night, love in torment or a lonely body, it touches the window-panes in vain, it abandons the street corners in tears.
§ grief with the door closed, grief opposite grief.
|| The closed door again.

introspective isolation, represented by the rooms in which he mentally confined himself and by the doors, walls and windows behind which he symbolically barricaded himself. His statement in *Égloga, elegía, oda* that

> Fatal extiende
> Su frontera insaciable el vasto muro
> Por la tiniebla fúnebre*   (p. 27)

acknowledged wearily that the solitude into which he deliberately withdrew was both a retreat and a cell. The 'repentina fuga estrellada en un muro'† which occurs in *Un río, un amor* (p. 46) destroys his hopes of escape and condemns him to his prison as tyrannically as Altolaguirre, who appeared in *Ejemplo* 'golpeando las paredes sordas'‡ (p. 40).

Implicit in his description of himself in *Donde habite el olvido* as a 'niño / Prisionero entre muros cambiantes'§ (p. 93) was his belief that life was a succession of cells and circles: oblivion lies within oblivion, solitude feeds on solitude and, as he stated bitterly in *Los placeres prohibidos*, 'Sales de un frío para entrar en otro'‖ (p. 79). The cold and snow which he transformed vividly in *Primeras poesías* into a choking reptile drove him into himself, freezing his body and his mind in a numb awareness of his solitude in a chill world:

> Y la fuga hacia dentro. Ciñe el frío,
> Lento reptil, sus furias congeladas;
> La soledad, tras las puertas cerradas,
> Abre la luz sobre el papel vacío.¶   (p. 15)

Cernuda chose lonely withdrawal into still contemplation, whose lethargy and gloom he summarized wearily in *Donde habite el olvido* as

> Cristal, soledades,
> La frente, la lámpara,**   (p. 94)

---

* The vast wall inexorably extends its insatiable frontier through the funereal darkness.   † sudden flight shattered on a wall.
‡ beating on the deaf walls.   § captive child amid changing walls.
‖ You leave one cold atmosphere only to enter another.
¶ And the flight within. The cold, a slow reptile, tightens its frozen furies. Solitude, behind the closed doors, opens the light onto the empty paper.
** Window-pane, solitudes, the brow, the lamp.

because his private thoughts, hopes and dreams were his only indulgence in and his only antidote to an existence he condemned as 'a demented fair' and 'a stupid carnival',[1] based, according to his bitter comment in *Un río, un amor*, on two lies: the lie of living and the lie of the flesh (p. 57).

What made Cernuda turn away from life and look, as he stated in *Los placeres prohibidos*, 'Más allá de la vida'* into death and 'Más allá del amor'† into oblivion (p. 84) was the conviction he shared with Bécquer's Manrique that love and glory are as unattainable as a moonbeam.[2] Salinas's discontent with reality, which he hinted at in his frequent use of *más allá*, *detrás* and *al otro lado* and which he defined in *Víspera del gozo* as his 'doctrinal and dogmatic dissatisfaction',[3] explains his frank hostility throughout his writings to order and symmetry. He contracted and kept the habit, described in *Fábula y signo*, of

> diciendo siempre que no
> a las formas y a los tiempos‡ (p. 127)

because, echoing Gide's creed that 'Paradise is still to be remade', he believed that 'the world is already made. And yet at the same time constantly to be made.'[4] Guillén's delight in the nude's 'Claridad aguzada entre perfiles'§ (p. 79) could never let him mourn like Salinas in *Fábula y signo* a woman 'encerrada entre medidas'‖ (p. 110), nor could his enjoyment of the panoramic views from his balcony tempt him to echo his friend's lament in *Presagios* that all he saw from his window was the unchanging order of the universe which he inherited at birth:

> Me lanzo a la ventana. Miro:
> cada cosa en su sitio, como siempre;
> la montaña, el poniente y la estrella primera,
> otra vez me confirman esa orden
> que al nacer entendí, sin nada nuevo.¶ (p. 40)

---

* Beyond life. † Beyond love.
‡ always saying no to forms and times.
§ Clarity sharpened amid profiles. ‖ confined within measurements.
¶ I rush to the window. I look: everything in its place, as always; the mountain, the sunset and the first star once more confirm to me that order which, with nothing new, I understood at birth.

Convinced like his character Aurelia in *El desnudo impecable* that
'chance is the poetry of the real',[1] Salinas explored a world of
mental adventure and make-believe. Because of his determination
to 'operate always on the inexplicable',[2] he preferred to sharp
contours and brilliant light the wispy vagueness of what he called
in *Todo más claro* (1949) 'los cendales de lo nunca visto'* (p. 385),
which blurred his world as consistently as the 'Cendal flotante de
leve bruma'† clouded Bécquer's.[3] Salinas's failure to glimpse the
mysterious figure lurking in the mist in 'Busca, encuentro' of
Seguro azar made him establish in the question 'La mirada, ¿ para
qué?'‡ (p. 82) his hostility to sight, which led him in the creed he
postulated in 'Vocación' of the same work to reject categorically
the perfect, symmetrical universe admired by Guillén in favour of
the fluid, virgin and flexible world of his imagination:

> Cerrar los ojos. Y ver
> incompleto, tembloroso,
> de será o de no será,
> —masas torpes, planos sordos—
> sin luz, sin gracia, sin orden
> un mundo sin acabar...§   (p. 52)

The freedom Salinas declared when he stated in *Presagios* that
'No hay nada afuera que me ponga linde'‖ (p. 32) was not a
passport to a world of uninhibited fantasy but a permit to drill his
mental agility, which after the tension, litheness and coherence of
La voz a ti debida stiffened into the automatic manœuvres of
Razón de amor. In his eagerness to censure 'the glacial psycho-
technical madrigals' of *La voz a ti debida*, Domenchina[4] forgot that,
although Salinas's intelligence was animated and sharpened by
love, the love about which he rhapsodized in his poems found its
stimulus in a woman's body, which he commemorated in his
voluptuous references to its lips and voice, to its 'carne tibia'
(p. 185) and 'tierno cuerpo rosado'¶ (p. 132). That the woman's

---

* the gauzes of the never seen.   † Floating gauze of light mist.
‡ The eyes: what use are they?
§ Close my eyes. And see incomplete, trembling, uncertain—torpid masses, dumb
planes—without light, without grace, without order, an unfinished world.
‖ There is nothing outside me that restricts me.
¶ warm flesh; tender pink body.

body was the foundation of the elaborate verbal structure Salinas
built around love is clear from the closing lines of *La voz a ti
debida*, where he predicted that the shadows which are the only
possible offspring of separation will have to return for regeneration

> a esta corporeidad mortal y rosa
> donde el amor inventa su infinito.*   (p. 206)

Despite his lingering memories of the pink body, it was with
the *infinito* that Salinas was more concerned. His definition of
happiness in *Presagios* as an 'alma sin cuerpo'† (p. 18) and his
description of the body in *Seguro azar* as 'sombra, engaño'‡
(p. 67) anticipated the mental surgery of *La voz a ti debida*, where,
as he explained in characteristically deliberate lines, he methodically amputated the woman's lips, destroyed her complexion and
stilled her arms and voice in order to live and love in a world free
from the exciting but troublesome presence of the flesh:

> Así
> mi amor está libre, suelto,
> con tu sombra descarnada.
> Y puedo vivir en ti
> sin temor
> a lo que yo más deseo,
> a tu beso, a tus abrazos.§   (p. 191)

Salinas's neat admission in *La voz a ti debida* that he was 'sin
ganas de ganar'‖ (p. 155) and his equally pert accusation in *Presagios* that 'Cierro brazos, tú los abres'¶ (p. 39) illustrate his
belief that to win a woman's body would end the timeless pleasures
generated by her form but sustained by his mind. His decision to
'vivirlo dentro'** (p. 136) forced him further and further away
from his sensual recollection, repeated as if in disbelief, that

> Ayer te besé en los labios.
> Te besé en los labios††   (p. 171)

---

* to this pink and mortal body where love invents its infinite.
† body without soul.   ‡ shadow, illusion.
§ Thus my love is free, loose, with your fleshless shadow. And I can live in you
  without fear of what I most desire, your kiss, your embraces.
‖ without wishing to win.   ¶ I close my arms, you open them.
** live it within.   †† Yesterday I kissed you on the lips. I kissed you on the lips.

until he found himself alone firstly 'kissing a kiss', and finally, as
he precisely explained to himself, kissing his memory of a kiss:

> Porque ya no es una carne
> ni una boca lo que beso,
> que se escapa, que me huye.
> No.
> Te estoy besando más lejos.* (p. 171)

When Salinas stated that 'por detrás de las gentes / te busco'†
(p. 134), he pointed to his search outside reality for a private
identity unseen by other people. His insistence that

> También detrás, más atrás
> de mí te busco. No eres
> lo que yo siento de ti‡ (p. 134)

reveals his clear distinction between the woman who inspired his
love and his love for her, suspended in a timeless, unmarked plane
which he imagined in lines reminiscent of Quevedo as a living
death:

> Vivir ya detrás de todo,
> al otro lado de todo
> —por encontrarte—,
> como si fuese morir.§ (p. 134)

To possess his *amada* would thwart Salinas's ambition to live
perpetually cocooned within a love from which he excluded the
banal data of time, place and circumstance. Rejecting the normal
senses in favour of new ones like the 'luz del tacto' (p. 63) and the
'luz del oír'‖ (p. 239), he detached himself from reality and particularly from his ubiquitous *amada*, who is so fully a creature of the
physical world that she appears unpredictably

> ...en los alfabetos,
> en las auroras, en los labios.¶ (p. 156)

---

* For it is no longer a flesh, nor a mouth that I kiss, which is escaping, is fleeing from
  me. No. I am kissing you from a distance.
† I seek you behind people.
‡ I also seek you behind me, way behind me. You are not what my senses tell me
  you are.
§ To live now behind everything, beyond everything—through finding you—as
  if it were death.
‖ light of touch; light of hearing.   ¶ in alphabets, in daybreaks, in lips.

Hostile to the roofs which weigh on him as heavily as they did on Altolaguirre, Salinas took himself in his fantasy to 'cielos / intemporales' (p. 150), where he and his *amada* drift as 'nadadores celestes'* (p. 170) in a rarefied atmosphere. His neat opposition of where he lived and where he refused to live, together with his precisely qualified specification of his chosen milieu, made his lines more reasoned and controlled than Prados's, more taut than Altolaguirre's plain statement that 'mi vida vuela celeste'† (p. 114):

> No en palacios de mármol,
> no en meses, no, ni en cifras,
> nunca pisando el suelo:
> en leves mundos frágiles
> hemos vivido juntos.
>
> . . . .
>
> Nos cobijaban techos,
> menos que techos, nubes;
> menos que nubes, cielos;
> aun menos, aire, nada.‡   (p. 200)

Determined to savour the 'delicia lenta / de gozar, de amar, sin nombre'§ (p. 140), Salinas opted for an existence kept pure, remote and impersonal by a screen of pronouns, summarized neatly in the phrase 'Yo te quiero, soy yo'‖ (p. 147). To use a name, which he imagined melodramatically as a dagger thrust into a pure breast (p. 141), would destroy the freedom of anonymity, which he celebrated in a joyful chant:

> Para vivir no quiero
> islas, palacios, torres.
> ¡Qué alegría más alta:
> vivir en los pronombres!¶   (p. 146)

---

* timeless heavens; celestial swimmers.
† my life flies celestial.
‡ Not in marble palaces, not in months, no, nor in numbers, never treading the earth: in light and fragile worlds have we lived together.
    We were sheltered by roofs, less than roofs, clouds; less than clouds, skies; even less, air, nothing.
§ slow delight of enjoying, of loving, without a name.
‖ I love you, it is I.
¶ In order to live I do not want islands, palaces, towers. What sublime joy: to live in pronouns!

His declarations that

> Entre figuraciones
> vivo, de ti, sin ti*   (p. 184)

and:

> Nosotros, sí, nosotros,
> amando, los amantes†   (p. 187)

outlined a simple situation which, although highly personal, was sterilized by anonymity and by the distance he maintained between her and himself. Clearly agreeing with Proust that 'as soon as one loves one no longer loves anyone',[1] Salinas stilled and silenced the woman while he hymned the love which she had stimulated. Love was not something he was prepared to share with a woman, whom he needed in order to begin loving but whom he purged from his thoughts in order to keep loving; his tribute to her was not the conventional praise of beauty, figure or elegance, but an epitaph to the separation which he enforced and maintained:

> Su gran obra de amor
> era dejarme solo.‡   (p. 183)

Love gave meaning to Salinas's life and coherence to *La voz a ti debida*, which, unimpeded by numbers or titles, moves with irresistible fluency as his thoughts revolve around love. Sharing Shelley's view of love as 'Thou Wonder, and thou Beauty, and thou Terror', as the epigraph makes clear, Salinas was more interested in probing and weighing its effects on his sensibility than in imagining what it could look like. His perfunctory description of falling in love as lightning (p. 143) is buried in lines that lack colour and image but are tense with precise and balanced arguments, whose movements hinge on such words as *sí, no, quizá, porque, ¿por qué?* and *si*, in which he posed in frequent questions problems like:

> ¿Abrazarme? ¿Con quién?
> ¿Seguir? ¿A quién?§   (p. 203)

* Without you I live among outlines of you.
† We, yes, we, the lovers loving.
‡ Her great work of love was to leave me alone.
§ Embrace? With whom? Follow? Whom?

Salinas's exclamation in *Seguro azar* that loving his *amada* was an

> ...ir y venir
> a ti misma de ti misma!* (p. 64)

placed her at the centre of his world and at the axis of his thoughts;
all haphazard movements are futile. In *La voz a ti debida* his precisely balanced formula and his solemn litany of disparate sites
emphasize that she was the fixed point to which he was chained:

> El ir y venir
> a los siglos, a las minas,
> a los sueños, es inútil.
> De ti salgo siempre, siempre
> tengo que volver a ti.† (p. 167)

When in his play *La bella durmiente* Soledad exalted anonymity and
enjoyed 'being unknown, escaping from the image which others
have of one',[1] she expressed Salinas's contempt for the public
identity adopted by his *amada* as she moves by instinct through a
cautiously charted life of predictable acts and physical sensations:

> Tú vives siempre en tus actos.
> Con la punta de tus dedos
> pulsas el mundo, le arrancas
> auroras, triunfos, colores,
> alegrías; es tu música.
> La vida es lo que tú tocas.
>
> De tus ojos, sólo de ellos,
> sale la luz que te guía
> los pasos. Andas
> por lo que ves. Nada más.‡ (p. 131)

Piercing the public image of a person whom other people expect
to be gay, Salinas refused to be dazed and deflected by her capri-

---

* coming and going to yourself from yourself!
† Coming and going to centuries, to mines, to dreams, is useless. I always depart
from you, I always have to return to you.
‡ You live always in your acts. With the tips of your fingers you touch the world,
you snatch from it daybreaks, triumphs, colours, joys; it is your music. The
intrument you play is life.
  From your eyes, and only from them, comes the light which guides your
steps. You walk through what you see. Nothing more.

cious gyrations, breathlessly captured in his indiscriminately sweeping censure of

> tus rostros, tus caprichos y tus besos,
> tus delicias volubles, tus contactos
> rápidos con el mundo,* (p. 157)

and went straight 'a lo desnudo y a lo perdurable't (p. 157), which he defined elsewhere in the work in phrases composed of pronouns and inelegant but emphatic adjectives as 'la irrefutable tú'‡ (p. 175) and 'pura, libre, / irreductible: tú'§ (p. 147).

Because Salinas observed the principle established by Proust that 'each one needs to find reasons for his passion',[1] *Razón de amor* suffered from what Ángel del Río properly diagnosed as 'a drop in poetic tension'.[2] Salinas seemed unable to recognize and therefore remedy the monotony caused by the impasse in his thoughts, in which the *amada* still occupied a central position as the immobile figure whose body he ignored in his pursuit of fleshless purity. Although he insisted in lines that echo the conclusion of *La voz a ti debida* that

> ...un sueño sólo es sueño
> verdadero
> cuando en materia mortal
> se desensueña y se encarna,‖ (p. 217)

he maintained his stubborn opposition to 'estas formas cansadas de este mundo'¶ (p. 283) in order to undertake a flight from life which he defined in the crisp title 'Suicidio hacia arriba'. Suspended in the heavens, the two lovers drift so freely that Salinas pitied those who are oppressed by roofs and choked by cobwebs,

> los que viven aún bajo techado,
> donde telas de araña se entretejen
> para cazar, para agostar los sueños...** (p. 285)

---

* your faces, your whims and your kisses, your voluble delights, your rapid contacts with the world.   † to the bare and the lasting.
‡ the irrefutable you.   § pure, free, irreducible: you.
‖ a dream is only a real dream when it shakes off its dream and embodies itself in mortal matter.   ¶ these weary forms of this world.
** those who still live beneath a roof, where cobwebs entwine to hunt, to wither dreams.

Eager to remain enclosed within a capsule where all that mattered to him was love and his thoughts about love, Salinas seemed to clench his teeth, steel his nerves and utter a challenge to himself as he expressed his determination to love and keep on loving:

> hay que querer sin dejarlo,
> querer y seguir queriendo.*   (p. 226)

But when he insisted in 'Suicidio hacia arriba'

> que nosotros estamos
> contentos, sí, contentos
> del cielo alto, de sus variaciones,†   (p. 285)

he appeared to feel the need to convince us by repetition of his contentment, to combat the tiredness caused by his conscious efforts to defy the stiffening of his thoughts, to keep the past alive and to maintain the tension and fluidity of *La voz a ti debida*.

The energetic delight in the 'trajín, ir, venir'‡ which animated *La voz a ti debida* (p. 204) evaporated in *Razón de amor* into a weariness with 'este vaivén,/este ir y venir'§ and a subdued search for 'un quererse quieto, quieto'‖ (p. 244). Unable to sustain in *Razón de amor* the élan of *La voz a ti debida*, Salinas composed a work at once discursive, emotionally inconsistent and structurally loose, in which digressions on water (pp. 246-8) and 'Una lágrima en mayo' (pp. 260-1) coexist with the vigorous affirmations of 'Suicidio hacia arriba' and 'Destino alegre'.

Love's search in *Razón de amor* for

> un más detrás de un más,
> otro cielo en su cielo¶   (p. 256)

signalled the determined pursuit of a private goal undertaken in their writings by Altolaguirre, Cernuda, Prados and Salinas. When they disengaged themselves from the outside world and focused on themselves, their pose of inactivity and their chants of

---

* one must love without let, love and carry on loving.
† that we are contented, yes, contented with the lofty heavens, with its variations.
‡ bustle, coming and going.
§ this fluctuation, this coming and going.   ‖ a still, still love.
¶ something more behind something more, another heaven in its heaven.

isolation should have led them ideally to compensate for their narrow range of theme with emotional intensity, imaginative power and verbal energy, for a hermit has to create interest in a narrative of solitude, a recital of his meditations and an exposure of his spiritual condition. Lacking intense feelings and an active fantasy, Altolaguirre, who was a competent and lucid manipulator of words, made a virtue out of sober dignity and staid, uncoloured precision. Feeling deeply and writing tensely, Prados appealed to the reader's stamina as he charted in his taut, nervous and spasmodic lines a mind caught in trance-like communion with itself. Salinas's disdain of direct contacts and direct sensations detached him consistently from reality and particularly his *amada*; accomplished by his intelligence when his emotions were tranquillized and his senses dormant, Salinas's graph of love's effects on him was a closely reasoned exercise in eloquence, dense and controlled in *La voz a ti debida*, loose and predictable in *Razón de amor*. Although Cernuda was deeply absorbed in himself and obeyed his dictum that 'The poet talks alone',[1] his spiritually honest recognition and avowal of his difference was framed within his censure of the world that choked him and crushed his dreams; in his poetry he used his vigorous imagination to paint a graphic and exemplary picture of a solitary aware of his complex, demanding nature and determined to be faithful to himself and to his dreams despite a society whose values and customs he found abhorrent. I hope that the next chapter will demonstrate Cernuda's ability to record his defiant solitude with a technique of poetic rebellion.

THE BROKEN RHYTHM

Si me preguntáis de dónde vengo, tengo que conversar con
  cosas rotas,
con utensilios demasiado amargos,
con grandes bestias a menudo podridas
y con mi acongojado corazón.*

Pablo Neruda, Residencia en la tierra (1925-35)

The 'cracked things' which Joyce invented in his nimble, resourceful mind and put into the head and mouth of Leopold
Bloom[1] challenge the reader to escape from orthodox expression
and embark on the literary adventure of *Ulysses*. This adventure
is as perplexing as the canvases of Dalí, Miró, Gris and Ernst, and
as provocative as the film Dalí and Buñuel made in 1928, *Un chien
andalou*, whose dissolving scenes of horror and violence, which
have been described as 'seventeen minutes of pure, scandalous,
dream-imagery', aroused great interest in Spain.[2] To understand
and savour the literary and artistic currents of the 1920s and 1930s,
the mind of the reader must be as flexible and his imagination as
lively as those of the writers and artists who dare him to jettison
his prejudices and follow them into what Ernst called in his description of one of his paintings 'an unknown—new and non-
conformist'.[3] It was because Lorca wanted people to explore the
unknown with him that he invited them to emulate his 'equestrian leap' from reality into fantasy, from the ordinary into the
mysterious, and accept without demur his bold imaginative statements in *El público* (1933) that 'A cat can be a frog. And the winter
moon can very well be a faggot covered with frozen worms'
(p. 1071).

The vigorous flight from the conventional and the fervent
search for new modes of expression, which in Spain stimulated

---

* If you ask me where I come from, I have to talk with broken things, with
utensils that are too bitter, with great beasts that are often putrid, and with my
grieving heart.

the tiresome verbiage of *ultraísmo* and the feeble rhetoric of *crea-cionismo*, found their most revolutionary formula in France in the explosive doctrines of surrealism. Louis Aragon's definition of surrealism as 'the wild and passionate use of the stupefying image'[1] demonstrated that the surrealist poets gave to the image a predominance and an autonomy which, when unsupported by theme and emotion, led, as Breton recognized in his manifestos, to 'a very high degree of *instant absurdity*' and a 'voluntary in-coherence'.[2] By obeying Breton's formula of 'pure psychic auto-matism', the French surrealist poets ruptured the conventional associations between words and objects and erupted in images and visions often too volcanic to be contained within the rigid moulds of verse forms. That the reader has to be a visionary to follow the capricious and unpredictable psychic leaps of poets hostile to reason is clear from Breton's blunt demand that 'he who still refuses, for instance, to *see* a horse galloping on a tomato should be looked upon as a cretin. A tomato is also a child's balloon—surrealism, I repeat, having suppressed the word "like".'[3] Anyone who looks at Dalí's paintings may legitimately wonder why he included in one of them his wife and a lamb-chop; Dalí's inability to explain with a brush what he revealed in his autobiography: that he did so because he liked his wife and lamb-chops,[4] makes the two motifs into a private and whimsical juxta-position, as disconcerting on a canvas as the eccentrically mated words set down on a printed page by poets like Breton, who wrote in a book aptly called *L'union libre* (1931):

> Ma femme à la chevelure de feu de bois
> Aux pensées d'éclairs de chaleur
> A la taille de sablier
> Ma femme à la taille de loutre entre les dents du tigre... *[5]

By making images the stimuli rather than the vehicles of thoughts and ideas, the French surrealists aspired to shape a new poetic consciousness that would be privileged to see through the flow of images an unsuspected vision of the world; Aragon's

---

* My wife with the hair of forest fire, with the thoughts of lightning flashes of heat, with the hour-glass figure, my wife with the figure of an otter between the tiger's teeth.

claim that 'each image at each blow forces you to revise the whole universe' was as grandiose as Diego's boast that *creacionismo* was the 'doorway or threshold of a whole new Art'.[1] But what some surrealist poets failed to realize as they incited their fantasies to create image after image, was that without the backbones of theme, form and emotion images become a shapeless parade of imaginative energy. In their search for novel and illuminating relationships between words and objects, they threw their images into the air 'like homing pigeons', as one critic has written, 'without bothering to find out if they would return at the right time to the dove-cot'.[2] Using a different metaphor, Antonio Machado tartly criticized the surrealists' cult of the haphazard when he suggested that Juan de Mairena would have remarked acidly that 'Those mules on the water-wheel have not yet realized that there is no water-wheel without water.'[3]

Just as Machado's deep-seated antipathy to image and metaphor blocked his understanding and acceptance of baroque and surrealist poetry, so did Guillén's limpid emotions and love of order dictate an instinctive hostility to surrealism, expressed in his trenchant statement that 'There is no babble quite so empty as that of the subconscious left to its triviality.'[4] His categoric assertion that 'In Spain no one was ever satisfied with the surrealist "document"'[5] belongs to the tangle of claims and counter-claims which obscure the supposed influence of French surrealism on Spanish poetry; one critic's statement that 'Neither Alberti, nor Cernuda, nor Lorca surrenders to automatism'[6] clashes with Cernuda's admission that 'surrealism, with its aims and technique, had won me over'.[7]

Some poets nervously flinched from the word 'surrealism' as if there were something sinister or shameful about it. In a letter he wrote in 1928 to Sebastián Gasch, one of the regular members of the self-styled 'groups of the surrealists' which met in Barcelona,[8] Lorca felt impelled to warn his friend that the 'new spiritualist manner' of poems like 'Oda al Santísimo Sacramento del Altar' 'is not surrealism' (p. 1594). And Alberti's contempt for what he called 'another new nickname'[9] led him to disclaim as rapidly as Lorca any influence of surrealism; he quickly followed his recollection that he wrote several poems of *Sobre los ángeles* in the grip of 'an unsolicited automatism, a spontaneous, trembling, feverish impulse' with the warning: 'But my song was not obscure...'[1]

Perhaps the only thing that emerges clearly from a tentative excursion into this no man's land of half-truth and contradiction is that, as they sought new modes of expression and exploited their mental vitality, Spanish writers in the 1920s responded in different degrees to a range of stimuli, from the aggressive dynamism of Marinetti to the imaginative excesses of the French surrealists. To describe the imagery of *Sobre los ángeles*, *Sermones y moradas*, *Un río, un amor*, *Los placeres prohibidos* and *Poeta en Nueva York* as surrealist is to abuse a label that, apart from contributing nothing to our comprehension of these works, gives Spanish poetry of the 1920s and 1930s a far too narrow frame of reference at a time when difficult and cryptic imagery was a phenomenon as international as the technique of chaotic enumeration and the revolt against traditional verse forms. It is not only in Spain that we find a type of poetry that, in its readiness to recognize any word as poetic and in its liberal use of the new and ever-increasing sense-data engendered by the technical advances of the twentieth century, aimed to suggest a climate of the mind rather than record a precise narrative of facts and feelings.

The interest shown by Spanish writers in French surrealism was so individual, uneven and sporadic that it did not crystallize into a programme or movement. But although surrealism did not exert a systematic influence on Spanish poets, it did repeat more vehemently the challenge already made by writers like Torre, Diego and Gómez de la Serna to explore the fantasy and liberate words from their outworn associations; as Cernuda pointed out, it offered him and Aleixandre a springboard for their pursuit of 'greater freedom of expression', 'and the important thing, as people know, is the athlete and not the springboard'.[2] The critical essays and translated extracts which appeared in Spanish magazines particularly in the 1920s[3] were evidence of contact and curiosity and a gentler and more insistent stimulus to artistic ferment than the strident and subversive harangue which Aragon delivered at the

Residencia de Estudiantes on 18 April 1925 and which Alberti recalled many years later;[1] posing as 'a germ-carrier, a public poisoner', Aragon announced 'the advent of a new spirit of revolt', threatened to 'make the blonde blood of the pavements gush' and warned that 'We are the agitators of the spirit.'[2]

That Spanish writers responded to these sporadic impulses is apparent in their curiosity about the workings and disorders of the mind. The aside Espina made in *Luna de copas*: '(see Freud)',[3] cited the inevitable authority on psychoanalysis whom the French surrealists revered and whose theories the dilettante bullfighter Ignacio Sánchez Mejías attempted to dramatize in his play entitled appropriately *Sinrazón* (1928), where Ballina states in a precise echo of Freud that 'A mad man is...a man who dreams continually. The dream, according to modern theories, is a desire repressed by our consciousness.'[4] Two characters of *Luna de copas*, Don Enrique, afflicted by 'plural nervousness', and Silvia, suffering from 'nervous excitement',[5] could have legitimately joined the 'Neuropaths' Club' which Domenchina founded in his novel *La túnica de Neso* (1929), where he paraded his enthusiasm for Freud and his interest in uninhibited sexual behaviour with the prurience he displayed in his poetry. The conviction he put into Dr Monje's mouth that 'Psychoanalysis is a splendid discovery for literature'[6] allowed him to join with the surrealists in exploring under the shelter of a science 'the in no way narrow possibilities of the absurd'[7] and to clothe his feverish obsession with sex in scientific fact as impressive as the symptoms Arturo listed to Dr Solesio:'—Paranoid obsession. Multiple phobias. Functional disorders in almost all the organs. And insomnia!'[8] By making Monje prescribe for Arturo 'A session of psychoanalysis and two of gymnastic eroticism, with changes of protagonist and posture,'[9] Domenchina ensured that the patient's punctilious observance would give him ample opportunity to narrate with relish rabid and at times grotesque sexual encounters.

Led to flaunt virility as a literary pose by his exhibitionist obsession with what he called in *Dédalo* (1931-2) the 'Carne cruda de la pasión sexual',*[10] Domenchina liberally peppered his prose

* Raw flesh of sexual passion.

and poetry, which he openly defined in *El tacto fervoroso* (1929–30) as 'Poemas del mal sabor de boca', with words normally found in medical works or manuals of erotica. Fascinated by the phallos and childishly determined to defy sexual taboos, he degraded to a vulgar licentiousness the literary freedom generated by *creacionismo*, *ultraísmo*, surrealism and psychoanalysis, interpreting the formula 'Palabras en libertad'*[1] as the liberty to use any words. When Moreno Villa insisted in *Carambas* (1931) that

> ...el veintitrés y la cómoda
> comulgan con el zapato y la oropéndola
> sin que noten anomalías en el discurso,†[2]

he too seemed to be advocating with his deliberately whimsical juxtapositions the wanton absurdity already displayed in Giménez Caballero's attempts to 'Shuffle my cards'[3] and in Dámaso Alonso's decision to think of 'absurd and amusing things'.[4] But what made Moreno Villa's poetry more valuable than a graph of literary fashion was his view of poetry as the 'confession' of authentic feelings.[5] Like Alberti, Cernuda and Lorca, Moreno Villa used poetry to purge himself of the 'asco y pesadez'‡ which led him to view himself as a 'miserable carrito'§ haunted by death.[6] His solitude and anguish forced him to see nothing but despair and ugliness around and within him, as he stated sadly in *Colección* (1924):

> He perdido el ritmo
> y sólo veo fealdad:
> ....
> He perdido el ritmo
> y sólo veo mi maldad.‖[7]

Domenchina, however, wallowed in his poetry in mud, slime and dung because he wanted to and not because they signified his revulsion against a life he chose to represent as unrelievedly

---

* Words in liberty.
† the number twenty-three and the chest of drawers commune with the shoe and the golden oriole without their noticing any anomalies in their speech.
‡ nausea and fatigue.   § wretched little cart.
‖ I have lost the rhythm, and I see only ugliness.
   I have lost the rhythm, and I see only my wickedness.

squalid. The artistic freedom used particularly by Alberti, Cernuda and Lorca to describe thoughts and feelings that defied expression in prose was distorted by Domenchina into a licence to shock, to display a crude vitality summarized in the childish formula he expounded in *La túnica de Neso*: 'I fart, therefore I exist.'[1] The advice Dr Solesio gave Arturo: 'Abstain from all criticism. And do not mortify yourself by giving literary shape or cohesion to what you say',[2] authorized Arturo's overheated thoughts and actions and allowed Domenchina to record salacious episodes without controlling his fantasy, his prurience or what Juan Ramón Jiménez called his 'frightful vocabulary'.[3]

Dreams and the subconscious also proved irresistible to Hinojosa, whom Cernuda, selecting a label as imprecise as it is contentious, went so far as to call 'the first Spanish surrealist':[4] he did not say whether he was referring to chronology or technique. As he nonchalantly tossed his thoughts into the air, Hinojosa put his trust in chance, for when they dropped on his head like 'snowflakes'[5] they fell into random sequences of images and visions as mystifying as the blend of real and unreal elements interwoven by the Catalan poet J. V. Foix in the prose poems of his *Diari 1918*:[6]

> Our intertwined hands fused with the young vine-
> branches on the bank of that river that had its bed
> full of pebbles in the form of white hearts at
> midnight when the lovers lose their blood through
> the only wound opened in love during sleep. And
> our white blood evaporated during sleep before
> consciousness formed with the blood marble statues
> or floating icebergs in these troubled waters
> peopled by lumps of skeletons and long smiles of
> redskins.[7]

Like the breathless rhetorical displays of Marinetti and Torre, Hinojosa's cult of chance, his effervescent images and his juxtaposition of objects as incongruous as three hearts and a billiard table tell us more about the currents of his age than about him;[8] the 'dark woman with aluminium breasts and dressed in wax tights' he created in *La flor de California*[9] was an anonymous plaything of his fantasy.

VI Aleixandre, Cernuda and Lorca in 1931

With his claim that Larrea relayed to Alberti, Aleixandre and Lorca 'a new literary technique', Cernuda tried to pinpoint the origin of a literary phenomenon whose roots were deep and complex.[1] Although Guillén's recollection that 'These poets talked through images'[2] neatly summarizes the fervour with which the poets of his age mined their imaginations, it does not distinguish between Alberti, Cernuda and Lorca on the one hand, who were forced to express through images thoughts and feelings that defied simple definition and precise analysis, and Aleixandre on the other, whose exuberant spawning of images was a manner and a mantle deliberately tailored to fit his vague and elastic creed that 'style is the poet'.[3] Aleixandre's passion for freedom, which explains his enjoyment in *Espadas como labios* of 'los no-límites'* (p. 230) and the paradoxical principle he established twenty-five years later that 'the universe of the poet is infinite but limited,'[4] led him to adopt and evolve a rhetoric of effusion. The tumult which in the restless pages of *Ámbito* rampaged rebelliously within the confines of verse-forms trampled down all formal barriers in his next three works as he assaulted the reader's sensibility with ecstatic enumerations and endlessly proliferating images drawn from inexhaustible sources of mental energy.

The work of Aleixandre that in aim, technique and achievement was closest to surrealism, as he himself has acknowledged,[5] is *Pasión de la tierra*, which is composed of densely textured and highly imaginative prose poems whose capricious fluidity he did not control and whose excesses of language and fantasy he did not correct. To record his vision of primeval chaos, Aleixandre wrote his 'poetry "in a nascent state"' out of the 'subconscious elements'[6] he harvested in the deep and inaccessible areas of his mind; this conscious pursuit of the mentally wayward and unformed made his original title *La evasión hacia el fondo* a more accurate label for an extravaganza that is one of the most unfathomable works of twentieth-century Spanish poetry.

Aleixandre's statement that 'Pensamientos, barcos, pesares pasan, entran por los ojos. Me soy, os soy'† (p. 208) shows that he

---

* non-limits.
† Thoughts, boats, sorrows pass through, come in by my eyes. I am I, I am you.

submerged his mind, senses and identity in what he himself called the 'mass in ebullition',[1] which paralysed him in an embryonic purity and rawness where he witnessed weird metamorphoses and savoured the strange perceptions and sensations of his 'conciencia sin funda'* (p. 163), whose freedom he celebrated in his boast that 'Mil bocas de heno fresco, mil paladares de mañana he tropezado en mi camino'† (p. 172). His faith that 'La consistencia del espíritu consiste sólo en olvidarse de los límites'‡ (p. 171) prompted him to put his trust in the chance prophecies and haphazard permutations of playing-cards, which in 'Fuga a caballo' he combined with the motif of the horse to illustrate his longing to be swept away

a otro reino, a la heroica capacidad de amar, a la bella guarda de todas las cajas, a los dados silvestres que se sienten en los dedos tristísimos cuando las rosas naufragan junto al puente tendido de la salvación.§

(p. 178)

It was because love can unite and so thwart the pitiless melting of things and creatures that in 'El mundo está bien hecho' Aleixandre followed the cries of '¡Ámame!'‖ made by the crickets and the cacti with the shouts of 'Muere, muere'¶ uttered by the serpent when it discovered the fact that delighted Guillén: 'el mundo está bien hecho'** (p. 206). Aleixandre's determination to let his mind roam freely through an effervescent world made him imagine love as a destructive power so fearful that it could transform a kiss into 'Un río de sangre, un mar de sangre'†† (p. 151). The whips, daggers and teeth which recur in *Pasión de la tierra* and other works of Aleixandre point to the brutality of a universe that, refusing to be divided or dominated, ferments as unpredictably as his prose, which, like these mysterious lines of 'La muerte o antesala de consulta', displays before the reader a mosaic of

* consciousness without a sheath.
† A thousand mouths of fresh hay, a thousand morning palates have I encountered on my way.
‡ The consistency of the spirit consists only in forgetting the limits.
§ to another kingdom, to the heroic ability to love, to the beautiful keeper of all the boxes, to the wild dice which are felt on the deeply sad fingers when the roses are shipwrecked near the outstretched bridge of salvation.   ‖ Love me.
¶ Die, die.   ** the world is well made.   †† A river of blood, a sea of blood.

fantasy, an impetuous sequence of changing planes, capricious associations, eccentric hypotheses and joltingly plain statements:

La hora grande se acercaba en la bruma. La sala cabeceaba sobre el mar de cáscaras de naranja. Remaríamos sin entrañas si los pulsos no estu-vieran en las muñecas. El mar es amargo. Tu beso me ha sentado mal al estómago. Se acerca la hora.

La puerta, presta a abrirse, se teñía de amarillo lóbrego lamentándose de su torpeza. Dónde encontrarte, oh sentido de la vida, si ya no hay tiempo. Todos los seres esperaban la voz de Jehová refulgente de metal blanco. Los amantes se besaban sobre los nombres. Los pañuelos eran narcóticos y restañaban la carne exangüe. Las siete y diez. La puerta volaba sin plumas y el ángel del Señor anunció a María. Puede pasar el primero.* (p. 154)

As Aleixandre played patience in 'El solitario', the pack plotted for him an erratic journey of mental adventure 'camino de lo des-caminado'† (p. 189); the reader may perhaps be forgiven for not following the labyrinthine paths that thread through this virgin territory. By observing his rule that 'un hombre que persigue perderá siempre sus bastones, su lento apoyo, enhebrado en la hermosura de su ceguera'‡ (p. 200), Aleixandre recorded the spurts of his volatile and insubordinate mind, whose mutiny, which he himself had incited, he was to subdue partly in his sub-sequent works. His comforting blanket assertions that poetry should 'communicate' and express not 'beauty' but 'emotion'[1] allowed him ample freedom to say what he liked and how he liked as he assaulted our sensibility. By courting chance and throwing 'las yemas al aire'§ (p. 198) in an action that paralleled

---

* The momentous hour approached in the fog. The room nodded on the sea of orange peel. We would row without entrails if the pulses were not in our wrists. The sea is bitter. Your kiss has upset my stomach. The hour approaches.

The door, ready to open, was tinged with lugubrious yellow lamenting its torpor. Where can I find you, o meaning of life, if there is no time. Everyone awaited the voice of Jehovah resplendent with white metal. The lovers kissed one another over the names. The handkerchiefs were narcotic and staunched the lifeless blood. Ten past seven. The door flew without feathers and the angel of the Lord announced Mary. The first one can go in.

† on the road to somewhere never traversed before.

‡ a man who pursues will always lose his walking-sticks, his slow support, tied to the beauty of his blindness.

§ the yolks in the air.

Hinojosa's carefree method, Aleixandre imagined the sudden transformation by which, after kissing the playing-cards, he changed into a gramophone record (p. 190). And his search for the 'expressive words' which came to him in his sleep (p. 181) and which he did not sift when awake unearthed such rare and resonant examples as *delicuescente, intercostal, vivíparo* and *carpeto-vetónico*, with which he seemed keen to justify his faith that 'poetry is not a *question of words*'.[1]

Aleixandre's belief that 'Every word is poetic if necessary'[2] fed the loquacity which he confessed disarmingly in *Pasión de la tierra* (p. 177) with an indiscriminate diet, often as graceless as his censure of words in *Espadas como labios* as a 'torpe vientre hinchado'* (p. 260). By prefacing *Espadas como labios* with Byron's definition of a poet as 'a babbler', Aleixandre suggested ominously that he was fulfilling the promise he made in *Pasión de la tierra*: 'No me ahorraré ni una sola palabra'† (p. 163). The strain of singing, as he twice insisted, with his whole body (pp. 251, 284) made him imagine in 'La palabra' smoke pouring out of his mouth as he ejaculated words in rapid lists, or raced, stopped for breath and impetuously changed the direction of his thoughts:

> El frío sueña
> con estampido-eternidad. La vida
> es un instante
> justo para decir María. Silencio.
> Una blancura, un rojo que no nace,
> ese roce de besos bajo el agua.
> Una orilla impasible donde rompen
> cuerpos u ondas, mares, o la frente.‡ (p. 259)

This irrepressible impulsiveness forced Aleixandre to recite catalogues of objects and creatures whose only link is their common membership of the universe; as he saw himself in 'La palabra' as nothing more than a tiny snail (p. 221), his awe and excitement at

* torpid swollen belly.
† I shall not save a single word.
‡ The cold dreams of explosion-eternity. Life is a moment just enough to say Mary. Silence. A whiteness, a red which is not born, that touch of kisses beneath the water. An impassive shore on which break bodies or waves, seas, or the brow.

being encompassed by the lush complexity of creation spilt into an indiscriminate roll-call of its components:

> Una mano de acero sobre el césped,
> un corazón, un juguete olvidado,
> un resorte, una lima, un beso, un vidrio.*   (p. 239)

His chant that 'he visto el mar, la mar, los mares, los no-límites'†
(p. 230) takes us on a crescendo of freedom from the single and the specific to the unlimited and undefined. *Pasión de la tierra* presented us not with an identifiable person but with the excited virginal consciousness of a poet exploring the mysteries of *lo descaminado*; *Espadas como labios* invited us to follow Aleixandre's imagination as it ranged exuberantly over the universe, whose awesome expanse he signposted constantly with the words *tierra, cielo, mar, río* and *nube*.

Although Aleixandre imagined himself as a cloud and a wasp in 'Acaba' (p. 250), where he dreamed like Altolaguirre and Prados of the freedom of the air, it was to the sea that he resorted most frequently in his fantasy. His repetition throughout *Espadas como labios* of the words *mar, playa, espuma, onda, marea, nave, navío, barco, lancha, vela, quilla, bogar* and *navegar* reveals in their variety and frequency his enthusiasm for an element that in its uncontrollable restlessness represents perfectly liberty of thought and action; in 'Resaca' his voice and his embraces are as free as the open sea, the flying spray and the billowing sail:

> Este ancho mar permite la clara voz nacida,
> la desplegada vela verde,
> ese batir de espumas a infinito,
> a la abierta envergadura de los dos brazos distantes.‡   (p. 241)

The freedom he demanded in 'Libertad' was liberty of mind and body; he wanted to drink in the sensations aroused by the world outside him and look within himself at areas that existed in his fantasy, virgin tracts visible only to his 'ojos no pisados'§ (p. 230).

---

* A steel hand on the grass, a heart, a forgotten toy, a spring, a file, a kiss, a piece of glass.   † I have seen the sea, the sea, the seas, the non-limits.
‡ This broad sea allows the clear new-born voice, the unfurled green sail, that whipping of foam to the infinite spaces, to the open span of the two distant arms.
§ untrodden eyes.

What Aleixandre's eyes sought and discovered in *Espadas como labios* as they turned away like Salinas from the obvious, 'lo más fácil', to the mysterious, 'un cuento'* (p. 252), was a world of surprise, whose sudden and capricious metamorphoses he documented in frequent records of odd transitions whose pivot is *o*:

> Yo aspiro a lo blanco o la pared, ¿quién sabe?
> Aspiro a mí o a ti o a lo llorado,
> aspiro a un eso que se va perdiendo
> como diez dedos, humo o lo ya atónito.† (p. 252)

The *o* which peppers these lines and Aleixandre's poetry as a whole links the acrobatic leaps of a mind where, according to his neat diagnosis, 'extremos navegan'‡ (p. 242). With strange phrases like 'una senda o jirafas de blancura'§ (p. 228) and 'vientres o conchas/o perezosas barcas'‖ (p. 274), Aleixandre challenged us to emulate his mental flexibility and supply for ourselves the unseen, suppressed links between objects grouped just as capriciously by *como*, which licenced comparisons as surprising as the 'dulce sonrisa abierta como un vidrio cortado'¶ (p. 257).

The disparate objects which Aleixandre gathered into clusters as eccentric as:

> Una música o nardo
> o unas telas de araña,
> un jarrón de cansancios
> y de polvos o nácar...** (p. 273)

were thrown together by 'the clearly differentiated psychic movements' which, Aleixandre maintained, 'give unity to each poem' of *Espadas como labios*.[1] But to claim that a complex of mental impulses gives coherence to a poem is to postulate unity in anarchy, is to suggest that cattle racing in four directions create the wholeness of a stampede. To perceive the truth and revelation Aleixandre

---

* the most facile; a tale.
† I aspire to white or the wall, who knows? I aspire to me or to you or to what has been mourned, I aspire to something that is being lost like ten fingers, smoke or the already astonished.   ‡ extremes sail.
§ a path or giraffes of whiteness.   ‖ bellies or shells or lazy boats.
¶ sweet smile opened like a cut piece of glass.
** A music or spikenard or some cobwebs, a jug of weariness and of powders or mother-of-pearl.

mentioned in his poems (pp. 244, 259), the reader has to destroy his inhibitions, cleanse his mind and prepare it for entry into a universe more intricate than simple titles like 'Muerte' and 'Río' would have us believe; he has to pick his way through a world of shifting planes, fleeting visions and changing shapes, where hands suddenly become mountains, as in 'Resaca' (p. 242), or where, as Aleixandre showed in 'Blancura', an open wound can become a bee and then a rose as it moves into the 'supersensible reality' which he regarded as the poet's province:[1]

> Universo tocado con la yema,
> donde una herida abierta
> ayer fue abeja, hoy rosa, ayer lo inseparable.*
>
> (p. 283)

Aleixandre's supple canon that

> Todo lo que está suficientemente visto
> no puede sorprender a nadie†   (p. 235)

guaranteed that his poetry would shock as well as disconcert and licenced his enthusiasm for the ugly elements of creation, whose role he defended in a vigorous stanza of 'Por último':

> Quiero un bosque, una luna, quiero todo,
> ¿ me entiendes? todo, hasta lo horrible,
> esos cabellos de saliva extensa.‡   (p. 252)

The lights shining through the armpits in 'Suicidio', where in a vision as horrid as Lorca's 'Martirio de Santa Olalla' a body hangs in the wind 'herido por las lenguas que chupan sus hormigas'§ (p. 276), illuminate Aleixandre's enjoyment of the macabre and repellent, which made 'el vello de los pubis'‖ (p. 235) as irresistible to him as 'las rosas del pubis'¶ were to Neruda.[2] And when Aleixandre wrote that

---

* Universe touched with the yolk, where an open wound was yesterday a bee, today a rose, yesterday what was inseparable.
† Everything that is sufficiently seen cannot surprise anyone.
‡ I want a forest, a moon, I want everything, do you understand me? everything, everything, even the horrible, those heads of hair of extensive spittle.
§ wounded by the tongues which lick its ants.
‖ the pubic hair.   ¶ the rose of the pubis.

...los caballeros abandonados de sus traseros
quieren atraer todas las miradas a la fuerza hacia sus bigotes,*

(p. 236)

he failed to recognize that without humour to redeem it his vision of men trying to divert attention from their fugitive buttocks to their moustache can only be a gratuitous display of poetic freedom containing the 'very high degree of *instant absurdity*' which Breton diagnosed in surrealist poems.[1]

Whitman's faith that 'Sex contains all, bodies, souls...'[2] was echoed in 'el whitmaniano vértigo'† which excited Domenchina[3] and in Aleixandre's belief that 'la idea es carne'‡ (p. 263). The neatly alliterative juxtaposition of 'clavos' and 'caricia'§ in one poem (p. 223) and the discovery of 'un tiburón en forma de cariño'‖ in another (p. 243) show that love for Aleixandre was a brutal passion which brought pain as well as pleasure, anguish as well as frenzy. The lips which obsessed him in *Espadas como labios* perpetutate the river of blood which, released by a kiss in *Pasión de la tierra* (p. 151), still flows in *La destrucción o el amor* as evidence of his steadfast attitude to love and consistent vision of it.

The mouth which in the strangely titled 'El más bello amor' of *Espadas como labios* Aleixandre likened to a 'bestial fruit', a dagger and a bite (p. 244) still haunted him in *La destrucción o el amor*, where his linking of kisses or lips with teeth and blood reinforced his vision of love as a brutal power as graphically as his conjunction of *amor* and many sharp weapons, from the *colmillo, garra, dientes* and *uñas* of the body to the *espada, hacha, flecha, dardo, clavo, látigo* and *cuchillo* used by the hand. His vehement statement that 'quiero matar o amar o morir o darte todo'¶ (p. 316) established love as a force so terrible that it allowed no middle course as it confronted him with the macabre choice between 'un cadáver o un beso'** (p. 323) and 'la muerte putrefacta o el beso'†† (p. 364).

---

* the gentlemen abandoned by their buttocks want to divert everyone's eyes to their moustaches.
† the Whitman-like vertigo.
‡ idea is flesh.   § nails; caress.
‖ a shark in the shape of affection.
¶ I want to kill or love or die or give you everything.
** a corpse or a kiss.   †† putrid death or the kiss.

The vigour contained within the beautiful form of a woman's body invited him to melt into the lava flowing through her veins and die suspended in ecstasy:

> Quiero amor o la muerte, quiero morir del todo,
> quiero ser tú, tu sangre, esa lava rugiente
> que regando encerrada bellos miembros extremos
> siente así los hermosos límites de la vida.*   (p. 308)

By confining his hungry eyes to these 'beautiful limits', Aleixandre realized his ambition to 'vivir en el fuego'† (p. 307); roaming in *La destrucción o el amor* over a woman's thighs, stomach, waist, throat, neck, lips and mouth, lingering over her breasts and hovering like Domenchina in *La túnica de Neso* over her armpits,[1] he catalogued feverishly the anatomical details of a form that, unlike Guillén's clinically reposed and asexual 'Desnudo', embodied the love which rules and enfolds the universe. His insistent use of 'es' and 'sé' at the end of his 'Triunfo del amor' organized into a rapturous litany his definition of love as a naked body whose habitat is the elements and nature and whose destiny is to savour the sensations it provokes:

> Es sólo ya el desnudo. Es la risa en los dientes.
> Es la luz o su gema fulgurante: los labios.
> Es el agua que besa unos pies adorados,
> como un misterio oculto a la noche vencida.
> . . . .
> Yo sé quien ama y vive, quien muere y gira y vuela.
> Sé que lunas se extinguen, renacen, viven, lloran.
> Sé que dos cuerpos aman, dos almas se confunden.‡   (p. 366)

While Guillén's crisp and controlled mind channelled his ecstatic enjoyment of creation into simple images, terse statements

---

* I want love or death, I want to die completely, I want to be you, your blood, that roaring lava which, irrigating the beautiful extreme limbs in which it is contained, feels thus the beautiful limits of life.   † live in fire.

‡ It is now only the nude. It is laughter on the teeth. It is light or its resplendent gem: the lips. It is water kissing some adored feet, like a mystery hidden to the conquered night.

I know who loves and lives, who dies and gyrates and flies. I know that moons are extinguished, are reborn, live, weep. I know that two bodies love, two souls melt into one.

and formal moulds, Aleixandre let his words and images stream erratically over the page as his volatile fantasy raced over the universe; too impulsive to linger in any one place, he wandered ceaselessly in *La destrucción o el amor* around the elements, from the earth, where he lay, as he pointed out with characteristic effusion, 'entre lo verde presente, entre lo siempre fresco'* (p. 353), to the sea, which he celebrated in 'Que así invade' (pp. 389–90), to the air, whose freedom entranced him so much that in 'Nube feliz' he imagined himself in lines reminiscent of 'Acaba' in *Espadas como labios* as a bird, a feather, a cloud and a breeze escaping from the world (pp. 397–8).

That *La destrucción o el amor* commemorated Aleixandre's recovery from tuberculosis, as he himself has reminded us,[1] is apparent in his eagerness to expose his senses to the exuberance of nature and go digging for sensations with an insistence charted in his enthusiastic use of repetition and enumeration:

> Dejadme, sí, dejadme cavar, cavar sin tregua,
> cavar hasta ese nido caliente o plumón tibio,
> hasta esa carne dulce donde duermen los pájaros,
> los amores de un día cuando el sol luce fuera.† (p. 314)

But the alternative of 'Un clamor o sollozo de alegría'‡ (p. 378) shows that Aleixandre's sensations ranged within limits as extreme as the contrasts which in his eyes composed creation. When he wrote that 'Musgo o luna es lo mismo, lo que a nadie sorprende'§ (p. 336), he tried casually to play down the eccentric relationships and control the 'imaginative contagions'[2] which in *Pasión de la tierra* and *Espadas como labios* had hardened into a mannered eccentricity. In *La destrucción o el amor* his forging of strange links was more of a tool than an end in itself; his desire to explore, exhibit and exalt the material richness of the universe led him in 'Quiero pisar' to follow his statement that 'Quiero muslos de acero' with

---

* amid the present green, amid the always fresh.
† Let me, yes, let me dig, dig without pause, dig down to that hot nest or warm feather, down to that sweet flesh where the birds sleep, the loves of a day when the sun shines outside.
‡ A shout or sob of gaiety.
§ Moss or moon is the same, a fact that surprises no-one.

the alternative 'acaso musgo tenue'* (p. 383); and the quick transformation of two hands into two mountains in 'Resaca' of *Espada como labios* (p. 242) was matched in 'Eterno secreto' of *La destrucción o el amor* by a rapid change of scenery whose elements are linked first by their initial 'p' and more loosely by their common membership of creation:

> en un bosque de palmas, de palomas dobladas,
> de picos que se traman como las piedras inmóviles.† (p. 356)

Aleixandre's faith in the unity of the world eliminated divisions and guaranteed, according to the titles of two poems, the presence of a 'Mar en la tierra' and the unity of 'La selva y el mar'. The sky of mud which appears in one poem (p. 393) and the metal feathers found in another (p. 401) illustrate both the fluid unity of creation and the flexibility of a mind that swung rapidly between earth and sky, sea and earth, beauty and horror, anguish and rapture, tenderness and savagery, life and death. But around these extremes of place, feeling and condition Aleixandre put, as if the universe were a woman's waist, an arm (p. 324), which he changed in 'Cobra' into a cobra encircling the chaotic richness of the universe (pp. 387–8). Predictably, in *La destrucción o el amor* Aleixandre paraded the lushness of creation in lists which, like the excitedly indiscriminate finale of 'Se querían', expose his dependence on a technique that aggravated the verbal diarrhoea from which he suffered in his attempts to achieve 'propagation':[1]

> Día, noche, ponientes, madrugadas, espacios,
> ondas nuevas, antiguas, fugitivas, perpetuas,
> mar o tierra, navío, lecho, pluma, cristal,
> metal, música, labio, silencio, vegetal,
> mundo, quietud, su forma. Se querían, sabedlo.‡ (p. 406)

When in *Mundo a solas* Aleixandre catalogued the 'remotas playas, nubes felices, un viento así dorado'§ (p. 429) and exalted

---

* I want thighs of steel; perhaps tenuous moss.

† in a forest of palms, of folded doves, of beaks which are woven like the motionless stones.

‡ Day, night, sunsets, daybreaks, spaces, new, old, fugitive, perpetual waves, sea or earth, ship, bed, feather, crystal, metal, music, lip, silence, vegetal, world, stillness, her form. They loved each other, know it.

§ remote beaches, happy clouds, a wind thus golden.

the '¡ Cielo redondo y claro donde vivir volando...!'* (p. 444), his enthusiastic tribute to the variety and freedom of the universe established between this work and *La destrucción o el amor* a link which was strengthened even further by the reappearance of love as a hammer smiting as cruelly here as it did in *Pasión de la tierra* (pp. 427, 165–6). But while anyone familiar with Aleixandre's poetry expects to find titles like 'Humano ardor', 'Al amor', 'Filo del amor', 'Tormento del amor' and 'El amor iracundo', he has to detect in the titles 'No existe el hombre', 'Ya no es posible' and 'Nadie' a deepening pessimism clearly signalled in the epigraph, for which he resorted significantly to Quevedo: 'Yace la vida envuelta en alto olvido.'† The confidence with which in his preceding works he had celebrated nature and sung his own role in it has crumbled into the doubt which made him echo with '¿Quién soy, quién eres, quién te sabe?'‡ (p. 452) the disturbing questions Alberti posed some eight years previously in 'El ángel desconocido' of *Sobre los ángeles*:

> Por las calles, ¿ quién se acuerda?
> ....
> Dime quién soy.§   (p. 250)

Aleixandre's melancholy insistence in *Mundo a solas* that 'Allí no existe el hombre' (p. 449) and that 'El hombre está muy lejos'‖ (p. 450) lamented the replacement of élan by the despair which had anguished Alberti, Cernuda and Lorca several years earlier. Now a passive bystander rather than a dynamic actor, Aleixandre has discovered painfully that the world is not a compact circle but a void; the 'cadáver en pie' (p. 423) and 'yertos hombres'¶ (p. 460) who people it represent his distress as simply and chillingly as the 'uninhabited body' which appears in *Sobre los ángeles* (pp. 250–4) and the 'grey man' and 'headless horsemen' whom Cernuda introduced into *Un río, un amor* (pp. 41, 60) as graphic comments on a life he found bleak, aimless and sterile.

---

* Round, clear sky where one can live in flight!
† Life lies enveloped in deep oblivion.
‡ Who am I, who are you, who knows of you?
§ As I walk through the streets, who remembers me? Tell me who I am.
‖ Man does not exist there; Man is very distant.   ¶ standing corpse; rigid men.

The irreconcilable conflict between Cernuda's imprisonment in a world composed of 'tedium, monotony, strange beings'[1] and his constant yearning 'for some impossible Golden Age'[2] of love, beauty and eternal youth suspended him in an incurable discontent, generated his angry attacks on mankind in general and family life in particular, and hardened his resolve to be faithful to himself at all costs, even if it meant violating orthodoxy. His pugnacious observance of his dictum: 'Cultivate what others censure in you, for that is your true self',[3] was a posture of defiance prompting his determined assault on social taboos, his flaunting of 'forbidden pleasures' and his explosive shout of anarchy in a poem of *Un río, un amor* sourly called '¿Son todos felices?', where the only survivor of the wanton destruction illustrated by the split head is defeat itself:

> Abajo pues la virtud, el orden, la miseria;
> Abajo todo, todo, excepto la derrota,
> Derrota hasta los dientes, hasta ese espacio helado
> De una cabeza abierta en dos a través de soledades,
> Sabiendo nada más que vivir es estar a solas con la muerte.*
>
> (p. 61)

With this vehement repudiation of order and perverse advocacy of defeat, Cernuda was voicing the malaise and rebelliousness which conditioned him to find in surrealism as much of a social protest as a poetic stimulus. His view of Spain towards the end of the 1920s as a 'decrepit country' crumbling under Primo de Rivera's dictatorship explains his enthusiastic absorption of 'a spiritual current' that incited and authorized him to fly in the face of the society he regarded as smug and unjust.[4]

It was in *Un río, un amor* and *Los placeres prohibidos* that Cernuda emulated and responded to the 'malaise and daring' which he sensed in the poetry of Aragon, Breton and René Crevel.[5] Faithful to 'the first impulse' pursued and advocated by the surrealists, he recorded 'at one go and without corrections'[6] the failure of love

---

* Down then with virtue, order, poverty; down with everything, everything except defeat, defeat right up to the teeth, right up to that frozen space of a head split in two across solitudes, knowing nothing more than that to live is to be alone with death.

and desire, which he nevertheless defended tenaciously as a value of life despite his collapsed ideals, frightening fantasies and the corrosive disillusion provoking his wistful hypotheses in *Los placeres prohibidos*:

Si el hombre pudiera decir lo que ama,
Si el hombre pudiera levantar su amor por el cielo
Como una nube en la luz;
Si como muros que se derrumban,
Para saludar la verdad erguida en medio,
Pudiera derrumbar su cuerpo, dejando sólo la verdad de su amor,
La verdad de sí mismo,
Que no se llama gloria, fortuna o ambición,
Sino amor o deseo,
Yo sería aquel que imaginaba.*   (pp. 72–3)

But what was a creative malaise in *Un río, un amor* and *Los placeres prohibidos* subsided in *Donde habite el olvido* and *Invocaciones* into a repetitive nostalgia, where such restrained, elegiac statements as 'He amado, ya no amo más'† (p. 91) perpetuated Cernuda's discontent with none of the boldness which in his previous two works had led him to reinforce his forthright laments like 'Estoy cansado de estar vivo'‡ (p. 49) with capricious constructions, surprising images, colloquial phrases and nightmare visions of phantoms and headless men who in *Un río, un amor* filed through his mind to enact his anguish:

Una angustia sin fondo aullaba entre las piedras;
Hacia el aire, hombres sordos,
La cabeza olvidada,
Pasaban a lo lejos como libres o muertos;
Vergonzoso cortejo de fantasmas
Con las cadenas rotas colgando de las manos.§   (p. 56)

---

* If man could say what he loves, if man could lift his love through the heavens like a cloud in the light; if like collapsing walls, in order to greet the truth erect in the middle, he could demolish his body, leaving only the truth of his love, the truth of himself, which is not called glory, fortune or ambition, but love or desire, I would be he who dreamed.

† I have loved, I no longer love.   ‡ I am tired of being alive.

§ A bottomless anguish howled among the stones; towards the air, deaf men, having forgotten their heads, passed in the distance as if free or dead; a shameful cortège of phantoms with broken chains dangling from their hands.

Although in *Un río, un amor* Cernuda imagined disconcertingly that 'la luna es madera'* (p. 60), he did not strain his fantasy to weave impenetrable thickets of images; in the alternatives he suggested in 'Perlas grises o acaso cenicientas estrellas't of the same work (p. 42), the link between pearls and stars on the one hand and grey and ashen on the other is visually much closer and more coherent than the connection between, for example, the 'steel thighs' and 'tenuous moss' in *La destrucción o el amor* (p. 383). Cernuda did not paint in his poems a canvas of fluid and dynamic nature, but presented a firm and purely functional back-cloth whose elements—night, mist, wind, clouds, sky, stars and sea—stiffened into a poetic code as they established and reflected his emotional climate. His description of himself as an extinguished star (p. 43) suggests that he was less interested in forging novel images than in finding for his emotions a simple and meaningful picture or, as he himself put it in Eliot's phrase, the 'objective correlative' of his experience.[1] When he wrote in *Los placeres prohibidos* that

Corazas infranqueables, lanzas o puñales,
Todo es bueno si deforma un cuerpo,‡   (p. 67)

he was reinforcing the savage feeling explicit in the second line in precisely the way he said Baudelaire did: 'through the object'.[2] The objects he placed repeatedly in his poems as he tried to give his emotions a shape and texture that can be felt and visualized without mental strain are deliberately humble and commonplace because of his belief that 'Such objects of supernatural experience do not need to be *a priori* 'poetic'; the more humble they appear at first sight, the more significant they are made by the experience which is objectified in them.'[3] By representing night as a whip (p. 46), flowers as iron (p. 67) and the world as wire (p. 62), he let three simple things depict his view of life as cruel and hard; his choice of a snake to describe insidious snow (p. 15) and of rags to describe cold (p. 53) guaranteed an emotional response in the reader, who visualizes the things without effort and detects through them Cernuda's chill feelings and horror of snow; and

---

* the moon is wood.   † Grey pearls or perhaps ashen stars.
‡ Impenetrable cuirasses, lances or daggers, everything is good if it deforms a body.

the stone which recurs constantly in his poems illustrates and strengthens with its simple associations of violence, weight and lifelessness Cernuda's crushed and restricted existence in a bleak world.

Hostile to the 'succulent and unusual language' which he censured with particular severity in Darío,[1] in *Un río, un amor* and *Los placeres prohibidos* particularly Cernuda relaxed the starched and sometimes strained phrasing of *Perfil del aire* as he tried to reproduce 'the spoken language and colloquial tone'.[2] His frequent and straightforward use of colours like *amarillo, gris, negro, verde, azul* and *blanco* reacted against artifice and opted for economy: while such contrived phrases of *Perfil del aire* as 'luz de alabastro' and 'ébano en sombra luciente'[*3] are paralysed on one level of meaning, simple and apparently effortless phrases of *Un río, un amor* like 'hombre gris' (p. 41), 'rojizo hastío' (p. 50) and 'labios amarillos'[†] (p. 61) are pictures that in their strangeness surprise the reader and illustrate Cernuda's disturbed feelings. And the apparently gratuitous conversational gambit with which he began 'Carne de mar' in *Un río, un amor*: 'Dentro de breves días será otoño en Virginia'[‡] (p. 58), together with such colloquial phrases as 'Es igual' (p. 79), 'quién sabe' (p. 55) and 'Qué más da'[§] (p. 80), underline his antipathy to grandiloquence and his fondness for conversational turns of phrase which took the sting out of his feelings but left a bitter taste in the mouth of the reader, who is uneasily conscious in lines like the following acceptance of destruction in *Un río, un amor* that out of despair, weariness or pique Cernuda sheltered behind expressions that leave much unsaid:

> Que derriben también imperios de una noche,
> Monarquías de un beso,
> No significa nada;
> Que derriben los ojos, que derriben las manos como estatuas vacías,
> Acaso dice menos.[||]
>
> (p. 55)

* alabaster light; ebony in shining shadow.
† grey man; reddish weariness; yellow lips.
‡ In a few days it will be autumn in Virginia.
§ It's all the same; who knows; What's the difference.
|| That they also demolish empires of a night, monarchies of a kiss, means nothing; that they demolish the eyes, that they demolish the hands like empty statues, perhaps says less.

With a defiant line of *Los placeres prohibidos*: 'Déjame esta voz que tengo'* (p. 76), Cernuda defended the uniqueness of his expression, even though he knew that his confinement within what Bécquer called 'the narrow circle of the word'[1] blocked his faithful transmission of his thoughts and emotions. His insistent and exasperated admission in *Un río, un amor* that

> ...él con sus labios,
> Con sus labios no sabe sino decir palabras;
> Palabras hacia el techo,
> Palabras hacia el suelo...† (pp. 51–2)

transformed 'palabras' into a term of disdain which he uttered with even greater pessimism in *Los placeres prohibidos*; when he said baldly:

> Palabras de demente o palabras de muerto,
> Es igual,‡ (p. 79)

the colloquial phrase sealed with a helpless shrug of the shoulders his bitter conviction that words, whether from the mouth of a corpse, madman or poet, can communicate nothing but meaningless, incoherent sounds.

Cernuda's belief in the ineptitude of words stopped him from translating the stimulus he received from the French surrealist poets into the creation of verbal extravaganzas; the springboard which he confessed he found in surrealism was, as Octavio Paz has aptly pointed out, 'something more than a lesson of style, more than a creed...: it was...a subversion'.[2] Realizing that he could not bemuse himself with or disguise himself in verbal arabesques, Cernuda plotted his mental impasse in a simple pattern of repetition where the first word recoiled on him and on the reader. Such phrases of *Un río, un amor* as 'Noche que no puede ser otra cosa sino noche'§ (p. 54), 'un hombre con su estigma de hombre'‖ (p. 55), 'Duda con manos de duda y pies de duda'¶ (p. 57) and

---

* Leave me this voice I have.
† he with his lips, with his lips knows only how to say words; words towards the ceiling, words towards the floor.
‡ Words of a madman or words of a corpse, it's all the same.
§ Night which cannot be anything other than night.
‖ a man with his stigma of man.
¶ Doubt with hands of doubt and feet of doubt.

'Espinas en lugar de espinas'* (p. 58) show that Cernuda's thoughts and feelings revolve impotently within an area as restricted as the parallel lines also deployed by a poet who did not surrender unconditionally to the dictates of automatic writing. When he wrote in *Un río, un amor*:

> Bajo la noche el mundo silencioso naufraga;
> Bajo la noche rostros fijos, muertos, se pierden† (p. 42)

and:

> Un grito acaso pueda ofrecer más encantos,
> Con el manto escarlata,
> Con el pecho escarlata,‡ (p. 54)

he channelled his obsession with night and the fascination of the sinister scarlet into a simple scheme as emphatic and resonant as the groups of similes which, like 'Vacío como pampa, como mar, como viento'§ of the same work (p. 41), reveal the desire he shared with Aleixandre to insist on a satisfactory equivalent.

Despite his antipathy to words and his professed enthusiasm for the techniques of surrealism, Cernuda was able with his circular phrases and parallel lines to give verbal shape to the doubt and disillusion undermining his existence and underlying his poetry. When in *Un río, un amor* the sea

> ...se volvió lentamente
> Adonde nadie
> Sabe nada de nadie,‖ (p. 53)

it returned voluntarily to a place whose mysteries are as insoluble as the crime summarized in a title reminiscent of countless detective stories as 'El caso del pájaro asesinado'. Intrigued and perplexed by the lights which once flickered ominously for a reason now known only to the waves, Cernuda recited a litany of doubt and mystery linked by his repetition of 'o', 'algo', 'acaso' and

---

* Thorns instead of thorns.
† Beneath the night the silent world is shipwrecked; beneath the night fixed, dead faces are lost.
‡ A shout can perhaps offer more delights, with the scarlet cloak, with the scarlet breast.
§ Empty as the pampa, as the sea, as the wind.
‖ returned slowly to where no-one knows anything about anyone.

'quizá' and by his futile use of *saber*. Faced with the formidable task of solving a crime which may or may not have been committed 'by no-one or by someone', Cernuda ascertained only one thing, which he knew already: that everything is uncertain:

> Fue un pájaro quizá asesinado;
> Nadie sabe. Por nadie
> O por alguien quizá triste en las piedras,
> En los muros del cielo.
>
> Mas de ello hoy nada se sabe.
> Sólo un temblor de luces levemente,
> Un color de miradas en las olas o en la brisa;
> También, acaso, un miedo.
> Todo, es verdad, inseguro.* (p. 49)

By postulating someone or no-one as the author of a crime, Cernuda let his mind swing through a full arc of doubt, posing himself an alternative as extreme as 'afirmaciones / O negaciones',† 'Verdades o mentiras'‡ in *Un río, un amor* (p. 58) and 'reinos perdidos o quizá ganados'§ in *Los placeres prohibidos* (p. 85). The ease with which he oscillated between truth and lies at the end of 'Dejadme solo' exposes his repetition of 'verdad' and 'verdades' at the beginning of the poem as an incantation gulling the reader to expect more than the poet's vision of man as a chill creature of snow:

> Una verdad es color de ceniza,
> Otra verdad es color de planeta;
> Mas todas las verdades, desde el suelo hasta el suelo,
> No valen la verdad sin color de verdades,
> La verdad ignorante de cómo el hombre suele
>   encarnarse en la nieve.‖ (p. 58)

---

* It was a bird perhaps assassinated; no-one knows. By no-one or by someone perhaps sad in the stones, in the walls of heaven.

  But today nothing is known about it. Only a tremor of lights lightly, a colour of glances in the waves or in the breeze; also, perhaps, a fear. Everything, it is true, is unsure.

† affirmations or denials.   ‡ Truths or lies.

§ kingdoms lost or perhaps won.

‖ One truth is the colour of ash, another truth is the colour of a planet; but all truths, from the ground to the ground, are not worth the colourless truth of truths, the ignorant truth of how man is wont to be incarnated in snow.

As he moved restlessly within the narrow confines of his mind and feelings, Cernuda could only mark time and lament in *Un río, un amor* 'No saber donde ir, donde volver'* (p. 62). Lines that appear to contain a logically developed sequence of thoughts curl into a circle around which we move uneasily from paradoxical openings like 'A través de una noche en pleno día'† of *Un río, un amor* (p. 47) to such carefully and disconcertingly casual endings as 'Comprendí por qué llaman prudente a un hombre sin cabeza'‡ of *Los placeres prohibidos* (p. 77), which corroborate Octavio Paz's perceptive comment that 'at times Cernuda "talks like a book"'.[1]

The *malestar* which attracted Cernuda to surrealism forced him to break out of the symmetrical patterns he employed in *Perfil del aire* and *Égloga, elegía, oda* and the alexandrines he used in the first four poems of *Un río, un amor*; instead, he adjusted the spasms of his thought to the variable, impulsive rhythms of everyday speech, whose informality, captured in phrases like 'En cuanto a' (p. 58), 'No sé por qué' (p. 47), 'Nunca sabremos, nunca' (p. 49) and 'Un gemido no es nada'§ (p. 54), reinforced his hostility to lush and resonant language and framed a complex of deeply personal experiences in phrases, constructions and inflexions familiar to the reader and listener, who is tricked by the formula opening 'Desdicha' in *Un río, un amor* into expecting a tale:

> Un día comprendió cómo sus brazos eran
> Solamente de nubes;
> Imposible con nubes estrechar hasta el fondo
> Un cuerpo, una fortuna.‖   (p. 51)

In *Un río, un amor* and *Los placeres prohibidos* especially the rhythms of spoken speech, broken by ifs, buts and ands, are attuned to the bewilderment and indecision which Cernuda depicted graphically in the title of a poem of *Los placeres prohibidos*: 'Telarañas cuelgan de la razón'; he named in the first five lines of

---

* Not knowing where to go, where to return.
† Through a night in full day.
‡ I understood why they call a headless man prudent.
§ As for; I don't know why; We shall never know, never; A groan is nothing.
‖ One day he understood how his arms were made only of clouds; impossible with clouds to clasp as tightly as one can a body, a fortune.

this poem five things—cobwebs, ashes, hurricane, birds and leaves
—out of which he created a picture of a mind reduced to dusty
dereliction and solitary disenchantment by the savage love which
has replaced the vital birds and leaves with ashes:

> Telarañas cuelgan de la razón
> En un paisaje de ceniza absorta;
> Ha pasado el huracán de amor,
> Ya ningún pájaro queda.
> Tampoco ninguna hoja...*   (pp. 68–9)

Convinced that life could offer nothing but the promise of despair
and death, in eight poems of *Los placeres prohibidos* Cernuda used
versicles to prophesy gravely and eloquently the disaster, oblivion
and decay to which he felt mankind is doomed; dividing his
periods into short and solemn clauses in 'Esperaba solo', Cernuda
related a strange episode with a restraint, directness and factual
precision that throw into relief the sinister details:

Esperaba algo, no sabía qué. Esperaba al anochecer, los sábados. Unos
me daban limosna, otros me miraban, otros pasaban de largo sin verme.

Tenía en la mano una flor; no recuerdo qué flor era. Pasó un adolescente que, sin mirar, la rozó con su sombra. Yo tenía la mano tendida.

Al caer, la flor se convirtió en un monte. Detrás se ponía un sol; no
recuerdo si era negro.

Mi mano quedó vacía. En su palma apareció una gota de sangre.†

Hooking our interest and bracing the poem with his repetition of
'Esperaba', 'otros', 'Tenía', 'mano' and 'flor', Cernuda narrated
with cinematographic concision a sequence of events which, however fantastic, highlight one thing: his solitude. The curiosity and
indifference of bystanders, the single adolescent bringing mem-

---

* Cobwebs hang from the mind in a landscape of absorbed ash; the hurricane of
love has passed, no bird remains. No leaf either.

† I was waiting for something, I did not know what. I would wait at nightfall, on
Saturdays. Some would give me alms, others would look at me, others would
pass by without seeing me.

I would hold a flower in my hand; I do not remember what flower it was.
An adolescent passed by who, without looking, brushed against it with his
shadow. I had my hand outstretched.

As it fell the flower changed into a mountain. Behind a sun was setting; I do
not remember if it was black.

My hand remained empty. In its palm appeared a drop of blood.

ories of a happier past, the sunset, the transformation of a nameless flower into a mountain, the drop of blood suddenly replacing the flower in his hand: all these compose a tableau rich in elements and situations whose one stable feature is the motionless and solitary poet.

Cernuda pursued the 'objective correlative' of his emotions and experiences with such enthusiasm that at times he deployed a complex of objects woven by a dominant theme or feeling into what C. Day Lewis has called a 'network of communication'.[1] The 'Había' which begins five of the six versicles of 'Había en el fondo del mar' introduces simply a series of things that, although as deliberately disparate as 'una estrella, una liga de hombre, un libro deteriorado y un violín diminuto'* (p. 84), are all at the bottom of the sea as useless and as detached from the world as the poet himself. By intertwining the motifs of railway tracks, birds and the snow-covered countryside in 'Nevada' of *Un río, un amor*, Cernuda transports us as swiftly as the birds that gave the railroads their names through bleakly unchanging landscape and monotonous time, which glides on the tracks underpinning the poem towards a future of rigidly prescribed moods and settings, in which sadness will follow joy, snow will fall on snow and trees will succeed trees:

> En el Estado de Nevada
> Los caminos de hierro tienen nombre de pájaro,
> Son de nieve los campos
> Y de nieve las horas.
>
> . . . .
>
> Los árboles abrazan árboles,
> Una canción besa otra canción;
> Por los caminos de hierro
> Pasa el dolor y la alegría.
>
> Siempre hay nieve dormida
> Sobre otra nieve, allá en Nevada.†   (pp. 44–5)

* a star, a man's garter, a damaged book and a minute violin.
† In the State of Nevada the railroads have names of birds, the fields are of snow and the hours are of snow.
   The trees embrace trees, a song kisses another song, grief and joy pass by on the railroad.
   There is always snow sleeping on other snow, there in Nevada.

Following the railroad as it points inflexibly—and with greater maturity than in *Perfil del aire*—towards a future that will be an exact replica of the unhappy present is the headless horsemen, whose quest in *Un río, un amor* for

> Llaves recién cortadas,
> Víboras seductoras, desastres suntuosos,
> Navíos para tierra lentamente de carne... *   (p. 60)

enacts Cernuda's faith in love and desire. As the headless horseman —and Cernuda—looked into the distance he saw a fire reducing memories to ashes (p. 60); when in 'Luna enemiga' of *Sobre los ángeles* Alberti peered into the future he foresaw with vividness and predicted with solemnity the certainty of oblivion; drifting in a kind of limbo, his body and achievements will survive only in faded clothes and pages and be commemorated only by yawns of boredom:

> Salvadme de los años en estado de nebulosa,
> de los espejos que pronuncian trajes y páginas desvanecidos,
> de las manos estampadas en los recuerdos que bostezan.†
>
> (p. 287)

In *Sobre los ángeles* Alberti is suspended without hope between the menace of an empty future and memories of a blissful past untroubled by thoughts of time and death. His elegiac first poem, 'Paraíso perdido', laments his entry into spiritual and emotional torment and his loss of the gaiety with which in his first four books of poetry he had sought themes outside himself and expressed them in manners which he had assimilated brilliantly. His interest in himself, heralded by the autobiographic 'Carta abierta' of *Cal y canto*, was a painful but poetically hygienic liberation of skills trapped in the splendid craftsmanship of *Cal y canto*; the volcanic emotional and spiritual crises which led to and are recorded in *Sobre los ángeles* have given him, as he focused all his attention on himself, full and independent possession of his own genius, an-

---

* Recently cut keys, seductive serpents, sumptuous disasters, ships to make slow landfall on flesh.
† Save me from the years in a state of nebulae, from the mirrors pronouncing vanished garments and pages, from the hands clamped on yawning memories.

nexed for so long by the poets and poetry he admired and eagerly emulated. In *Sobre los ángeles* Alberti was no longer a prisoner of the exact verse forms which almost petrified his feelings in *Cal y canto*; casting off the self-imposed discipline of sonnets, tercets and ballads, he subordinated form to poetic purpose, using parallelism if it suited him, as it does in '5' (p. 264), and passing within the same work, as he himself recalled, 'from the controlled, disciplined short line...to a longer line, more adaptable to the movement of my imagination at that time'.[1]

Juan Ramón Jiménez's blind and splenetic attacks on Alberti's 'satanism of obscene aesthetic, of black mass'[2] reveals his failure to understand why the author of *Marinero en tierra*, which he had praised so highly, could have changed into the poet Salinas has remembered as 'Rafael the tormented',[3] whose use of imagery was not another impressive display of poetic virtuosity but a means of discharging and illustrating thoughts, fears and feelings which would otherwise have been bottled up within him or documented in the cold, confidential prose of a psychiatrist's file. When Alberti reminisced some thirty years later about *Sobre los ángeles*, he recited an apparently endless list of impulses, motifs, anxieties and physical troubles which, although offering the circumstantial starting-point of several poems, throws into relief his masterful achievement in giving poetic shape and expression to a complex crisis that defies cold analysis and sits uneasily in prose:

Impossible love, battered and betrayed in the best hours of submission and confidence; the most rabid jealousy, capable of plotting in the insomnia of the night the cold, calculated crime; the melancholy shadow of the suicide friend...; unconfessed envy and hatred, struggling to emerge, to explode like an imprisoned underground bomb; empty pockets, useless even to warm my hands; endless rambling walks in wind, rain and heat; the family, indifferent to or silent at this great battle, which showed on my face, in my whole being...; childhood fears, invading me in gusts which still brought me remorse, doubt, dread of hell, sombre echoes of that Jesuit college which I loved and suffered in my Cadiz bay; discontent with my previous work, my haste, something that impelled me ceaselessly never to stop, never to take a moment's breath; all this, and many other contradictory, inexplicable, labyrinthine things.[4]

Although *Sobre los ángeles* is an intricate web of motifs and impulses, Alberti did not surrender his imagination to the wayward fancies of psychic dictation; the images procreated by his rich and energetic fantasy were a poet's escape from total silence and complete incoherence. To represent his thoughts and feelings Alberti now incorporated into his poems images he found striking and drew with words the pictures he once made—and still makes —with a brush. His statement that '*Sobre los ángeles* marks in my work very different affinities: the biblical poets Ezekiel, Isaiah and St John; Baudelaire, Rimbaud and Bécquer'[1] is not an invitation to track down sources but an avowal of spiritual kinship with writers whose experiences paralleled his own and whose words at times graphically expressed similar feelings. Less important than the discovery and identification of a source or reminiscence is the question why, for example, Alberti shared Rimbaud's revulsion against life and obsession with hell, or why he saw in Quevedo's vision of the body and soul as empty dwellings a visually attractive motif.

The burning coal which Alberti transposed from the Old Testament to 'El cuerpo deshabitado' (p. 250) is one of the easily imaginable spiritual references which frame the tragedy of a man whose soul is the battleground of Saint Michael and Lucifer in 'Los dos ángeles' (p. 263) and who is mocked in 'Can de llamas' by the dog of St Dominic de Guzmán into whose mouth he put the flaming torch given it by religious lore (pp. 270–1). Reduced in 'El ángel desconocido' from the stature of his namesake Saint Raphael, who appeared in his traditional role as the guardian of travellers in *Marinero en tierra* (pp. 46, 54) and *Cal y canto* (p. 211), to the insignificance of a faceless nobody in a crowd, Alberti recorded in *Sobre los ángeles* an emotional anguish and a spiritual collapse so devastating that in 'Muerte y juicio' he stood back and, judging himself as solemnly as a priest delivering his Lenten sermons on Death and Judgment, pronounced his melancholy verdict: 'Para ir al infierno no hace falta cambiar de sitio ni postura'* (p. 284).

Alberti was so obsessed with his imprisonment within a hell on

* To go to hell there is no need to change position or posture.

earth that he illustrated his exile from grace with details as precise as the

alas rotas, laúdes, cuerdas de arpas,
restos de ángeles* (p. 274)

hurled from heaven in 'El alma en pena' and with figures as dominant and visually appealing as the angels. His transformation of the latter into what he called 'blind reincarnations of everything that was bloody, desolate, agonizing, terrible and at times good within me'[1] created a highly flexible poetic code that denoted the complex feelings seething inside him. As the 'angel of anger' kicked a stone lying amid the nettles (p. 268), it condensed in one gratuitous act and one moment of spontaneous rage the wrath that gave the 'envious angel' a tongue as sharp as axes (p. 269). When the angels of light and darkness clash in 'Los dos ángeles', they enacted a scene of the emotional autobiography which Alberti, painting a backcloth of universal anarchy, dramatized in acts of violence for which he chose weapons as savage as the axe, sword, wire, tine, sickle and revolver.

Alberti suddenly found himself locked in a world of rough justice, where the 'vengeful angels' petulantly interrogate the hapless stranger whose intrusion into their jealously guarded kingdom they resent and punish with ruthless liquidation; only the poet, who is as solitary and misunderstood as the anonymous stranger, takes no part in his thinly motivated and coldly described murder. The brutality of the 'cruel angels' ensures that nature, ravaged by violent winds, will never bloom into leaf or flower and that the birds will never again be able to soar freely over

la mar, los campos, las nubes,
el árbol, el arbolillo...† (p. 266)

The red-hot wire with which the angels pierce the birds' beaks is a frightening illustration of the savagery whose unpredictable and menacing irruptions are deliberately provoked by the subversive 'angel of ashes'. Parodying the mission and character of Christ, Ceniciento, whose ashen body is a clear index of destruc-

---

* broken wings, lutes, harp strings, angels' remains.
† the sea, the fields, the clouds, the tree, the sapling.

tion and death, comes down not to spread light and preach love but to unleash the fury of nature, to set element against element, to foment on earth Lucifer's rebellion in heaven to which Alberti referred in 'Tres recuerdos del cielo' (p. 279) and 'El ángel de arena' (p. 280). Proving that his vision of universal turmoil is compatible with an architectural sense of form, Alberti contained the disorder he visualized around him within a beautifully compact and disciplined frame, where two octosyllabic quatrains and two parallel couplets are poised around the pivotal summary of Ceniciento's nature:

> Precipitadas las luces
> por los derrumbos del cielo,
> en la barca de las nieblas
> bajaste tú, Ceniciento.
>
> Para romper cadenas
> y enfrentar a la tierra contra el viento.
>
> Iracundo, ciego.
>
> Para romper cadenas
> y enfrentar a los mares contra el fuego.
>
> Dando bandazos el mundo,
> por la nada rodó, muerto.
> No se enteraron los hombres.
> Sólo tú y yo, Ceniciento.* (p. 260)

A similar sense of balance, apparent in the subtitle '(Norte, Sur)', made Alberti oppose in the second and third stanzas of 'Los ángeles bélicos' the cities of the south wind and cities of the north wind before they are entangled in stanza four in the violent mêlée of battle, which fuses identities into the corporate anonymity of 'Gentío' and reduces bodies to capsules of rage:

---

* As the lights had been hurled over the precipices of heaven, you came down in the boat of mist, Ceniciento.
   To break chains and set the earth against the wind.
   Angry, blind.
   To break chains and set the seas against fire.
   Lurching, the world rolled dead through the void. Mankind did not realize this. Only you and I did, Ceniciento.

> Gentío de mar y tierra,
> nombres, preguntas, recuerdos,
> frente a frente.
> Balumbas de frío encono,
> cuerpo a cuerpo.*   (p. 256)

As the 'warlike angels' battle around him, Alberti, who depicted himself twice in this poem as a 'torre sin mando, en medio',† cannot check but can only watch the turmoil as impotently as the 'hound of flames' which fails to unite his body and soul, to which he gave the cosmic proportions of south and north. Before the regular order of south–centre–north is disrupted to north–south–centre, Alberti placed at the centre of the poem two magnificent lines in which we hear the dog's anguished howls and visualize the flaming torch clamped between teeth whose sharpness we sense in 'dentados' and 'agudos':

> Riegan los aires aullidos
> dentados de agudos fuegos.‡   (p. 271)

As its howls rend the air with shrill regularity, the dog mourns its own immediate failure to prevent the savage confrontation of north and south and Alberti's inability to quell the anarchy of his personal crisis, which, shattering the paradise evoked with such nostalgia in 'Tres recuerdos del cielo' (pp. 278–80), explodes into the bullets, abduction, telegram, blood and death which illustrate in a solemn catalogue the mysterious treachery he mentioned in 'El mal minuto':

> Ese minuto fue el de las balas perdidas,
> el del secuestro, por el mar, de los hombres que quisieron ser pájaros,
> el del telegrama a deshora y el hallazgo de sangre,
> el de la muerte del agua que siempre miró al cielo.§   (p. 281)

---

* People of sea and earth, names, questions, memories, brow to brow. Bulks of cold rage, body to body.
† uncaptained tower, in the middle.
‡ The air is irrigated by jagged howls of sharp fires.
§ That minute was the minute of the lost bullets, of the abduction by sea of the men who wanted to be birds, of the inopportune telegram and the discovery of blood, of the death of the water which always looked at the heavens.

Studding 'Luna enemiga' with a complementary cluster of associations, Alberti chose colliding stars, a hostile moon, burning blood and rebellious kings to depict his violent plunge into the oblivion of faded clothes and pages, which, to judge from the restrained pairing of 'Una hoja, un hombre'* (p. 287), is as commonplace and unnoticed as a leaf falling from a tree. The celestial turmoil into which he inflated his personal disorders condemned him to live on and under the earth; his fate is that of the wine in 'El ángel de las bodegas', which, sealed within barrels, is denied the chance of ever seeing sea and snow and of enjoying the salon pleasures illustrated with ironic precision by tea and a grand piano:

> La flor del vino, muerta en los toneles,
> sin haber visto nunca la mar, la nieve.

> La flor del vino, sin probar el té,
> sin haber visto nunca un piano de cola.†   (p. 281)

The abysses, caves, mines, tunnels, vaults and wells which form part of the scenery of *Sobre los ángeles* illustrate the belief Alberti shared with Rimbaud that 'Theology is serious, hell is certainly *below*—and heaven above.'[1] Like Bécquer, whose anguish he evoked sympathetically in 1931 in terms he had already used of himself in *Sobre los ángeles*, Alberti in his imagination 'has descended to the bottom of the wells and has returned from the abysses with his soul deranged with fear'.[2] Failing to elicit from his dead and useless guardian angel any response to his question concerning the whereabouts of Paradise, he started in 'Paraíso perdido' a journey into despair, wandering blind and aimless amid a universal silence and perpetual darkness which, simply described, seal him in painful solitude:

> Ciudades sin respuesta,
> ríos sin habla, cumbres
> sin ecos, mares mudos.
> . . . .

---

* A leaf, a man.

† The cream of the wine, dead in the barrels, without ever having seen the sea, the snow.

   The cream of the wine, without tasting tea, without ever having seen a grand piano.

Silencio. Más silencio.
Inmóviles los pulsos
del sinfín de la noche.

¡ Paraíso perdido !
Perdido por buscarte,
yo, sin luz para siempre.*   (pp. 247–8)

Because Alberti felt shunned by humanity and banished from his previous angelic innocence, he cast himself in 'Los ángeles sonámbulos' as 'un rey en tinieblas't (p. 276) harassed in his nightmare by rebellious eyes and ears, and in 'El ángel desconocido' as a neglected figure whose sorrowful thoughts of past glory are embittered by his sad awareness of his present insignificance; cloaked in anonymity by the uniform of the mass, the figure identified by sandals, tunic and wings as the erstwhile St Raphael has to remind himself of the past splendour which no-one remembers:

Vestido como en el mundo,
ya no se me ven las alas.
Nadie sabe cómo fui.
No me conocen.

Por las calles, ¿ quién se acuerda?
Zapatos son mis sandalias.
Mi túnica, pantalones
y chaqueta inglesa.
Dime quién soy.‡   (p. 250)

The streets in which Alberti encountered the 'foolish angels' (p. 272) and the 'dumb angels' (p. 273) provide a physical setting for the erratic movements of his mind, forced by jaundiced hindsight to see the origins of his present despair and bewilderment in

---

* Cities without reply, rivers without speech, peaks without echoes, dumb seas. Silence. More silence. Motionless are the pulses of endless night. Paradise lost! Lost because I sought you, I, without light for ever.
† a king in darkness.
‡ Dressed as a mortal, no-one can now see my wings. No-one knows how I once was. They do not know me.

In the streets, who remembers? Shoes are my sandals. My tunic is now trousers and English jacket. Tell me who I am.

his childhood. His realization in 'Muerte y juicio' that the 'billetes de inocencia'* (p. 283) once stuffed into his pockets have been replaced by what Rimbaud called in *Une saison en enfer* his 'notebook of the damned',[1] forced to the surface memories of his schooldays, which he vivified and incorporated into his present complex of troubles. On the blackboard that constitutes the easily imaginable backcloth of 'El ángel de los números' is enacted a scene of disorder, for the illumination brought by the easy movements of the numbers has been destroyed by their paralysis and the angel's death, leaving the world and the poet clouded in doubt and mist:

> Tizas frías y esponjas
> rayaban y borraban
> la luz de los espacios.
>
> Ni sol, luna, ni estrellas,
> ni el repentino verde
> del rayo y el relámpago,
> ni el aire. Sólo nieblas.†   (p. 257)

The routine recorded in 'Los ángeles colegiales' of closing compasses in the afternoon and opening books in the morning (p. 285) was as rigid and numbing as the automatic and indiscriminate memorizing of facts, which so overloaded his soul that in 'Muerte y juicio' he imagined it sinking under their weight to the bottom of the sea:

> Perdido entre ecuaciones, triángulos, fórmulas y precipitados azules,
> entre el suceso de la sangre, los escombros y las coronas caídas,
> cuando los cazadores de oro y el asalto a la banca,
> en el rubor tardío de las azoteas
> voces de ángeles te anunciaron la botadura y pérdida de tu alma.‡
>   (p. 283)

---

* tickets of innocence.
† Cold chalks and sponges crossed out and erased the light of space.
   Neither sun, moon nor stars, nor the sudden green of lightning and thunder, nor air. Only mists.
‡ Lost amid equations, triangles, formulae and blue precipitates, amid the bloody succession, the ruins and the fallen crowns, at the time of the hunters of gold and the attack on the bank, in the tardy glow of the rooftops angels' voices told you of the launching and loss of your soul.

Mourning in 'El ángel de las bodegas' his chill discovery that 'un alma oculta frío y escaleras'* (p. 281), Alberti used the reminiscence of Quevedo I mentioned in chapter 1 to depict himself in 'Desahucio' as an empty house to be let and vacated at the whim of cruel angels (p. 249), and in 'El cuerpo deshabitado' as an empty body from which he had driven his unwanted tenant with a live coal (p. 250). Like Bécquer's Manrique, who mistook the elusive moonbeam for the ideal woman, Alberti was detached from mankind by his hopeless pursuit of the impossible, be it truth in 'Paraíso perdido' (p. 248), the sources of heaven in 'Muerte y juicio (p. 283), the phantom 'no-one' in the fourth part of 'El cuerpo deshabitado' (p. 252), or the purchase of heaven desired crazily by the 'avaricious angel':

> Ese hombre está muerto
> y no lo sabe.
> Quiere asaltar la banca,
> robar nubes, estrellas, cometas de oro,
> comprar lo más difícil:
> el cielo.
> Y ese hombre está muerto.†   (p. 276)

In *Sobre los ángeles* Alberti chronicled his transformation into a spectre, unseen and unseeing, unknown and unknowing, who in two graphic lines of 'El cuerpo deshabitado' imagined himself crucified into the rigidity of plaster at the very edge of the world, from which he could fall only into the void:

> Solo, en el filo del mundo,
> clavado ya, de yeso.‡   (p. 253)

The precise parallel lines of '5' compose a narrative of petrification which relates with factual coldness the sudden and systematic attack on the poet by five ashen hands which, destroying his senses one by one in a sequence he was to duplicate in his *auto*

---

* a soul conceals cold and staircases.
† That man is dead and does not know it. He wants to attack the bank, steal clouds, stars, gold comets, buy what is most difficult to buy: heaven. And that man is dead.
‡ Alone and of plaster, now nailed on the edge of the world.

El hombre deshabitado, leave him, like the Uninhabited Man, 'as if
dead in life, or as if alive in death':[1]

> Y no viste.
> Era su luz la que cayó primero.
> Mírala, seca, en el suelo.
>
> Y no oíste.
> Era su voz la que alargada hirieron.
> Óyela muda, en el eco.
>
> Y no oliste.
> Era su esencia la que hendió el silencio.
> Huélela fría, en el viento.
>
> Y no gustaste.
> Era su nombre el que rodó deshecho.
> Gústalo en tu lengua, muerto.
>
> Y no tocaste.
> El desaparecido era su cuerpo.
> Tócalo en la nada, yelo.*   (p. 264)

Frozen into a robot existence, Alberti can make no contact
with mankind. The 'dumb angels', sealed by their muteness in an
anxious solitude, must remain mystified by the supernatural divi-
sion of the poet into two forms; they can only long with an impotent despair marked by the litany of 'quieren, quisieran, querrían'†
(p. 273) to halt this wandering figure and illuminate his murky
soul—as if it were a cupboard or a cellar—with a match:

> Hombres, mujeres, mudos, querrían ver claro,
> asomarse a mi alma,

---

* And you did not see. It was the light of his eyes that fell first. Look at it dry on
the ground.
 And you did not hear. It was his voice that they stretched and wounded.
Hear it dumb in the echo.
 And you did not smell. It was his essence that cleft the silence. Smell it cold
in the wind.
 And you did not taste. It was his name that rolled in pieces. Taste it dead on
your tongue.
 And you did not touch. It was his body that had vanished. Touch it icy in the
void.
† want to, would like to, would wish to.

> acercarle una cerilla
> por ver si es la misma.
> Quieren, quisieran...* (p. 273)

Alberti now imagined himself locked within a world peopled not
by human beings but by the 'Hombres de cinc, alquitrán y
plomo't he introduced into 'Los ángeles de las ruinas' (p. 290), a
world that with its ovens, ammonia, gall, lime, molten lead, nitric
acid, petroleum, pitch, sealing wax and sulphur burns as savagely
as the hell he described in *De un momento a otro* (1934–9), where he
gave his Jesuit school those frightening features seared on his
mind—and on the mind of Joyce's Stephen Dedalus—by fiery
sermons:

> (Hay allá abajo una cisterna,
> un hondo aljibe de demonios,
> una orza de azufre,
> de negra pez hirviendo.
> Hay un triste colegio de fuego,
> sin salida.)‡ (p. 373)

Just as the collapse of a room in Alberti's play *De un momento a
otro* (1938–9) represented Gabriel's failure to combat the prejudices and incomprehension of his family, so do the ruins littering
'Los ángeles muertos' illustrate Alberti's imprisonment in an existence he now found fragmented and pointless. The débris briefly
visible through the mist, the brick fallen from a tower or cart, the
collapsing chimneys, dilapidated furniture and dusty letters are all
signs of curtailed activity and creeping decay. His precise indica-
tion at the end of the poem that the 'dead angels' can be sought

> Cerca del casco perdido de una botella,
> de una suela extraviada en la nieve,
> de una navaja de afeitar abandonada al borde de un precipicio§
> (p. 291)

* Dumb men and women would like to see clearly, peer into my soul, take a
  match to it to see if it is the same. They want, they would like....
† Men of zinc, pitch and lead.
‡ Down below there is cistern, a deep tank of demons, a crock of sulphur, of
  boiling black pitch. There is a sad school of fire, without an exit.
§ Near a lost bottle-top, the sole of a shoe astray in the snow, a razor abandoned
  at the edge of a precipice.

lists some of the carelessly discarded rubbish surrounding Alberti as he viewed himself trapped within a private hell on earth. The poems of *Sobre los ángeles* emerged from a mind feverishly engaged in illustrating its own insecurity, despair and bewilderment; it was a happy accident that one of the most imaginatively vital works of twentieth-century Spanish poetry was an attempt to describe spiritual and emotional sterility and to illustrate Alberti's vision of himself as a being who, like his thwarted hero Gabriel, was 'Useless, null, broken, trapped!'[1]

The survival in 'El ángel superviviente' of one maimed and wingless angel (p. 292) ended Alberti's battle but not his bitterness; with a self-righteousness implicit in the religious overtones of the title, he uttered in *Sermones y moradas* a volley of acrid recriminations and strident self-justifications which, seething anarchically in endlessly flowing lines, fail to engage completely our emotions or involve us in his difficulties. Alberti tried in *Sermones y moradas* to repeat the unrepeatable, but produced instead of another masterpiece a shrill protest in which he overstrained his imagination and struck defiant, theatrical postures. That this work grew out of *Sobre los ángeles* is clear from his reference to his confrontation of 'un batallón de ángeles'* (p. 313), from his concern for his soul and from his obsession with death, which led him to write elegies to Garcilaso and Villalón and to appear as 'un muerto más entre las tumbas'† (p. 315), who in 'Espantapájaros' particularly was burdened like Quevedo with the death of all mankind:

Ya en mi alma pesaban de tal modo los muertos futuros
que no podía andar ni un solo paso sin que las piedras revelaran
   sus entrañas.‡   (p. 303)

Although these links between *Sobre los ángeles* and *Sermones y moradas* demonstrate the depth and strength of Alberti's malaise, he had by now moved so far away from the original impulses that the inevitable cooling of fervour and stiffening of attitudes made *Sermones y moradas* into an uneasy sequel as subordinate to *Sobre los*

---

* a battalion of angels.   † one more corpse among the tombs.
‡ The future dead now weighed so heavily on my soul that I could not take a single step without the stones revealing their entrails.

ángeles as *Razón de amor* is to *La voz a ti debida*. While in *Sobre los ángeles* Alberti was concerned to record a complex experience in all its confused rawness and heat, in *Sermones y moradas* he attempted to justify his experience with an ardour more simulated than authentic. 'Sin más remedio', for example, will disappoint those in search of clues and explanations; while *Sobre los ángeles* was a moving and richly illustrated cry of solitude and exile from the normal world, in this poem he merely tells us that he had to exile himself and lament:

> Tenía yo que salir de la tierra,
> la tierra tenía que escupirme de una vez para siempre como
> un hijo bastardo,
> como un hijo temido a quien no esperan nunca reconocer las
> ciudades.
>
> ....
>
> Había que expatriarse involuntariamente,
> dejar ciertas alcobas,
> ciertos ecos,
> ciertos ojos vacíos.*   (p. 301)

When Alberti toasted 'la devastación absoluta de los astros'† in the poem he called ironically 'Morada del alma que espera la paz' (p. 313), which resounds with shouts of war and death, he not only transformed destruction from a symptom of his emotions into an end in itself but rehearsed in poetry the shout which he uttered with the romantic defiance of Rivas's Don Alvaro after the first performance of *El hombre deshabitado* on 26 February 1931: 'Long live extermination! Death to the rottenness of all the contemporary Spanish theatre!'[1] His belief—which in the 1930s acquired a social and political bias with his growing commitment to communism—that the shattering of this world must precede 'la perfección de los cielos'‡ (p. 298) led him to encrust his poems with tokens of death and violence, from the stone bullets and

* I had to depart from the earth, the earth had to spit me out once and for all like a bastard son, like a dreaded son whom the cities never expect to recognize. I had to go into exile against my will, leave certain rooms, certain echoes, certain empty eyes.
† the absolute devastation of the stars.
‡ the perfection of the heavens.

boiling oil of the first piece (p. 295) to the haemorrhage of the last (p. 315).

It was the disintegration of the universe Alberti sought and recorded so enthusiastically in *Sermones y moradas* that made him remark casually: 'Ya a mí no me hace falta para nada comprobar la redondez de la Tierra'* (p. 303); the unity and wholeness so precious to Guillén exploded into a chaos of débris and detritus which Alberti observed attentively and hymned solemnly in 'Elegías', where his recital of objects chosen with random relish illustrates his revulsion against a filthy and fragmented world as emphatically as the acrid barrage of his 'Índice de familia burguesa española', written in 1933, indicted his family for their bourgeois complacency:[1]

1. —La pena de los jarros sin agua caídos en el destierro de los objetos difuntos.
2. —La noticia del crimen de la noche, abandonada entre cardos, muelles rotos y latones viejos.
3. —La botella que no se rompío al caer y vive con el gollete clavado en los oasis de las basuras.
4. —La venda rota de una herida, arrastrada por las hormigas de las tres de la tarde....† (p. 312)

Unfortunately for the poetic success of *Sermones y moradas*, the shock-tactics Alberti employed repel rather than stun the reader, who is put in mind of *Cal y canto* by Alberti's determination to mystify and astound and by his indiscriminate enjoyment of the imaginative richness which in *Sobre los ángeles* he mined deeply and controlled expertly. Whereas in *Sobre los ángeles* his dignity and measure invited us to recognize in his loss of faith a great personal tragedy, in *Sermones y moradas* he forfeits our sympathy by souring his faithlessness with an irreverence as distasteful as his

---

* I no longer have any need to verify the roundness of the Earth.
† 1. —The sorrow of the waterless jugs fallen into the exile of dead objects.
  2. —The news of the crime of the night, abandoned among thistles, broken springs and old tins.
  3. —The bottle that did not break when it fell and lives with the neck nailed in the oases of the refuse.
  4. —The broken bandage of a wound, dragged along by the ants that appear at three in the afternoon.

vision of the Holy Spirit submerging bodies 'en el sulfuro de los volcanes'* (p. 297) and with his bitter reference to dove number 948, which in his eyes brings as little hope as the previous nine hundred and forty-seven:

Soy inmortal: no tengo quien me hiera.

Y ahora me aburro ante las posturas desesperadas de los muertos que
    sueñan inútilmente con la resurrección de la carne.

Mas he aquí la paloma 948.†   (p. 313)

In *Sermones y moradas* the deep disturbances which motivated and were documented in *Sobre los ángeles* upset Alberti's poetic balance and blurred the dividing line between freedom and anarchy, authentic bewilderment and the cultivated perplexity he displayed in many questions, some of which are so eccentric and protracted as to be unanswerable. Alberti's confession that 'he perdido mi jaca'‡ (p. 306) and his statement that 'la electricidad corre por mi esqueleto'§ (p. 308) illustrate the erratic surges of poetic activity in which he seemed to be the plaything of his turbulent blood, which in 'Sermón de la sangre' 'Me llama, me grita, me advierte, me despeña y me alza...'‖ (p. 303). A willing victim of the 'delirious insomnia' he crisply diagnosed in the Lorca of *Poeta en Nueva York*,[1] he invites us to sense the meaning hidden in cryptic assertions like 'Una lata de conservas siempre hace más frío el frío de un esqueleto'¶ (p. 309) and to follow submissively the volcanic flow of lines that seem to stretch endlessly in displays of imaginative stamina.

The rhetorical extravaganzas of *Sermones y moradas* were a desperate attempt to maintain the emotional impetus and surpass the imaginative suppleness of *Sobre los ángeles*; but having once made

---

* in the sulphur of the volcanoes.
† I am immortal: there is no-one to wound me.
    And now I get bored before the desperate postures of the dead who dream uselessly of the resurrection of the flesh.
    But here is dove 948.
‡ I have lost my nag.
§ electricity runs through my skeleton.
‖ Calls me, shouts to me, warns me, throws me down, lifts me up.
¶ A tin of preserves always makes the cold of a skeleton colder.

his angels enact and frame his anguish, Alberti's redeployment of his despair without the cohesion of such an energetic cast was an anti-climactic exercise in fantasy and parade of bitterness. Although *Sobre los ángeles* was necessary for Alberti's mental and poetic health, it did not cure him of the ills which he exhibited in *Sermones y moradas* with a defiant and acrimonious independence; giving his cry of pain the sharp edge of denunciation, he offered us instead of the emotional tautness and imaginative control of *Sobre los ángeles* a supercharged tension, which, although clearly symptomatic of his deep-seated malaise, his bewilderment and his isolation in a world whose values he no longer respected, can only disappoint those who find supremely exemplified in *Sobre los ángeles* a visually appealing expression of a complex spiritual and emotional crisis.

Alberti's comment that in *Poeta en Nueva York* Lorca 'staggers like a drunk'[1] summarizes neatly the erratic movements of mind, feeling and fantasy which Lorca translated into the word-pictures of *Poeta en Nueva York* and sought to transpose into the fading and disconnected images of the film for which he hurriedly drafted a screenplay in New York, *Un viaje a la luna*.[2] Lorca's revulsion against America in general and New York in particular made the tortured pages of *Poeta en Nueva York* so different from the sensuous games of *Poema del cante jondo* and *Romancero gitano* that several critics, reluctant to free him from the oppressive '*myth of the gipsy*'[3] and unable to come to terms with his new tense and cryptic manner, have censured him for penning 'artificial hieroglyphics' and 'delirious visions'.[4] It was left to the poet who described in *Sobre los ángeles* experiences akin to those Lorca recorded in *Poeta en Nueva York* to remind us that, as the latter was trying to document the indefinable with the language of a poet, 'hermeticism is licit'.[5]

In *Poeta en Nueva York* Lorca resorted with desperate vigour to images, which now exhibit his feelings as well as his volatile fantasy. Although the rapid beating of his heart sometimes sent a rush of blood to his head and clouded his reason, it made him detonate the emotional charge within him in salvos of images, many of which are so consistently linked by the 'poetic logic' which, according to his essay on 'Imaginación, inspiración, evasión' (1928), comes with inspiration (p. 1546) that they offer us welcome guidelines through a work where Lorca undertook a purge as necessary for his poetic and emotional health as *Sobre los ángeles* was for Alberti's. The poetry he wrote between it and *Romancero gitano* which he defined significantly in a letter to Jorge Zalamea written in 1928 as 'poetry of OPENING ONE'S VEINS' (p. 1598), shows that *Poeta en Nueva York* was not a sudden surge of anguish but the painful birth of the malaise which had been conceived by mysterious emotional troubles, accelerated by his growing dissatisfaction with his work and intensified by his awareness that he must change and explore milieux other than those in which he was deeply rooted. The 'acute longing to get away from Spain' which he confessed to Guillén in 1926[1] was a desire to escape from unspecified personal troubles, to seek new stimulus outside Andalusia and to translate into action the ideal of change and development he postulated in 'Imaginación, inspiración, evasión', where he maintained that 'The light of the poet is contradiction' (p. 1548).

Resenting that his poetic prose of *un gitano legítimo* had hardened into a legend, Lorca turned away from the spectacular world of gipsies framed by picturesque Andalusia and presented himself instead as a lost, dazed and dismembered being whose moss-covered temples (p. 416) and decision to let his hair grow (p. 399) related him to Eliot's vacant and indecisive figure who resolved in *The Waste Land* to 'rush out as I am, and walk the street / With my hair down, so' (ll. 132–3). With his despairing cry of 'mi rostro, ¡ mi rostro !, ¡ ay, mi comido rostro !'* (p. 442), Lorca illustrated the crumbling of his once harmonious personality now doomed, to use a line of *El público*, to 'A cluster of wounds and a complete confusion' (p. 1076). When he described himself as a 'poeta sin brazos perdido / entre la multitud que vomita't (p. 416), he translated into two simple pictures his solitude and impotence amid disgusting humanity, represented in *Poeta en Nueva York* by an unpleasant cast, for his jaundiced eye picked out drunks; the fat

* my face, my face, oh, my eaten face !
† an armless poet lost amid the vomiting multitude.

woman who in an act of grotesque frenzy turns octopuses inside
out (p. 415); the faceless robots who stagger 'como recién salidas
de un naufragio de sangre'* (p. 425); the cooks and waiters who in
a repellent vision of servility lick the wounds of millionaires
(p. 409); and the pansies whose aberrations he set against the lusty
virility of the Walt Whitman revered by Domenchina:

> ...por las azoteas,
> agrupados en los bares,
> saliendo en racimos de las alcantarillas,
> temblando entre las piernas de los chauffeurs
> o girando en las plataformas del ajenjo,
> los maricas, Walt Whitman, te soñaban.† (p. 452)

Lorca's insistence that the two poems he sent to Sebastián Gasch
in 1928 'respond to my new *spiritualist* manner' (p. 1594) marked
his abandonment of a literary masquerade and his need once again
to expose his feelings in poetry, as he did in *Libro de poemas*. An
example of this 'spiritualist manner' which with its sharp focus on
the unpleasant elements of life heralded the chaotic tableaux and
strident denunciations of *Poeta en Nueva York* is his 'Oda al Santísimo Sacramento del Altar';[1] as he turned to the broken, anarchic
world in the second half of the poem, starkly called 'Mundo',
Lorca heard not the accordions played by seraphim and gipsies in
'Muerto de amor' but harsh shouts and babbling tongues, saw not
gipsy heroes, erotic winds and the Civil Guard but prostitutes,
decapitated heads and a frightening anonymous army which has
come to kill the nightingale:

> Escribientes dormidos en el piso catorce.
> Ramera con los senos de cristal arañado.
> Cables y media luna con temblores de insecto.
> Bares sin gente. Gritos. Cabezas por el agua.
>
> Para el asesinato del ruiseñor, venían
> tres mil hombres armados de lucientes cuchillos.

---

* as if recently emerged from a shipwreck of blood.
† on the rooftops, gathered in the bars, emerging in clusters from the sewers,
trembling between the legs of the chauffeurs or gyrating on the platforms of
wormwood, the pansies dreamed of you, Walt Whitman.

Viejas y sacerdotes lloraban resistiendo
una lluvia de lenguas y hormigas voladoras.* (p. 556)

The playfully ironic announcement made by a gramophone in
El paseo de Buster Keaton (1928): 'In America there are nightingales' (p. 806), changed in *Poeta en Nueva York* into graphic visions
of maimed and murdered birds. The bird whose neck was to be
twisted in the forty-ninth scene of *Un viaje a la luna* was in
Lorca's imagination the victim of universal brutality at odds with
the love and peace preached automatically by the remote and
idealistic ancient in 'Grito hacia Roma':

Pero el viejo de las manos traslúcidas
dirá: Amor, amor, amor,
aclamado por millones de moribundos;
....
dirá: paz, paz, paz,
entre el tirite de cuchillos y melones de dinamita;...† (p. 449)

The 'pequeñas golondrinas con muletas'‡ found in the kitchens
by idiot children in one poem (p. 423) and the dove on which a
man urinates in another (p. 448) are persecuted by an inhuman
civilization that denies Christ, whose agony on the cross Lorca
sang with compassion in 'Oda al Santísimo Sacramento del Altar'.
The suffering Christ of flesh and blood has been replaced in
'Nacimiento de Cristo' by a clay figure whose birth is celebrated
not by angelic voices but by wolves, toads and disembodied
voices (p. 424) as shrill and tuneless as the hollow cries of '¡ ale-
luya!' uttered by the decapitated sailor in 'Navidad en el Hudson'
(p. 420), who discovers painfully that the season of good will is
one of instinctive savagery.

* Scribes sleeping on the fourteenth floor. A whore with breasts of scratched
crystal. Cables and a half-moon with insect tremors. Empty bars. Shouts.
Heads through the water.
  For the murder of the nightingale came three thousand men armed with
shining knives. Old women and priests wept as they resisted a rain of tongues
and flying ants.
† But the old man with the translucent hands will say: Love, love, love, acclaimed
by millions of dying people; he will say: peace, peace, peace, amid the shiver of
knives and melons of dynamite.
‡ tiny larks with crutches.

In his attempt to elude the 'passions' and 'great *sentimental crisis*' he confessed enigmatically to Sebastián Gasch in 1927,[1] Lorca collided with something far more catastrophic than what he tried to escape from. In the last section of *Poeta en Nueva York*, which he called significantly 'Huída de Nueva York. Dos valses hacia la civilización', he danced away with obvious relief from a city and country which, embittered and stunned by the Depression, assumed the frightening aspect of a hell on earth, barbaric in its crushing of the individual and pagan in its homage to the god of money, amply represented in these poems by Wall Street, coins, numbers and millionaires. With its gigantic buildings, jagged skyline, seedy ghettoes, polluted rivers and dizzy speed, New York offered Lorca a backcloth, a framework and a standard against which to measure and denounce humanity; in the interview he gave to L. Méndez Domínguez in 1933 he emphasized that, as he did not want to 'draw New York from the outside', 'My observation must then be lyrical' (pp. 1614-15). Because the grotesque capers of the mask amid a chorus of howls and groans signify graphically that America, appropriately close to the Arctic cold, was possessed by jungle savagery, its *danse macabre* transcended New York, as Lorca made clear in his indictment of '¡...salvaje Norteamérica!':

No es extraño este sitio para la danza, yo lo digo.
El mascarón bailará entre columnas de sangre y de números,
entre huracanes de oro y gemidos de obreros parados
que aullarán, noche oscura, por tu tiempo sin luces,
¡ oh salvaje Norteamérica! ¡ oh impúdica! ¡ oh salvaje,
tendida en la frontera de la nieve!*   (p. 414)

Marooned in a city he associated in 'Oda a Walt Whitman' with mud, wire and death (p. 451), Lorca recorded in poetry the intense shock produced on his emotions and on his sensibility by a city and a country with which he hardly came into contact. Suddenly

---

* I say that this place is not strange for the dance. The mask will dance amid columns of blood and numbers, amid hurricanes of gold and groans of unemployed workmen who will in the black night howl their laments for your dark era, o savage, shameless, savage North America, stretched out on your frontier of snow!

detached from his small and peaceful Granada, he saw only the surface of American life, depending for company on Spaniards like Ángel del Río and Federico de Onís. There is a simpler reason for Lorca's loneliness in New York than Larrea's grandiose suggestion that he was 'inadaptable';[1] his failure to learn English isolated him amid a multitude of strangers whose words were so rapid and incomprehensible that he imagined them graphically as having 'hormigas en las palabras'* (p. 437). His ears could capture only sounds that know no linguistic barriers: moaning, vomiting, weeping and the shrieks of pain inflicted sadistically by the cruel, persistent probe which he transplanted from 'Asesinato' to the end of *Bodas de sangre*:

> Un alfiler que bucea
> hasta encontrar las raicillas del grito.†   (p. 419)

What Lorca set down in the poems of *Poeta en Nueva York* was a mass of sensuous visions and impressions which he coloured with prejudice and filtered through his imagination in order to shape an anguished indictment of a way of life to which he was instinctively alien. His melancholy conviction that 'la vida no es noble, ni buena, ni sagrada'‡ (p. 453) made him acutely sensitive to the suffering of a world he described in the same poem as 'agonía, agonía' (p. 453). Haunted in New York, as he told Gil Benumeya in 1931, by 'A pathetic symbol: Suffering' (p. 1608), he now saw a hideous summary of mankind's torment in the Great War, whose horrors he mourned in 'Iglesia abandonada (Balada de la Gran Guerra)', where the father's elegy to his son is as pathetic and vivid as Remarque's *All Quiet on the Western Front*, which, according to Ángel del Río,[2] Lorca knew in the translation of Benjamín Jarnés and Eduardo Foertsch, *Sin novedad en el frente*, published in Madrid in 1929. In its stoic simplicity and submissive reference to impersonal authority, the father's statement that 'Sé muy bien que me darán una manga o la corbata'§ (p. 411) throws

---

* ants in their words.
† A pin which probes till it finds the tiny roots of the yell.
‡ life is not noble, or good, or sacred.
§ I know very well that they will give me a sleeve or the tie.

into relief the brutalities of war, which in Remarque's words 'is a cause of death like cancer and tuberculosis, like influenza and dysentery. The deaths are merely more frequent, more varied and terrible.'[1]

The 'sympathetic understanding of the persecuted' which Lorca professed to Gil Benumeya (p. 1609) explains both his poetic exaltation of the gipsies and his compassionate lament for the negroes, contained within Harlem as tightly as their king is imprisoned within the degrading uniform of a janitor, which in Lorca's eyes is the ultimate stigma of the slavery and anguish he solemnly defined in 'Oda al rey de Harlem':

> ¡ Ay, Harlem ! ¡ Ay, Harlem ! ¡ Ay, Harlem !
> ¡ No hay angustia comparable a tus ojos oprimidos,
> a tu sangre estremecida dentro del eclipse oscuro,
> a tu violencia granate sordomuda en la penumbra,
> a tu gran rey prisionero con un traje de conserje !* (p. 407)

Lorca now visualized life as a hell on earth: negroes are condemned to the 'dark eclipse' of Harlem; doves are banished to the sewers (p. 430); and to feed the dying, unseen slaughterers kill each day with mathematical precision and ritual coldness so many animals that the figure of three hundred licenced in *Romancero gitano* by the traditional ballads was inflated astronomically in 'New York. Oficina y denuncia' to

> cuatro millones de patos,
> cinco millones de cerdos,
> dos mil palomas por el gusto de los agonizantes,
> un millón de vacas,
> un millón de corderos
> y dos millones de gallos,
> que dejan los cielos hechos añicos.†   (pp. 443–4)

---

* O Harlem, Harlem, Harlem ! There is no anguish that can be compared to your oppressed eyes, to your blood trembling in the dark eclipse, to your garnet violence deaf and dumb in the penumbra, to your great king captive in a janitor's suit.

† four million ducks, five million pigs, two thousand doves to indulge the dying, one million cows, one million lambs and two million chickens, whose cries splinter the heavens.

Lorca's cry of '¡ Oh mi Stanton, idiota y bello entre los pequeños animalitos... !'* (p. 430) expressed simply his pity for a suffering child doomed like the birds and cows consistently tortured in this work to a life of persecution and pain inflicted by the hungry cancer, to which he gave a sinister life as it prowls at the appropriate hour of midnight through corridors, conversing with the worms which have riddled the documents as methodically as the disease is consuming Stanton:

> A las doce de la noche el cáncer salía por los pasillos
> y hablaba con los caracoles vacíos de los documentos,
> el vivísimo cáncer lleno de nubes y termómetros
> con su casto afán de manzana para que lo piquen los ruiseñores.†
>
> (p. 429)

With his bleakly hyperbolic prophecy in 'Grito hacia Roma' of one million carpenters making chains for unborn children (pp. 448–9), Lorca impressed on us his melancholy conviction that the latter are condemned before birth to the misery and death predicted simply by the child in his play *Así que pasen cinco años*:

> Nunca veremos la luz,
> ni las nubes que se levantan,
> ni los grillos en la hierba,
> ni el viento como una espada.‡   (p. 977)

Pierced by pins, wires and coins, the children Lorca presented in *Poeta en Nueva York* are the helpless victims of robot brutality, which he stressed with many verbs of violence, with dangerous animals like alligators, crocodiles, iguanas and serpents and with such weapons as daggers, knives, needles, pins, swords and whips. His eyes jaundiced by emotional and spiritual troubles, Lorca saw no beauty in life and no dignity in death; the million grey rats he mentioned in 'Oda a Walt Whitman' (p. 453) illustrate his revulsion as graphically as the 'corpse-rats' described by Remarque[1]

---

* Oh my Stanton, idiotic and beautiful amid the tiny little animals... !
† At midnight the cancer sallied through the corridors and talked with the empty snails of the documents, the lively cancer full of clouds and thermometers with its chaste longing for an apple to be pecked by the nightingales.
‡ We shall never see the light, or the rising clouds, or the crickets in the grass, or the sword-sharp wind.

and the 'rats' alley / where the dead men lost their bones' imagined by Eliot in *The Waste Land* (ll. 115–16). The cemeteries, coffins, mummies, skeletons, skulls and tombs which recur in *Poeta en Nueva York* are the grimly ubiquitous tokens of the cosmic destructiveness which in 1934 claimed his bullfighter friend Ignacio Sánchez Mejías.

Like the poems of *Poeta en Nueva York*, Lorca's *Llanto por Ignacio Sánchez Mejías* was composed of what he called in the last stanza of his elegy 'palabras que gimen'* (p. 473). Lorca's funereal chanting, throughout the first section, of the first line of the poem, 'A las cinco de la tarde'† (p. 465), engraves on our minds the precise hour when death cut down the man whom Lorca eulogized in a *romance* of the second part with hyperbolic tributes that give him the stature of an epic hero:

> No hubo príncipe en Sevilla
> que comparársele pueda,
> ni espada como su espada
> ni corazón tan de veras.
> Como un río de leones
> su maravillosa fuerza...‡   (p. 469)

The broken body of Ignacio, corrupted in the first section by gangrene and death laying eggs in his wounds (p. 466), is in the third part of the poem a still form on a clinically cold slab. The corpse prostrate before the grieving poet, together with the blood still flowing in section two, is persistent and tangible evidence of the event whose finality Lorca indicated in the first part with his use of past tenses. His cry of '¡Que no quiero verla!'§ (p. 467) which resounds throughout the second section expresses his horror at the thought of Ignacio's blood flowing in the arena; as he stands before the corpse in the third section, his nostrils are filled with the stench of death and his eyes are hypnotized by the punctured and yellowing remains of the once lithe figure:

* words that groan.   † At five o'clock in the afternoon.
‡ There was no prince in Seville who can be compared with him, nor was there a sword like his sword nor such a true heart. Like a river of lions was his marvellous strength.
§ I do not want to see it!

> Ya está sobre la piedra Ignacio el bien nacido.
> Ya se acabó; ¿qué pasa? Contemplad su figura:
> la muerte le ha cubierto de pálidos azufres
> y le ha puesto cabeza de oscuro minotauro.
> . . . .
> ¿Qué dicen? Un silencio con hedores reposa.
> Estamos con un cuerpo presente que se esfuma,
> con una forma clara que tuvo ruiseñores
> y la vemos llenarse de agujeros sin fondo.* (p. 471)

The shroud and the cloths swathing Ignacio in the third part of the poem impress on Lorca a fact he lamented in the painful refrain of the last section: 'porque te has muerto para siempre'† (p. 472). Although Lorca predicted bitterly that Ignacio would be thrown like all the forgotten dead 'en un montón de perros apagados'‡ (p. 472), Sánchez Mejías will long be remembered outside Spain as the person who inspired a magnificent elegy. Lorca's anguish and sorrow; his impotent complaints about an injustice he could do nothing to remedy; his determination to evoke the death and decomposition of his friend in neatly plotted and metrically dignified stages, made his *Llanto por Ignacio Sánchez Mejías* into an eloquent comment on his spiritual condition in 1935 and into a tribute more emotionally charged and structurally coherent than Alberti's *Verte y no verte*, which was less a deeply felt lament for Sánchez Mejías than a dutiful display of poetic virtuosity prompted by his death.

Lorca was clearly forced by the pain of personal loss to write his elegy on Sánchez Mejías, whose sudden and violent end justified the bitter prophecies he made in *Poeta en Nueva York*, where death became in his eyes an event as routine and commonplace as eating a meal. The horror of his prediction in 'Pequeño poema infinito':

---

* Now Ignacio the noble lies on the slab. It is all over; what is happening? Look at him: death has covered him with pale sulphurs and has put on him the head of a dark minotaur.
What are they saying? The air is heavy with a stench-filled silence. We are in the presence of a body which is fading away, with a clear form that once had nightingales and now we see it being filled with bottomless holes.
† because you have died for ever.
‡ on a heap of dead dogs.

'tendremos que pacer sin descanso las hierbas de los cementerios'*
(p. 460) was intensified by his vision in 'Fábula y rueda de los tres
amigos' of 'los blancos derribos de Júpiter donde meriendan
muerte los borrachos'† (p. 402). When in 'Vaca' he imagined
once more

> ...el derribo de los cielos yertos
> donde meriendan muerte los borrachos,‡   (p. 432)

he stressed in the drunks' hideous diet his revulsion against men
brutified by alcohol and offered evidence of his retentive and
impressionable mind; Guillén has recalled that his son Claudio,
when he was three, once said in Lorca's presence on seeing a
stretch of waste-ground littered with débris that 'Drunks lunch
on death there.'[1] The fancy of a child's mind was implemented by
the imagination of an anguished poet to describe a life feeding
endlessly and hideously on death, whose macabre banality Eliot
indicated in *The Waste Land* with the horrifying questions:

> 'That corpse you planted last year in your garden,
>   'Has it begun to sprout? Will it bloom this year?' (ll. 71–2)

The hope Lorca expressed in 'Ciudad sin sueño':

> Haya un panorama de ojos abiertos
> y amargas llagas encendidas,§   (p. 422)

signalled his refusal to shelter behind a façade or remain encapsu-
lated within the childhood innocence he commemorated in '1910
(Intermedio)' when, as he emphasized in a solemn list, his eyes had
not yet been opened to the horrors of death and suffering imagined
as a festival of ashes:

> Aquellos ojos míos de mil novecientos diez
> no vieron enterrar a los muertos,
> ni la feria de ceniza del que llora por la madrugada,
> ni el corazón que tiembla arrinconado como un caballito de mar.‖
>
> (p. 400)

* we will have to graze without respite on the grass of the cemeteries.
† the white waste-grounds of Jupiter where the drunks lunch on death.
‡ the waste-ground of the stiff heavens where the drunks lunch on death.
§ May there be a panorama of open eyes and bitter inflamed sores.
‖ Those eyes of mine of nineteen hundred and ten did not see the burial of the
dead, or the ashen fair of him who weeps at dawn, or the trembling heart
cornered like a tiny sea-horse.

His confession that 'sé del horror de unos ojos despiertos'* (p. 427) reveals that in his insomnia, marked by the recurrence of *noche* and *nocturno*, his eyes were open wide to the nightmares around and within him; in 'New York. Oficina y denuncia' he insisted in clipped periods that, although he knew he could escape to the remote security of the mountains and filter what he saw through distorting 'spectacles of wisdom', he wanted to witness the blood of life and record unflinchingly, as he told Gil Benumeya, the collision of his 'poetic world with the poetic world of New York' (p. 1608):

> Existen las montañas. Lo sé.
> Y los anteojos para la sabiduría.
> Lo sé. Pero yo no he venido a ver el cielo.
> Yo he venido para ver la turbia sangre.† (p. 443)

Lorca's conviction that 'Será preciso viajar por los ojos de los idiotas'‡ (p. 418) warns us that he did not view the world with the eyes of a sane person or reproduce it with the lens of a camera. Sharing Aragon's belief that 'The only poetry is the poetry of the concrete',[1] he consistently organized the 'objects, landscapes, numbers, planets' which he postulated in 'Imaginación, inspiración, evasión' as the raw material of the poetic imagination (p. 1544) into new groupings joined by links visible only in the poet's mind. The critics who have written of Lorca's 'poetic automatism' and the 'obvious surrealism' of *Poeta en Nueva York*[2] forgot that the French surrealists did not discover poetic freedom, even though they built a creed around it. What was an earnestly pursued doctrinal licence in them was in Lorca an explosion of his already energetic fantasy detonated by the intense emotional pressures which led to and were recorded in *Poeta en Nueva York*. How much Lorca knew of French surrealism is still, so far as I know, a matter of conjecture; his nervous reminder that the poetry he sent to Gasch 'is not surrealism' (p. 1594) suggests that he knew enough about the movement to reject its label. Guillén pointed to a bridge between Lorca and surrealism with his recollection that 'Salvador

---

* I know about the horror of open eyes.
† Mountains exist. I know. And spectacles for wisdom. I know. But I have not come to see the sky. I have come to see the turbid blood.
‡ It will be necessary to travel through idiots' eyes.

Dalí and Federico live together intimately in the Residencia de Estudiantes. Luis Buñuel is also a companion of theirs';[1] the fact that Lorca wrote the screenplay of *Un viaje a la luna* after discussing *Un chien andalou* with a Mexican he met in New York, Emilio Amero, shows that, just as Dalí and Buñuel put their quaint thoughts and visions into eccentric verse, Lorca sought to complement his drawings with a cinematographic expression of his fantasies.[2]

Lorca's statement in his story 'Nadadora sumergida' (1928) that 'It is necessary for the elephant to have partridge's eyes and the partridge to have unicorn's hooves' (p. 32) advocated the mental liberty which he had used in *Libro de poemas* to describe a presentiment as a 'nose of the heart' (p. 141) and which he exploited in 'Oda al rey de Harlem' to create a weird picture of the negro king using a spoon to pull out crocodiles' eyes and beat monkey's buttocks. Even if his strange claim that 'Cojos perros fumaban sus pipas'* (p. 460) may be a recollection, as one critic has suggested,[3] of an advertisement for an American tobacco whose trademark was a smoking dog, what matters is that with the possessive adjective 'sus' Lorca made the fantastic idea of dogs smoking into a routine activity with which they while away time and console themselves for the immobility forced on them by their lameness. And when he imagined that wet-nurses give children 'ríos de musgo y amargura de pie'† (p. 430), or when he asserted that 'mi corazón tiene la forma de una milenaria boñiga de toro'‡ (p. 440), he was trying with these strange images to shock our sensibilities and inviting us to visualize those unsuspected relationships forged by a poetic fantasy under stress.

To penetrate the dense verbal texture of *Poeta en Nueva York* the reader has to generate his own imaginative energy and find his own way through capriciously connected visions and nouns set down in staccato series. The

> colmillos, girasoles, alfabetos
> y una pila de Volta con avispas ahogadas§   (p. 409)

---

* Lame dogs were smoking their pipes.   † rivers of moss and standing bitterness.
‡ my heart has the form of millenary bull's dung.
§ fangs, sunflowers, alphabets and a voltaic cell with drowned wasps.

carried off by the south wind in 'Oda al rey de Harlem' lament in their haphazard mixture of natural life, means of communication and mechanical energy the indiscriminate destruction which Lorca saw all around him. His catalogue in 'Paisaje de la multitud que orina' of

> ¡ La luna ! Los policías. ¡ Las sirenas de los transatlánticos !
> Fachada de crin, de humo; anémonas, guantes de goma*
>
> (p. 418)

not only illustrates Alberti's point that 'Live things and dead things throng around him',[1] but offers a complex of interdependent objects which hint disturbingly at a mysterious journey on horseback and on ships whose ambiguous sirens imperil an existence already menaced by the police, the moon and the suggestion implicit in rubber gloves of a sinister surgical operation.

The anemones which Lorca inserted into these lines as a simple tribute to a life threatened constantly by pain and death reappear on the offertory in 'Iglesia abandonada' as an epitaph to the universal cruelty which he indicted in a series of frightening visions introduced simply by 'comprendí', 'tenía' and 'vi':

> Saqué una pata de gallina por detrás de la luna y luego
> comprendí que mi niña era un pez
> por donde se alejan las carretas.
> Yo tenía una niña.
> Yo tenía un pez muerto bajo las cenizas de los incensarios.
> Yo tenía un mar. ¿ De qué? ¡ Dios mío ! ¡ Un mar !
> Subí a tocar las campanas, pero las frutas tenían gusanos
> y las cerillas apagadas
> se comían los trigos de la primavera.
> Yo vi la transparente cigüeña de alcohol
> mondar las negras cabezas de los soldados agonizantes
> y vi las cabañas de goma
> donde giraban las copas llenas de lágrimas.†   (p. 411)

---

* The moon ! The police. The sirens of the liners! Façade of horsehair, of smoke; anemones, rubber gloves.

† I took a hen's foot from behind the moon and then I understood that my daughter was a fish through which the carts depart. I had a daughter. I had a dead fish beneath the ashes of the censers. I had a sea. Of what? My God ! A sea ! I went up to ring the bells but the fruit had worms and the burned-out

By using 'era' and repeating 'Yo tenía', the father lives sorrow-fully in the past and corroborates the death of his son and daughter in a series of desperately eccentric actions signalled by 'Saqué' and 'Subí'. His pathos is intensified by his awareness that religion, whose bells can toll only for death and whose censers produce ash which buries his dead child, cannot console him for the loss of life which he had engendered, represented by the fish and the sea. As Lorca looked through the eyes of a grief-stricken father, he saw evidence of death and decay in the tree disease known as *pata de gallina*; in the corpse-carrying carts; in the ashes of the censers; in the worm-eaten fruit and consumed wheat; and in the blackened heads of the dying soldiers numbed into fighting robots by alcohol which corrodes their minds and bodies just as storks feed on vermin.

The difficulty of the poems of *Poeta en Nueva York* is that they permit no single, secure interpretation but will strike different chords and associations in each reader. Although Lorca's images sometimes strayed so far from his subject and therefore from the reader's experience that, to use C. Day Lewis's words, they collide rather than collude,[1] his feelings of rage, impotence, nausea and compassion gave the work an emotional coherence framed by the five movements into which the ten sections of *Poeta en Nueva York* fall. With the first section, 'Poemas de la soledad en Columbia University', Lorca focused attention on his solitude and on his radically changed moods and preoccupations. In sections II and III, 'Los negros', 'Calle y sueños', he sought victims of and a setting for mankind's inhumanity, condensed into the Great War. Sections IV, V and VI, 'Poemas del lago Edem Mills', 'En la cabaña del Farmer (Campo de Newburg)' and 'Introducción a la muerte. Poemas de la soledad en Vermont' compose a pastoral interlude, marked by his epigraph from Garcilaso, where he was still haunted by death and sunk in despair. Having taken fresh breath in the countryside, he returned in sections VII and VIII, 'Vuelta a la ciudad' and 'Dos odas', to New York and a shrill

---

matches ate the spring wheat. I saw the transparent stork of alcohol peel the black heads of the dying soldiers and I saw the rubber shelters where glasses full of tears circled.

denunciation of its soullessness. Finally, with quickened pulse he recorded in sections IX and X, 'Huída de Nueva York. Dos valses hacia la civilización' and 'El poeta llega a La Habana', his escape from America and his return to hispanic civilization.

By setting down in poetry what he acknowledged to be a 'personal interpretation' of New York (p. 1608), Lorca produced an eloquent poetic document challenging in its imaginative vigour, disturbing in its tensions and ferociously explosive in its condemnation of American life. Unlike Aleixandre, who relished the role of babbler, Lorca, Alberti and Cernuda were forced to express themselves through images by a malaise so subverting and so comprehensive that it defied simple definition and precise diagnosis. Looking through 'idiots' eyes', Alberti, Cernuda and Lorca illustrated their anguished isolation and bitter hostility to a world they condemned and represented as absurd, cold, hostile and corrupt, producing a deeply felt and densely textured poetry that, as it expressed old fears and emotions in a new and taxing way, tests the reader's suppleness of feeling and fantasy. While Spanish literature in the 1920s was littered with the miscarriages of fevered minds straining to be novel, *Sobre los ángeles*, *Un río, un amor* and *Poeta en Nueva York* in particular emerged from the difficult union of deep spiritual troubles and original, creative imaginations. In purging themselves through poetry, Alberti, Cernuda and Lorca reached an extreme of poetic challenge and a peak of poetic activity which they would never attain again.

AFTER THE WAR

¿ Es que llegamos al final del fin
o que algo nuevo comienza?*

Alberti, *Vida bilingüe de un refugiado*
español en Francia (1939–40)

The Spanish Civil War scattered over the American Continent
many of the writers I have mentioned in these pages; some chose
exile rather than a political system they found abhorrent; others,
like Alberti, were forced by their political allegiance to flee. Of the
eight poets who dominate this book only Lorca failed tragically
to survive the war and only Aleixandre remained in Spain. The
savage conflict left a legacy of bitterness and upheaval which had
to change but could not curtail the activities of poets who after the
war continued to demonstrate their versatility and confidence
with plays, novels, short stories and critical essays. Although varied,
the writings of these seven poets since 1939 have been uneven in
quantity and quality; the least active, Altolaguirre, strayed little
from the paths he marked for himself before the war; on the
other hand, Alberti's memoirs, plays and prolific poetry reveal an
energy not always matched by self-control and critical acumen.

In the poetry they have written since 1939 most of these seven
poets live despite themselves in the past, rarely breaking out of the
elegiac mould whose common denominators are the themes of
loss, oblivion, distance, death—particularly the death of Lorca—
and old age, illustrated constantly by dust, autumn, fallen leaves
and skeletons. The lines, images, topics, techniques and forms
which some of these poets transposed from their earlier works
into their post-war poems points the reader to the past and not to
the future, which Alberti described in *Pleamar* (1942–4) as 'frozen'
(p. 568).

Although the Civil War does not appear in Aleixandre's poems,
it confined to the past and condemned to his memory the virginal

* Are we reaching the end of the end or is something new beginning?

Eden whose uninhibited pleasures he celebrated nostalgically in
Sombra del paraíso (1939–43):   Miré por dentro

> los ramos, las cañadas luminosas, las alas variantes,
> y un vuelo de plumajes de color, de encendidos
> presentes me embriagó...*   (p. 478)

War and age may have corrected his excesses of style and stilled
the raptures recorded in *La destrucción o el amor*, but it did not oust
from his mind memories of the brilliant sunlight, blonde hair,
strong colours and the radiant springtime vital with flowers, birds
and rivers. The naked figure who moves through *Sombra del
paraíso* was the model of those nude creatures who in *Nacimiento
último* (1925–52) still cavort in

>   ...los silenciosos prados,
> los festivales bosques
> y las umbrías florestas donde el sol se aplastaba con un frenético beso
> prematuro de estío.†   (p. 649)

In *Historia del corazón* (1945–53) Aleixandre again orchestrated
every detail of the body, which, like the 'Vagabundo continuo'
who appears in the same work, represents his fidelity since *Ámbito*
to his sensual fantasies:

> He aquí los senos, el vientre, su redondo muslo,
> su acabado pie,
> y arriba los hombros, el cuello de suave pluma reciente...‡ (p. 681)

His effusive tributes to love in *Historia del corazón*—a title that
points us to the past—do not conceal his realization that, although
love and lovers should in his view be immortal, age is braking and
death will end all erotic frenzies. Despite his sad awareness of
approaching death in such poems as 'El viejo y el sol', 'El niño y el
hombre' and 'Ante el espejo', he could still generate the poetic
energy to celebrate in *En un vasto dominio* (1962) parts of the body
and hair that remains resolutely blonde.

---

* I looked inside the bouquets, the luminous dales, the changing wings, and a
flight of coloured feathers, of burning gifts intoxicated me.
† the silent meadows, the festival forests and the shaded arbours where the sun
flattened itself with a frenzied premature kiss of summer.
‡ Here are the breasts, the belly, its round thigh, its finished foot, and, above, the
shoulders, the neck of gentle recent down.

Although Aleixandre's tenacious rhapsodies to love are repetitive, at least they were written with a vigour, fluency and confidence which deserted him when he wrote of people, places and things he saw in the world around him. His statement in *En un vasto dominio* that 'Para todos escribo'*1 struck a new note for a poet who has constantly explored his fantasy and consistently indulged his senses. His poems about a shepherd, or a threshing-floor, or 'Lope, en su casa', are occasional pieces which, lacking the coherence of a common purpose, are as flabby as the series of pen-portraits which disrupted the unity of *Nacimiento último*. The tributes to friends and family he has gathered into *Retratos con nombre* (1965), which complement the volume of prose reminiscences he published in 1958 under the title of *Los encuentros*, are pen-portraits flawed by dispirited diction and the sentimentality that made his poem to his still-born sister, 'Que nació muerta (Mi hermana Sofía)', an exercise in bathos.

Although *Retratos con nombre* is dominated by the memories of dead relatives and ageing friends, the 'cuerpos ligeros en el aire'†2 which appear in it perpetuate his resilient vision of eternal youth, which he retains in his mind as tenaciously as Altolaguirre maintained the posture he adopted when he first started writing poetry. Small in volume and repetitive in content, manner and mood, the poetry Altolaguirre wrote between 1939 and his death twenty years later invites one to diagnose in him a reluctance to look beyond himself and a lack of stamina illustrated by his reproduction in *Poemas en América* (1955) under the title of 'Mi forma inerte' of a poem originally included in *Nube temporal* (1939), 'Cuando te sueño'. The *dentro* and *hacia dentro* which recur in his poems led to the private capsule whose immobility Altolaguirre exalted in *Fin de un amor* (1949):

> Calla, sepulta en ti tu pensamiento,
> que, mejor que un jardín, patria es la mina
> y mejor la quietud que el movimiento.‡ (p. 173)

* I write for everyone.
† light bodies in the air.
‡ Silence, bury your thoughts within you, for, better than a garden, the mine is a homeland and stillness is better than movement.

However, in *Nube temporal* Altolaguirre's solitude and self-sufficiency were clouded by his awareness of death and briefly disturbed by nostalgic thoughts of Spain. Lorca, whom he mourned in *Nube temporal* (pp. 137–8), and Saturnino Ruiz, who worked in his printing press and whom he lamented in *Más poemas de las islas invitadas* (p. 159), were victims of time, whose power he acknowledged in his description of himself in *Nuevos poemas* (1946) as 'decrépito y cansado'* (p. 166). His hackneyed mention of 'el abismo de la muerte't (p. 142) and his repetition of the outworn metaphor 'agua de olvido'‡ (pp. 169, 208) suggest that he did not find in exile the verbal power and imaginative vigour he lacked before 1936. The clouds, trees, open fields and rivers with which he gave his pre-war poems a natural framework reappear as a reliable base on which he built poems that make few demands on the reader. His description of irrigation conduits in *Fin de un amor* as

> chorro preso en metal, que destapado
> blasfema espumas en su desvarío§   (p. 184)

is a surge of rhetorical vigour rare in a poet whose habit of explaining the significance of his symbols simplifies even further our passage through a poetry that present few challenges to the imagination.

The poetry Prados wrote after 1939 holds few surprises for anyone familiar with the poetry he wrote before the Civil War. His longing for Spain which he expressed in *Penumbras* (1939–41) in the haunting line 'Cuando era primavera en España'‖ (p. 141) only briefly postponed his resuscitation of nature and night as settings against which to project the tremors of his sensibility, rippling in *Jardín cerrado* (1946) into his insistence that

> De noche voy
> de noche,
> a buscar lo que perdí
> de noche.¶   (p. 193)

---

* decrepit and tired.   † the abyss of death.   ‡ water of oblivion.
§ a gush captive in metal, which, opened, blasphemes foam in its madness.
‖ When it was spring in Spain.
¶ By night I go by night, to seek what I lost at night.

In duplicating the circular repetitions of the past, Prados showed that he was no more able to shake off his obsession with night than his preoccupation with death and *la nada*, which made him ask in *Jardín cerrado* as he did in *Cuerpo perseguido*: '¿no seré yo el que está muerto?'* (p. 179).

Prados's uninhibited use of repetition, refrains, parentheses and exclamations form between the poetry he wrote before and after the Civil War a bridge strengthened by the reappearance of the ubiquitous verbs beginning with *des-* and of motifs as central to his poetry as flight, unity, nakedness and bleeding. His statement in *Jardín cerrado* that 'Mi cuerpo estaba huyendo'† (p. 207) and his mention in *Signos del ser* (1962) of 'mi constante huir'‡[1] are examples of the 'Pensamiento en círculo'§ he diagnosed succinctly in *La piedra escrita* (1961).[2]

That Prados was the pivot of his own poetic activity around which he ceaselessly revolved is demonstrated by a number of lines where his apparent playing with words and coining of para-doxes accurately chart his circular movements; in *Río natural* (1953) his unwittingly humorous affirmation that

> Así me voy caminando:
> yo delante y yo detrás... || (p. 280)

was echoed in *Signos del ser* by one of the *soleares* of which he was so fond:

> Delante de mí me acerco
> a mí; voy pasando a ser
> camino hacia mí: me alejo.¶[3]

But the dense grove and closed garden which Prados chose to depict his soul prove to be a maze from which neither he nor the reader can escape. His preoccupations with nature, solitude and the mirror are signs of a faithful poetic stance which made his poetry into a coherent and tightly knit record of a delicate sensibility.

Cernuda's admission in *Como quien espera el alba* (1941-4) that

---

* is it not I who am dead?   † My body was fleeing.
‡ my constant flight.   § Thoughts in a circle.
|| Thus do I go, with me in front and me behind.
¶ In front of me I approach me; I am becoming myself as I get near to me: I move away.

'Amo más que la vida este sosiego a solas'* (p. 227) maintained his love of solitude which he affirmed in *Perfil del aire*. Although his statement in *Las nubes* (1937–40) that

> Es tarde y nace el frío.
> Cerrada está la puerta,
> Alumbrando la lámpara†   (p. 162)

reproduced the chill and cheerless setting found in his first work as directly as poem titles like 'El indolente', 'Jardín antiguo' and 'Jardín', he was not immune like Prados to the world outside himself. Cernuda's unhappy exile in London, in 'that hateful Scotland'¹ and in America intensified the bitterness stirred in him by thoughts of Spain, marriage and a God so indifferent to man's suffering that in *Como quien espera el alba* he observed in his icily epigrammatic way that

> Para morir el hombre de Dios no necesita,
> Mas Dios para vivir necesita del hombre.‡   (p. 213)

Cernuda's determination to be faithful to himself permitted him to set himself above mankind and to comment immodestly in *Las nubes* that it is a sad fate to be born a gifted being (p. 136). The incurable dissatisfaction which he recorded throughout his work—and which is summarized neatly in the title of his last book of poetry, *Desolación de la quimera* (1956–62)—deadens his poems with a predominantly elegiac mood intensified by his thoughts of, and longing for, an ideal, immortal world of beauty. Although he commanded himself in *Vivir sin estar viviendo* (1944–9) not to look back (p. 268), he mused wistfully in *Las nubes* about a lost Eden (p. 160), and was haunted in *Desolación de la quimera* by the timeless innocence of childhood which he evoked in the prose poems of *Ocnos*.²

But Cernuda's realization in *Vivir sin estar viviendo* that memories represent nothing more than the futility of desire (p. 279) deepened the elegiac mood of his writings; the 'amada forma

---

* I love more than life this solitary peace.
† It is late and the cold is born. The door is closed, the lamp lights [the room].
‡ To die man does not need God, but God needs man to live.

esbelta'* which appears in *Como quien espera el alba* (p. 231) is, like Aleixandre's naked figures, a reminder of a perfect, innocent world now submerged beneath such evidence of mortality as broken flowers, ruins, the death of Lorca and the cemeteries which recur in *Las nubes*, *Como quien espera el alba* and *Vivir sin estar viviendo*. In one of the dramatic monologues of *Las nubes*, which show his versatility and articulate control of a new form, Cernuda cast himself as Lazarus bitterly resentful of his return to life; he felt so besieged and threatened by death that, echoing his vision of himself in *Los placeres prohibidos* as a figure who 'estaba muerto y andaba entre los muertos'† (p. 70), he described himself through Lazarus's mouth as 'un muerto / Andando entre los muertos'‡ (p. 167).

Alberti's stark statement in *Poemas escénicos* (1962) that 'Estoy ya muerto. Sí'§ shows that he could not visualize his burial with the waggish fantasy he displayed in *Cal y canto*; like Cernuda he cast himself as a corpse whose solitude in death reflects his loneliness in exile. That Alberti is 'cargado de muertos'‖ (p. 490), as he claimed in *Entre el clavel y la espada* (1939–40) in an echo of *Sermones y moradas*, is demonstrated by his elegies to Lorca, Miró, Salinas and Miguel Hernández and by the recurrence in his postwar poetry of dead soldiers and the bleeding bull, which represents for him Spain's agony. The empty future compels Alberti to live in the past, which acts both as a balm and an irritant. His constant memories of his childhood, of people he knew, of Spain and particularly of the Atlantic he celebrated in *Ora marítima* (1953), focus our attention on a happier age remote in time and distance as sharply as certain images remind us of *Sobre los ángeles*; the 'vestido sin esperanza'¶ (p. 826) and 'cueva sin aire y sin salida'** (p. 831) found in *Retornos de lo vivo lejano* (1948–56), the 'niño ya de piedra, muerto'†† (p. 948) who appears in *Ora marítima* and the 'cuerpo deshabitado'‡‡ (p. 1003) which recurs in *Baladas y*

---

* beloved slender form.
† was dead and walked among the dead.
‡ a dead man walking among the dead. § I am now dead. Yes.
‖ loaded with the dead. ¶ garment without hope.
** airless, exitless cave. †† child now of stone, dead.
‡‡ uninhabited body.

canciones del Paraná (1953–4), are epitaphs to a time of poetic confidence and vigour weakened by the weariness of exile and dissipated by Alberti's irrepressible penning of verse.

Like the withered prostitute who in two poems of *Poemas escénicos* represents the decay of beauty and strength, Alberti wearily but stubbornly plies his trade. The tired skeleton who figures in this work[1] still insists as Alberti did in *Baladas y canciones del Paraná* that 'yo tengo que seguir cantando'* (p. 994). The strain of resolutely singing even when he has little to sing about has made the poetry Alberti has written since the Civil War uneven in quality, repetitive in theme and—with its surfeit of refrains, *coplas* and epigrams—predictable in style; with disarming frankness he admitted in *Coplas de Juan Panadero* that

> En lo que vengo a cantar,
> de diez palabras a veces
> sobran más de la mitad.† (p. 872)

With no risk to his reputation Alberti could certainly have suppressed the well-lubricated but hollow resonance of *Buenos Aires en tinta china* (1950) and many of the verbal doodlings about people, places, poetry and the minutiae of life which, gathered into arbitrary collections like *Poemas diversos* (1945–59), *Poemas de Punta del Este* (1945–56) and *Baladas y canciones del Paraná*, are mechanical and spiritless. And if his voice is, as he lamented in *Baladas y canciones del Paraná*, dry (p. 982), it is because in *Signos del día* (1945–55), *Coplas de Juan Panadero* and *La primavera de los pueblos* (1955–7) the poet relapsed into the political propagandist still deeply committed to communism and still determined to keep old rancours alive.

Fortunately, Alberti will be remembered and celebrated not for his damp, lifeless epigrams and crudely doctrinaire attacks on Franco, the Falange and the United States, but for the disciplined eloquence and imaginative vigour which made *Retornos de lo vivo lejano*, *A la pintura* (1945–52) and—to a lesser extent—*Poemas escénicos* into coherent and eloquent works that represent the peaks

---

* I have to carry on singing.
† In what I come to sing, sometimes of every ten words I use half are superfluous.

of his poetic activity since 1936. In his tribute to painting particularly the verbal power which he has wilfully dissipated since 1939 animated his poems on colours, tools, materials and painters as different as Corot and Bosch, whose grotesque vitality he captured in a series of breathless enumerations:

> Barrigas, narices,
> lagartos, lombrices,
> delfines volantes,
> orejas rodantes,
> ojos boquiabiertos,
> escobas perdidas,
> barcas aturdidas,
> vómitos, heridas,
> muertos.* (p. 646)

It is a pity that a man capable of doing with words what painters achieve with a brush could not have recognized in his seemingly endless and undistinctive verses about his dog, daughter and politics a recurrent poetic exhaustion which self-discipline and discrimination could have cured.

In *Maremágnum* (1957), the first of the three books that compose *Clamor*, Guillén's attacks on Franco and the bitter choruses he put into the mouths of the police, the Falange and the clergy were prescribed not by a political stance but by a humanitarian hostility to injustice and cruelty. Because he could not remain oblivious of or indifferent to a civilization moved and menaced in his eyes by evil, he chose for *Clamor* the subtitle of *Tiempo de historia*. Guillén is no longer able to blind himself to the wrongs or stop his ears to the hubbub of the world where, as he succinctly put it in *A la altura de las circunstancias* (1963),

> Inquietud de metal
> Nos escupe superflua algarabía.†¹

In *Clamor* a hostile, savage and strident world squeezed and threatened Guillén as vigorously as it besieged the garden where

---

* Bellies, noses, lizards, worms, flying dolphins, rolling ears, gaping eyes, lost brooms, stunned boats, vomit, wounds and corpses.
† Metal anxiety spits superfluous clamour at us.

in ... *Que van a dar en la mar* (1960) Calisto and Melibea try to abstract themselves from time as they enjoy pleasures that must end. Calisto's longing that

> ¡ Oh si ya no existiese
> Más mundo que este huerto !*[1]

is, Guillén knows, impossible; the hints of violence and confusion which appeared in *Cántico* in such poems as 'A vista de hombre', 'Cara a cara' and 'Estación del Norte' swelled in *Clamor* into a crescendo of anguish and a tableau of chaos. 'That there is in *Cántico* a part of *Clamor* just as in *Clamor* there is a part of *Cántico*', as Guillén has claimed,[2] puts the work on two ends of a line, where the similarities—such as the use of the *décima* and *romance*—are less striking than the differences. In *Cántico* Guillén could never have written a poem about graffiti on the walls of a men's lavatory, as he did in *Maremágnum* (p. 186).

The 'Profunda profusión / De red'† which is found in *A la altura de las circunstancias*[3] takes us back in motif and alliteration to the 'red de rumbos'‡ which thrilled Guillén in *Cántico* (p. 33), just as the 'aires-auras / De Castilla'§ found in ... *Que van a dar en la mar* remind us of the prose-piece he published in 1923 under the title of 'Aire-aura'.[4] Although in *Maremágnum* the statue of the horseman is still 'Fornidamente gallardo'‖ and to breathe remains 'la mayor aventura',¶[5] the harmony of which he is still aware is constantly menaced by evil, which in a graphic censure 'Alza mansión con pútrida bodega',**[6] and by the erratic assaults of chance, which Guillén represented in *A la altura de las circunstancias* as dust covering man like a nuclear fall-out:

> Gime un polvo de caos pobre
> Con sus alimañas-peleles
> Dentro de la selva del hombre.††[7]

The thieves who erupt in 'Los atracadores' of *Maremágnum* represent for Guillén a life of danger as dramatically as the crash of

---

* Oh if only no more world existed than this orchard !
† Profound profusion of network.   ‡ Network of routes.
§ breezes-dawns of Castile.   ‖ Lustily bold.
¶ the greatest adventure.   ** Erects a mansion with a putrid cellar.
†† A wretched dust of chaos groans with its idiot-beasts inside man's jungle.

the racing car in 'Carrera' of *A la altura de las circunstancias* exemplifies the sudden and wanton destruction which, advocated by the devil throughout *Clamor*, liquidated Anne Frank and flattened Rotterdam. When he wrote in *A la altura de las circunstancias* that

> Sí, vomité, rechacé,
> Mundo, lo que nos sobraba.
> Pero te guardé mi fe,*[1]

he recorded the tenacious faith of a man forced to purge himself of the anguish and nausea which in *Maremágnum* he imagined as a

> ...lucha con la inmundicia
> Que dentro de mí padezco.†[2]

A new strain in *Clamor* is the worldly-wise tartness which embitters the comments on life, injustice and death Guillén has made in the groups of epigrams he called *tréboles*, some of which are pithy and pugnacious, others of which are flawed by rhymes as forced as 'Jesús' and 'orange-juice' and 'da' and 'bah'.[3] Time, whose power and passage he lamented in titles like 'Muerte de la rosa', 'Polvo del olvido', 'Los pobres muertos', 'Envejecer' and 'El hondo muerto', has eroded his former resigned acceptance of death, which has now given way to a series of anguished questions: '¿Yo, polvo sobre el polvo de una tierra?'‡ he asked in ...*Que van a dar en la mar*; '¿Qué futuro?'§ he wondered chillingly in *A la altura de las circunstancias*; and, most desperate of all, '¿Cremación de mi cadáver?'‖ he asked with incredulous terror in *Homenaje* (1967).[4]

What Guillén offers us in *Clamor* is not only an acrid indictment of a world moved by chance and ruled by threat but the shudders of a once confident and buoyant man slowly overcome by thoughts of imminent death. As he faces up in words he has borrowed from Quevedo to 'La ley de mi edad, tan dura',¶[5] he chants with simple dignity the pathetic dirge of old age:

---

* Yes, I vomited, I rejected, world, what we had left over. But I kept my faith in you.
† struggle with the filth which I suffer inside me.
‡ I, dust on the dust of an earth?   § What future?
‖ Cremation of my corpse?   ¶ The law of my age, so harsh.

El amanecer. Yo y la escarcha.
Frío el día, corto el vivir.
¡ Ay, mi edad, mi labor en marcha !*[1]

Like Guillén, Salinas felt 'the profound horror of our time',[2] which overwhelmed him in *Todo más claro* (1949) after he had celebrated in *El contemplado* (1946) his rediscovery of nature and the regeneration of his poetic energies dormant since he published *Razón de amor* ten years previously. In *El contemplado* his description of waves as 'bailarinas' (p. 302) and 'apuntes de Afrodita't (p. 314) signalled his delight in the Caribbean with images that take us back in spirit and fantasy to *Seguro azar* and *Fábula y signo*; and to state enthusiastically that 'Refulgen gozos, júbilos destellan't (p. 309) was to share Guillén's enjoyment of the world in phrases strongly reminiscent of *Cántico*.

But even the rapturous poems of *El contemplado* contain hints of disaster; when he referred to 'la gran ciudad de los negocios, / la ciudad enemiga'§ (p. 321) and stated that 'la nada tiene prisa'‖ (p. 322), he indicated his hostility to the mechanical soullessness of the twentieth century which he expanded in *Todo más claro* into a condemnation of a civilization that uses its laboratories and technical skills to plan the destruction of mankind. In 'Pasajero en museo' he envied the creatures which, sealed within their glass cases, do not have to worry about the future. Casting himself as an impotent but anguished spectator, he appears in 'Hombre en la orilla' as a man who, stupefied by 'Ruedas, sólo ruedas, ruedas'¶ (p. 352), stands not merely on the pavement's edge but on the brink of disaster, which he represented as a nought whose only exit is atomic death:

Tan sólo por una muerte
tiene salida la O.** (p. 361)

---

* Daybreak. I and the frost. The day is cold, life is short. Alas, my age, my departing toil!
† dancers; Aphrodite's notes.   ‡ Joys shine, delights sparkle.
§ the greaty city of business, the enemy city.
‖ nothingness is in a hurry.
¶ Wheels, only wheels, wheels.
** Only through a nought can death escape.

In 'Cero', which complemented his splendidly imaginative and devastatingly satirical novel *La bomba increíble* (1950) and his play *Caín o una gloria científica*, Salinas was so haunted by the ruins and torn flesh caused by the atom bomb—which he never named— that, like the dog howling pitifully for its master at the end of the poem, he sang a moving lament for the needless dead in lines for which he went, as did Guillén to write that 'No me podrán quitar el dolorido / Sentir',*[1] to Garcilaso:

> Invitación al llanto. Esto es un llanto,
> ojos, sin fin, llorando...†   (p. 403)

Salinas was led by his fear of atomic annihilation to predict the end of mankind and to see in the mirror his own skeleton, which is, as he warned us with the chill conciseness of Quevedo, the destiny of man: '(Último aquí del hombre: su esqueleto)'‡ (p. 384). But Salinas's indictment of man and his laboratories did not weaken his faith in the world; he combated the despair of *Todo más claro* to reaffirm in *Confianza* (1954) in terms that are again significantly reminiscent of Guillén his faith in love and his delight in the perfume of a rose and a bird's song.

With his poems on 'Verbo' and 'La vocación' and his determination to breathe and write

> Mientras haya
> alguna ventana abierta...,§   (p. 464)

Salinas ended his poetic career by reaffirming his faith in poetry and in life, even though both had been changed by the physical circumstance and the spiritual consequence of exile. The disruption or deplacement caused by the Spanish Civil War not only tested the resilience of Alberti, Aleixandre, Altolaguirre, Cernuda, Guillén, Prados and Salinas as most of them, to quote Salinas's eloquent phrase, 'rot in accursed exile',[2] but challenged them to emulate their pre-war vitality. The aftermath of the Civil War imposed on these seven poets limitations of subject, emotion and initiative

---

* They will not be able to take my sorrowful feelings from me.
† Invitation to tears. This is a lament, eyes ceaselessly weeping.
‡ The last residence of man is his skeleton.
§ As long as there is an open window.

which throw into relief the adventurous and confident variety of theme, form, fantasy and language of the works they wrote up to 1936. Respect for their fidelity to poetry since 1939 need not dilute or conflict with enthusiasm for their pre-war writings. Although, as Aleixandre lamented in *Nacimiento último*, 'Todos partieron, todos juntos en un momento, para muy diferentes caminos'* (p. 628), they left behind them a legacy of brilliant achievements which made the years 1920–36 into one of the densest, most varied and most rewarding periods in Spanish poetry; one cannot ask for more.

* They all left, all together at one moment, on very different paths.

NOTES

Introduction: 'The Brilliant Pleiad'

PAGE 1

1 Guillén, *Language and Poetry. Some Poets of Spain* (Cambridge, Mass., 1961), p. 214.

PAGE 2

1 Alberti, *La arboleda perdida. Libros I y II de memorias* (Buenos Aires, 1959), p. 162.

PAGE 3

1 C. Couffon, *Dos encuentros con Jorge Guillén* (Paris [1963]), p. 13.
2 Alberti, 'Federico García Lorca: *Poeta en Nueva York*', *Sur*, vol. IX (1940), no. 75, p. 149.
3 Cernuda, 'Recuerdo de Pierre Reverdy', in *Poesía y literatura II* (Barcelona, 1964), p. 201; 'Miguel de Unamuno', in *Estudios sobre poesía española contemporánea* (Madrid, 1959), p. 99.

PAGE 4

1 Guillén, *Federico en persona: semblanza y epistolario* (Buenos Aires, 1959), p. 64.
2 Bécquer, 'Entre sueños', in *Obras completas*, 11th ed. (Madrid, 1964), p. 764.
3 C. Bousoño, *La poesía de Vicente Aleixandre. Imagen. Estilo. Mundo poético*, 2nd ed. (Madrid, 1956), p. 16.
4 Darío, 'Prefacio' to *Cantos de vida y esperanza*, in *Poesías completas* (Madrid, 1954), p. 703.
5 Cernuda, 'Experimento en Rubén Darío', in *Poesía y literatura II*, p. 78.

PAGE 5

1 D. F. Fogelquist, *The Literary Collaboration and the Personal Correspondence of Rubén Darío and Juan Ramón Jiménez* (Coral Gables, Florida, 1956), p. 21.
2 *Ibid.* p. 16.
3 R. Gullón, *Cartas de Antonio Machado a Juan Ramón Jiménez* (San Juan, Puerto Rico, 1959), p. 32.
4 Couffon, *Dos encuentros con Jorge Guillén*, p. 11.

PAGE 6

1 Alberti, *La poesía popular en la lírica española contemporánea* (Jena and Leipzig, 1933), p. 12.
2 Altolaguirre, 'Cartas a Juan Ramón Jiménez', *Papeles de Son Armadans*, vol. XXXVIII (1965), no. CXIV, p. 273.
3 Salinas, 'Poética', in Gerardo Diego, *Poesía española contemporánea. Antología*, Nueva edición completa (Madrid, 1959), p. 319.
4 Jiménez, *Tercera antolojía poética (1898–1953)* (Madrid, 1957), p. 526.
5 D. Alonso, *Poemas puros. Poemillas de la ciudad* (Madrid, 1921), p. 31.

PAGE 7

1 A. Machado, *Los complementarios y otras prosas póstumas* (Buenos Aires, 1957), p. 38.
2 Unamuno, *Cancionero. Diario poético* (Buenos Aires, 1953), no. 339, p. 122.
3 Machado, *Los complementarios*, p. 40.
4 A. Machado, *Abel Martín*, 2nd ed. (Buenos Aires, 1953), pp. 44–9.
5 Recalled by Bergamín, *Al volver* (Barcelona, 1962), p. 111.
6 Unamuno, *Cancionero. Diario poético*, no. 915, p. 269; the verse is dated 14 March 1929.

PAGE 8

1 Gómez de Baquero, *Pen Club. I. Los poetas*, in *Obras completas*, vol. II (Madrid, 1929–30), p. 119.
2 Alberti, *La arboleda perdida*, p. 237.
3 Altolaguirre, 'Vida y poesía. Cuatro poetas íntimos', *Lyceum*, vol. IV (1939), no. 14, p. 15.
4 Guillén, *Federico en persona*, p. 111.
5 Altolaguirre, 'El caballo griego', *Papeles de Son Armadans*, vol. X (1958), no. XXX, p. 294.

PAGE 9

1 Guillén, *Federico en persona*, p. 82.
2 Concha Méndez, 'Luis Cernuda', *Ínsula*, no. 207 (February 1964).
3 Alberti, *La arboleda perdida*, pp. 172–3; *Imagen primera de...* (Buenos Aires, 1945), p. 21.
4 Guillén, *Language and Poetry*, p. 211.

PAGE 10

1 Recalled by Dámaso Alonso, 'Rafael entre su arboleda', *Ínsula*, no. 198 (May 1963); reprinted in D. Alonso, *Poetas españoles contemporáneos*, Tercera edición aumentada (Madrid, 1965), pp. 179–87.
2 Ortega y Gasset, *La deshumanización del arte y otros ensayos estéticos*, 4th ed. (Madrid, 1956), p. 32.
3 Jiménez, 'Acento. Poetas de antro y dianche', *La Gaceta Literaria*, no. 94 (November 1930).
4 Jiménez, *Cartas (primera serie)* (Madrid, 1962), p. 381.
5 Alberti, *La arboleda perdida*, p. 262.
6 Jiménez, 'Pedro Salinas', in *Españoles de tres mundos* (Madrid, 1960), p. 179; *Cartas (primera serie)*, p. 382.

PAGE 11

1 Jiménez, *Cartas (primera serie)*, pp. 305, 307.
2 *Ibid.* p. 273.
3 Alberti, *La arboleda perdida*, p. 168.
4 Torre, *Literaturas europeas de vanguardia* (Madrid, 1923), p. 59.
5 Diego, *Imagen. Poemas (1918–1921)* (Madrid, 1922), p. 45.

6 Marinetti, 'Fundación y manifiesto del futurismo', *Prometeo*, no. 4 (February 1909), pp. 65–73; *El futurismo* [tr. G. Gómez de la Mata and N. Hernández Luquero] (Valencia, 1911?).

PAGE 12

1 Jacob, *El cubilete de dados* (Madrid, 1924), p. 28.
2 Alberti, *La arboleda perdida*, p. 239.

PAGE 13

1 Alberti, *El poeta en la España de 1931* (Buenos Aires, 1942), p. 9.

Chapter 1: Old Poetry, New Poets

PAGE 17

1 J.G.O., 'María Teresa Montoya y el auto de la creación del mundo "El hombre deshabitado", del poeta Rafael Alberti', *Heraldo de Madrid* (26 February 1931), p. 5.
2 Alberti, 'Poética', in Diego, *Antología*, p. 447.
3 E. M. Wilson, 'Studies in Modern Spanish Poetry. I. Guillén and Quevedo on Death. Postscript', *Atlante*, vol. II (1954), no. 4, p. 237.
4 J. M. Blecua, 'Una charla con Pedro Salinas', *Ínsula*, no. 70 (October 1951).

PAGE 18

1 Cernuda, 'El crítico, el amigo y el poeta', in *Poesía y literatura* (Barcelona, 1960), p. 224.
2 The first number of *Carmen* (December 1927) contained Bartolomé Leonardo de Argensola's 'Nieve de mesa'; and numbers 6–7 (June 1928) included Bocángel's prologue to his *Rimas*, Jáuregui's 'Medusa' and an essay by J. M. de Cossío on Rioja called 'Llamas, sangre'.
3 For example: Alberti, *Imagen primera de...*; Cernuda's two volumes called *Poesía y literatura*; Guillén's *Language and Poetry*; Lorca's lectures on 'La imagen poética en don Luis de Góngora' given in Granada in 1927, on 'Las nanas infantiles' given at Vassar College in 1930, and on 'Arquitectura del cante jondo' given in Corunna in 1931; Salinas's *Reality and the Poet in Spanish Poetry* and *Ensayos de literatura hispánica*; and Altolaguirre's biography of Garcilaso, published in Madrid in 1933.
4 Alberti, *Lope de Vega y la poesía contemporánea, seguido de La pájara pinta* (Paris, 1964), p. 36.
5 E. Trépanier, 'García Lorca et La Barraca', *Revue d'Histoire du Théâtre*, vol. XVIII (1966), pp. 170–1. See too F. Masini, *Federico García Lorca e La Barraca* (San Casciano, Cappelli, 1966).
6 Cernuda, 'Historial', in *Poesía y literatura*, p. 241.

PAGE 19

1 Diego, 'La vuelta a la estrofa', *Carmen*, no. 1 (December 1927). Jarnés, *Ejercicios* (Madrid, 1927), p. 85.
2 Guillén, *Language and Poetry*, p. 213.

3 Salinas, *Víspera del gozo* (Madrid, 1926), p. 124; 'La palma y la frente', *España*, no. 79 (27 July 1916), p. 9.

PAGE 20

1 Alberti, *La arboleda perdida*, p. 162.
2 Cernuda, 'Historial', in *Poesía y literatura*, p. 241.
3 Diego, 'Emilio Prados: *Vuelta*', *Revista de Occidente*, vol. XVII (1927), no. LI, p. 386.
4 *Obras no dramáticas de Lope de Vega Carpio, Biblioteca de Autores Españoles*, vol. XXXVIII, p. 227*b*.
5 Guillén, *Federico en persona*, p. 137.
6 Diego, 'Don Luis de Góngora y Argote', *Revista de Occidente*, vol. IX (1925), no. XXVI, p. 250. For the incidence of 'décimas' see for example: Max Aub, 'Luna', *Carmen*, nos. 6–7 (June 1928); Bergamín, 'Décima', *Litoral*, nos. 5, 6, 7 (October 1927), p. 19; Domenchina, 'Décimas', *Revista de Occidente*, vol. XXXV (1932), no. CV, pp. 278–81.
7 Góngora, *Obras completas*, 4th ed. (Madrid, 1956), no. 200, p. 399.
8 *Obras no dramáticas de Lope de Vega Carpio, Biblioteca de Autores Españoles*, vol. XXXVIII, p. 232*a*.

PAGE 21

1 Cernuda, 'El crítico, el amigo y el poeta', in *Poesía y literatura*, p. 223.
2 R. Lida, 'Sobre las décimas de Jorge Guillén', *Cuadernos Americanos*, vol. C (1958), p. 476.

PAGE 22

1 Diego, 'Réplica', *Lola*, nos. 3–4 (March 1928).
2 Guillén, *Federico en persona*, p. 89.
3 Diego, 'Crónica del centenario de Góngora (1627–1927)', *Lola*, no. 1 (December 1927), and no. 2 (January 1928).

PAGE 23

1 Diego, 'Poema a Jorge Guillén (animándole a la edición de las *Octavas* de Góngora y a la de sus propias poesías)', *La Gaceta Literaria*, no. 3 (February 1927); 'A Rafael Alberti', *Verso y Prosa*, vol. I (1927), no. 2.
2 D. Alonso, 'Una generación poética', in *Poetas españoles contemporáneos*, 3rd ed., p. 169.

PAGE 24

1 L.-P. Thomas, *Étude sur Góngora et le gongorisme considérés dans leurs rapports avec le marinisme* (Brussels, 1910); A. Reyes, *Cuestiones gongorinas...* (Paris, 1918). See for example: 'Góngora y El Greco', *Índice*, no. 1 (1921), pp. 17–18; Góngora's 'Al nacimiento de Cristo Nuestro Señor', *Índice*, no. 3 (1921), p. 64; E. Díez Canedo, 'Góngora en francés', *España*, no. 297 (8 January 1921).
2 Cernuda, 'Historial', in *Poesía y literatura*, p. 240.
3 Cernuda, 'Yeats', in *Poesía y literatura II*, p. 169.
4 F. Rodríguez Marín, *El alma de Andalucía en sus mejores coplas amorosas* (Madrid, 1929), no. 1023, p. 284.

PAGE 25

1   See E. Asensio, 'Los cantares paralelísticos castellanos. Tradición y originali-
    dad', in *Poética y realidad en el cancionero peninsular de la Edad Media* (Madrid,
    1957), pp. 189–90, 208–9.
2   D. Alonso and J. M. Blecua, *Antología de la poesía española. Poesía de tipo
    tradicional* (Madrid, 1956), no. 141, p. 61.

PAGE 26

1   J. Cejador y Frauca, *La verdadera poesía castellana* (Madrid, 1921–6), vol. I,
    no. 80, p. 93.
2   *Ibid.* vol. I, no. 92, p. 94.
3   Alonso and Blecua, *Poesía de tipo tradicional*, no. 165, p. 71.
4   *La verdadera poesía castellana*, vol. I, no. 1025, pp. 268–9.
5   Alberti, *Lope de Vega*, p. 16.

PAGE 27

1   Lope de Vega, *Poesías líricas* (Madrid, 1951–2), vol. I, p. 71.
2   *La verdadera poesía castellana*, vol. I, no. 196, p. 111.
3   Guillén, *Federico en persona*, p. 129.
4   Lope, *Poesías líricas*, vol. I, p. 70.   5   Alberti, *Imagen primera de...*, p. 20.

PAGE 28

1   A. and M. Machado, *Obras completas* (Madrid, 1962), p. 152.
2   'Itinerarios jóvenes de España. Rafael Alberti', *La Gaceta Literaria*, no. 49
    (January 1929).
3   A. and M. Machado, *Obras completas*, pp. 115–16.

PAGE 29

1   Rodríguez Marín, *El alma de Andalucía*, no. 808, p. 239.
2   *Ibid.* no. 678, p. 211.   3   *Ibid.* no. 135, p. 92.

PAGE 30

1   A. Machado, *Poesías completas*, 6th ed. (Buenos Aires, 1952), p. 234.
2   A. Machado, *Juan de Mairena*, 3rd ed. (Buenos Aires, 1957), vol. II, p. 53.
3   'Itinerarios jóvenes de España. Rafael Alberti', *La Gaceta Literaria*, no. 49
    (January 1929).
4   Rodríguez Marín, *Cantos populares españoles* (Seville, 1882–3), vol. II, no. 2558,
    p. 294. Alberti mentioned this anthology in *La arboleda perdida*, p. 25.
5   *Marinero en tierra*, p. 27; *Cantos populares españoles*, vol. I, no. 150, p. 66.
6   Alberti, *La poesía popular*, p. 5.

PAGE 31

1   F. Asenjo Barbieri, *Cancionero musical de los siglos XV y XVI* (Madrid, 1890),
    no. 143, p. 101; also in Alonso and Blecua, *Poesía de tipo tradicional*, no. 38,
    p. 21.
2   Alonso and Blecua, *Poesía de tipo tradicional*, no. 227, p. 91.

PAGE 32

1   *La verdadera poesía castellana*, vol. I, no. 794, p. 218; no. 965, p. 256.

PAGE 34

1   Salinas, 'Nueve o diez poetas', in *Ensayos de literatura hispánica*, 3rd ed. (Madrid, 1967), p. 368.
2   Unamuno, *Cancionero. Diario poético*, no. 274, p. 101.
3   *La verdadera poesía castellana*, vol. II, no. 1286, p. 185.

PAGE 35

1   Asenjo Barbieri, *Cancionero musical*, no. 237, p. 132; also in Alonso and Blecua, *Poesía de tipo tradicional*, no. 44, p. 23.

PAGE 37

1   Alberti, *La poesía popular*, p. 14.
2   *Ibid.* p. 15.
3   I. and P. Opie, *The Lore and Language of Schoolchildren* (Oxford Paperbacks, 1967), p. 23.

PAGE 38

1   *Cantos populares españoles*, vol. I, no. 181, pp. 76–7; translated in the 'Double Surrealist Number' of *Contemporary Poetry and Prose*, no. 2 (June 1936).

PAGE 39

1   Lope, *Poesías líricas*, vol. I, p. 82.

PAGE 40

1   Alberti, *La arboleda perdida*, p. 22.
2   Alberti, *Lope de Vega*, p. 34.

PAGE 41

1   Alonso and Blecua, *Poesía de tipo tradicional*, no. 183, p. 76.
2   *La verdadera poesía castellana*, vol. I, no. 87, p. 94.

PAGE 43

1   A. Machado y Álvarez, *Cantes flamencos* (Buenos Aires, 1947), p. 136.
2   *Cantos populares españoles*, vol. III, no. 3794, pp. 82–3.
3   Quevedo, *Poesía original* (Barcelona, 1963), no. 412, p. 441.
4   *La verdadera poesía castellana*, vol. II, no. 1183, p. 93.

PAGE 44

1   *Cantos populares españoles*, vol. III, no. 3864, p. 94; *Cantes flamencos*, p. 120.

PAGE 45

1   *Cantos populares españoles*, vol. III, no. 5100, p. 370.
2   Guillén, *Federico en persona*, p. 105.

PAGE 46

1   A. Machado, *Poesías completas*, 6th ed., p. 245.

PAGE 47

1   D. Devoto, 'Notas sobre el elemento tradicional en la obra de García Lorca', *Filología*, vol. II (1950), pp. 292–341; 'Lecturas de García Lorca', *Revue de Littérature Comparée*, vol. XXXIII (1959), pp. 518–28.

PAGE 48

1   *La verdadera poesía castellana*, vol. I, no. 27, p. 84.

PAGE 49

1   Guillén, *Federico en persona*, p. 18.

PAGE 50

1   *Cantos populares españoles*, vol. I, no. 189, p. 83.
2   F. Llorca, *Lo que cantan los niños* (Valencia, n.d.), p. 36.
3   S. Córdova y Oña, *Cancionero infantil español* (Santander, 1948), no. 4, p. 26.

PAGE 51

1   *Cantos populares españoles*, vol. II, no. 1983, p. 180.

PAGE 52

1   Lope, *Poesías líricas*, vol. I, p. 73.
2   See for example: *Cantos populares españoles*, vol. IV, no. 6500, p. 164; Alonso and Blecua, *Poesía de tipo tradicional*, no. 286, p. 114.
3   *Cantos populares españoles*, vol. IV, no. 6524, p. 168.

PAGE 53

1   *Cantos populares españoles*, vol. IV, no. 6494, p. 162.
2   Guillén, *Federico en persona*, p. 84; letter of 3 March 1926.
3   *Cantos populares españoles*, vol. IV, no. 6144, p. 75.
4   *Ibid.* no. 6068, p. 62.

PAGE 54

1   Salinas, 'El romancismo y el siglo XX', in *Ensayos de literatura hispánica*, 3rd ed., p. 326.
2   Jiménez, *Tercera antolojía poética*, p. 35.

PAGE 56

1   Guillén, *Cántico*, 2nd ed. (Madrid, 1936), p. 292; *Cántico*, Primera edición completa (Buenos Aires, 1950), p. 478.
2   *Ibid.* (1936), p. 265; *ibid.* (1950), p. 465.

PAGE 57

1   Guillén *Cántico* (1936), pp. 291–2; *ibid.* (1950), pp. 477–8.
2   Salinas, 'El romancismo y el siglo XX', in *Ensayos de literatura hispánica*, 3rd. ed., p. 346.

PAGE 58

1 Guillén, *Cántico* (1936), p. 288; *ibid.* (1950), p. 476.
2 *Ibid.* (1936), p. 293; *ibid.* (1950), p. 478.

PAGE 59

1 Jiménez, *Tercera antolojía poética*, p. 76.
2 Guillén, 'Poniente de bronce', *Índice*, no. 2 (1921), pp. 30–1.
3 Guillén, *Federico en persona*, p. 84.

PAGE 62

1 Francisco García Lorca, 'Introduction' to Lorca, *Three Tragedies* (Harmonds-worth, 1967), p. 21.

PAGE 63

1 J. M. de Cossío, *Romances de tradición oral* (Buenos Aires, 1947), no. 2, p. 19.
2 Guillén, *Federico en persona*, p. 84.
3 Recalled by Guillén, *ibid.* p. 39.

PAGE 64

1 Alonso and Blecua, *Poesía de tipo tradicional*, no. 50, p. 26.
2 Guillén, *Federico en persona*, p. 84.
3 C. C. Smith, *Spanish Ballads* (Oxford, 1964), no. 14, p. 88; no. 16, p. 91.

PAGE 65

1 Cossío, *Romances de tradición oral*, no. 53, p. 128.
2 See for example the 'Romance de la amiga de Bernal Francia', in R. Menén-dez Pidal, *Flor nueva de romances viejos*, 10th ed. (Madrid, 1955), p. 122.
3 Smith, *Spanish Ballads*, no. 24, p. 107; no. 44, p. 150; no. 54, pp. 171, 172.

PAGE 66

1 Cossío, *Romances de tradición oral*, no. 54, p. 129. See too no. 17, p. 50; no. 20, p. 60; no. 34, pp. 91–2; no. 42, pp. 110, 111.
2 Smith, *Spanish Ballads*, no. 67, p. 203.
3 See R. Marrast, *Aspects du théâtre de Rafael Alberti* (Paris, 1967), pp. 21–2.
4 Menéndez Pidal, *Flor nueva de romances viejos*, 10th ed., p. 63.
5 Salinas, 'El romancismo y el siglo XX', in *Ensayos de literatura hispánica*, 3rd ed., p. 351.
6 Smith, *Spanish Ballads*, no. 53, p. 169.

PAGE 67

1 Smith, *Spanish Ballads*, no. 64, p. 197.
2 Góngora, *Obras completas*, 4th ed., no. 32, p. 111.
3 *Ibid.* no. 70, p. 194.

PAGE 69

1 Smith, *Spanish Ballads*, no. 54, p. 173.
2 Quevedo, *Poesía original*, no. 803, p. 1131.
3 Guillén, *Federico en persona*, p. 128.

PAGE 70

1 Góngora, *Obras completas*, 4th ed., no. 32, p. 111.
2 Quevedo, *Poesía original*, no. 701, p. 813.
3 *Ibid.* no. 880, p. 1294.

PAGE 72

1 Espinosa, *Obras* (Madrid, 1909), p. 181.
2 Domenchina, 'Lecturas. Poetas españoles del 13 al 31', *El Sol* (19 March 1933).

PAGE 73

1 Alberti, *La arboleda perdida*, p. 257. Diego, 'Fragmento de la Fábula de Equis y Zeda', *Litoral*, nos. 5, 6, 7 (October 1927), pp. 25–8.
2 A. Machado, *Abel Martín*, 2nd ed., p. 44.
3 Alberti, *La arboleda perdida*, p. 241.

PAGE 74

1 Espinosa, *Obras*, p. 26.

PAGE 75

1 Alberti, *La arboleda perdida*, p. 239.

PAGE 76

1 Quevedo, *Poesía original*, no. 837, p. 1185.
2 A. Machado, *Juan de Mairena*, 3rd ed., vol. II, p. 165.
3 Villalón, *Poesías* (Madrid, 1944), p. 117.
4 Guillén, 'La sala pequeña', *España*, no. 361 (17 March 1923), p. 5; 'El cisne', *Cántico* (1928), p. 80.
5 Góngora, *Obras completas*, 4th ed., no. 14, p. 63.
6 Salinas, *Reality and the Poet in Spanish Poetry* (Baltimore, 1966), p. 146.
7 Quevedo, *Poesía original*, no. 684, p. 761.

PAGE 77

1 Guillén, *Cántico* (1936), p. 249; *Cántico* (1950), p. 281. Quevedo, *Poesía original*, no. 30, p. 32.
2 E. M. Wilson, 'Guillén and Quevedo on Death. Postscript', *Atlante*, vol. II (1954), no. 4, p. 237.
3 Quevedo, *Poesía original*, no. 149, p. 153.
4 *Ibid.* no. 110, p. 91.

PAGE 78

1 Cernuda, *Perfil del aire* (Málaga, 1927), p. 22. Quevedo, *Poesía original*, no. 39, p. 39.

PAGE 79

1 Quevedo, *Poesía original*, no. 1, p. 3; no. 2, p. 4. See San Juan de la Cruz, *Obras* (Barcelona, 1965), pp. 821, 935.
2 Quevedo, *Poesía original*, no. 31, p. 33.

3 Quevedo, *Poesía original*, no. 30, p. 32; no. 14, p. 20; no. 6, p. 7.
4 Cernuda, *Ocnos*, 3rd ed. (Xalapa, 1963), p. 159.
5 Cernuda, *Perfil del aire*, p. 30.   6 Cernuda, *Ocnos*, 3rd ed., p. 101.

PAGE 80

1 Quevedo, *Poesía original*, no. 478, p. 516.
2 *Ibid.* no. 358, p. 378.   3 *Ibid.* no. 118, p. 96.
4 Alberti, *Teatro* (Buenos Aires, 1959–64), vol. I, p. 11.

Chapter 2: The Game of Poetry

PAGE 82

1 Espina, *Luna de copas* (Madrid, 1929), p. 33.
2 Giménez Caballero, *Julepe de menta* (Madrid, 1929), p. 85.
3 Giménez Caballero, 'Cartel de la nueva literatura', *La Gaceta Literaria*, no. 32 (April 1928).
4 Espina, *Pájaro pinto* (Madrid, 1927), p. 140.

PAGE 83

1 'Gómez de la Serna y la generación poética de 1925', in Cernuda, *Estudios*, p. 174.
2 'Declinación de Chabás', *Lola*, no. 2 (January 1928); 'Tontología', nos. 6–7 (June 1928).
3 Alberti, *La arboleda perdida*, pp. 218–19.
4 Moreno Villa, *Vida en claro. Autobiografía* (Mexico, 1944), p. 114.
5 Tzara, 'Proclama sin pretensión. Dada 1919', *Cervantes* (August 1919), p. 52.
6 Edmund Wilson, *Axel's Castle* (New York–London, 1934), p. 253.
7 R. Lacôte, *Tristan Tzara* (Paris, 1952), p. 106.

PAGE 84

1 Espina, *Luna de copas*, p. 9.
2 Gómez de la Serna, *Ismos* (Madrid, 1931), p. 185.
3 Moreno Villa, *La música que llevaba* [1913–47] (Buenos Aires, 1949), p. 215.
4 Postcard to Higinio Capote of 12 November 1928, reproduced in 'Cartas de Luis Cernuda (1926–1929)', *Ínsula*, no. 207 (February 1964). See 'Historial', in *Poesía y literatura*, p. 245.
5 Cernuda, 'Historial', in *Poesía y literatura*, pp. 245–6.
6 Giménez Caballero, *Julepe de menta*, p. 29.
7 Espina, *Pájaro pinto*, p. 17.
8 Moreno Villa, *La música que llevaba*, p. 227.

PAGE 85

1 Torre, *Hélices. Poemas 1918–1922* (Madrid, 1923), p. 108.
2 *Ibid.* p. 34.
3 Huidobro, *Poesía y prosa* (Madrid, 1957), p. 205.

PAGE 86

1 Espina, *Pájaro pinto*, p. 87.
2 Marinetti, *El futurismo*, pp. 58, 59, 72.
3 Marinetti, 'España veloz. Poema en palabra libre (Fragmento)', *La Gaceta Literaria*, no. 39 (August 1928).
4 Bacarisse, *El esfuerzo* (Madrid, 1917), p. 82; 'Ebrio de dinamismo', p. 131.
5 Bacarisse, *El paraíso desdeñado* (Madrid, 1928), p. 40.
6 Guillén, *Cántico* (1936), p. 208; *Cántico* (1950), p. 319.

PAGE 87

1 Torre, 'Poema ultraísta. Émbolo', *Grecia*, no. XXII (20 July 1919), p. 4.
2 Torre, *Literaturas europeas de vanguardia*, p. 251.
3 *Ibid.* p. 59.
4 E. López Parra, 'Canción nueva', *Ultra*, vol. I (1921), no. 4.
5 Torre, *Literaturas europeas de vanguardia*, p. 282.
6 Pedro Raida, 'Confesión', *Grecia*, no. XIV (30 April 1919), p. 19.
7 Torre, *Hélices*, p. 62.

PAGE 88

1 Torre, *Literaturas europeas de vanguardia*, p. 61.
2 *Ultra*, vol. I (1921), no. 4, p. 3.
3 Torre, *Literaturas europeas de vanguardia*, p. 283.
4 See G. Videla, *El ultraísmo. Estudios sobre movimientos poéticos de vanguardia en España* (Madrid, 1963), p. 114.
5 *Lola*, nos. 3–4 (March 1928).
6 Quevedo, *Poesía original*, no. 846, p. 1199.
7 Torre entitled the fourth section of *Hélices* 'Palabras en libertad'.

PAGE 89

1 Moreno Villa, 'Señales', *España*, no. 246 (22 January 1920), p. 9.
2 Giménez Caballero, *Yo, inspector de alcantarillas* (Madrid, 1928), p. 156.
3 Espina, *Luna de copas*, pp. 44, 43.
4 Hinojosa, *La flor de California* (Málaga, 1928), p. 117.
5 D. Alonso, 'Cédula de eternidad', *Revista de Occidente*, vol. XX (1928), no. LVIII, pp. 1, 14.
6 D. Alonso, 'Acuario en virgo', *Verso y Prosa*, vol. I (1927), no. 3.
7 Alonso, 'Cédula de eternidad', *Revista de Occidente*, vol. XX (1928), no. LVIII, p. 2.

PAGE 90

1 Joyce, *Ulysses* (London, 1960), p. 354.
2 Espina, 'Concéntricas', *España*, no. 298 (15 January 1921); reproduced in *Signario* (Madrid, 1923), p. 43.
3 Ortega y Gasset, *La deshumanización del arte*, 4th ed., p. 22.
4 Giménez Caballero, *Yo, inspector de alcantarillas*, pp. 9, 199.
5 Bergamín, *Enemigo que huye* (Madrid, 1927), p. 79.

PAGE 91

1 Bergamín, *Caballito del diablo* (Buenos Aires, 1942), p. 94.
2 Bergamín, 'Aforística persistente', *Alfar*, vol. v (1925), no. 47, p. 3.
3 Bergamín, *Enemigo que huye*, p. 15.
4 Jarnés, *Ejercicios*, p. 60.
5 Cernuda, *Variaciones sobre tema mexicano* (Mexico, 1952), p. 48.
6 Ortega y Gasset, *La deshumanización del arte*, 4th ed., pp. 31, 50.
7 'Manifiesto antiartístico', *Gallo*, no. 2 (April 1928); reproduced in M.
   Laffranque, *Les idées esthétiques de Federico García Lorca* (Paris, 1967), pp. 325–7.
8 Espina, *Luna de copas*, pp. 45–6.

PAGE 92

1 Jacob, *El cubilete de dados*, pp. 28, 48, 61, 55.
2 Gómez de la Serna, *Greguerías* (Valencia [1923]), pp. 30, 141, ix.
3 Gómez de la Serna, *Disparates* (Madrid, 1921), p. 5.
4 Gómez de la Serna, *Greguerías*, p. 202.
5 *Ibid.* pp. 128, 42, 165.
6 Cernuda, 'Gómez de la Serna y la generación poética de 1925', in *Estudios*,
   p. 168.

PAGE 93

1 Espina, *Luna de copas*, p. 112.
2 A. Machado, *Los complementarios*, p. 40.
3 Guillén, *Language and Poetry*, p. 207.
4 Diego, *Imagen*, p. 10.
5 *Ibid.* p. 45.   6 *Ibid.* p. 11.
7 *Ibid.* p. 45.

PAGE 94

1 Diego, *Imagen*, pp. 71, 114.
2 Diego, 'Posibilidades creacionistas', *Cervantes* (October 1919), p. 24.
3 Gómez de la Serna, *Greguerías*, p. 124.
4 Huidobro, *Poesía y prosa*, p. 230.
5 Anon., 'Gerardo Diego: *Imagen*', *España*, no. 321 (20 May 1922), p. 16.
6 Diego, *Imagen*, p. 55.

PAGE 95

1 Chabás, *Espejos. 1919—Verso—1920* (Madrid, 1921), p. 35.
2 Garfias, *El ala del sur* (Seville, 1926), [p. 77].
3 Diego, 'Espejo', *Grecia*, no. xxx (20 October 1919), p. 15.
4 Larrea, 'Evasión', *Grecia*, no. xxxi (30 October 1919), p. 2.
5 Larrea, 'Locura del Charlestón', in Diego, *Antología*, p. 390.

PAGE 96

1 Cernuda, 'Generación de 1925', in *Estudios*, p. 185.
2 Cernuda, *Perfil del aire*, p. 48.
3 Cernuda, 'Carta abierta a Dámaso Alonso', *Ínsula*, no. 35 (November 1948).
4 Cernuda, *Perfil del aire*, pp. 27, 45.

PAGE 97

1 Guillén, 'Cinco florinatas', *España*, no. 354 (27 January 1923), p. 8.
2 Guillén, 'Ventoleras. La mujer de viento en el viento', *Índice*, no. 3 (1921), p. 52.

PAGE 98

1 Guillén, 'El paraguas en el viento', *La Verdad*, no. 57 (August 1926).
2 Guillén, 'Rigor', *La Pluma*, no. 30 (November 1922), p. 347.
3 Guillén, 'Poesías', *La Pluma*, no. 36 (May 1923), p. 361.
4 Guillén, 'Oda inicial', *España*, no. 382 (11 August 1923), p. 8.

PAGE 99

1 Guillén, 'Rigor', *La Pluma*, no. 30 (November 1922), p. 345.
2 Guillén, *Cántico* (1950), p. 146.
3 Guillén, 'Encarnaciones', *La Pluma*, no. 15 (August 1921), p. 110; 'Antilógica', *España*, no. 271 (10 July 1921), p. 18. Diego, 'Antipoema', in *Imagen*, p. 105.

PAGE 100

1 Guillén, 'Poesía', *España*, no. 386 (8 September 1923), p. 4.
2 See D. Devoto, 'García Lorca y Darío', *Asomante*, vol. XXIII (1967), no. 2, pp. 24–5.

PAGE 101

1 Guillén, 'Cinco florinatas', *España*, no. 354 (27 January 1923), p. 8.

PAGE 102

1 Joyce, *Ulysses*, p. 570.

PAGE 103

1 Guillén, *Federico en persona*, p. 13.
2 *Ibid.* pp. 96, 97.

PAGE 105

1 Mª. T. León, *Rosa-fría, patinadora de la luna (Cuentos)* (Madrid, 1934).
2 Bergamín, 'El alegre (Rafael Alberti)', in Alberti, *Poesías completas*, p. 87. See too Bergamín, 'De veras y de burlas', *La Gaceta Literaria*, no. 71 (December 1929).

PAGE 107

1 Alberti, *La arboleda perdida*, p. 279.
2 *Ibid.* pp. 287, 288.
3 *Ibid.* p. 288.
4 'Un "suceso" literario. La conferencia de Rafael Alberti', *La Gaceta Literaria*, no. 71 (December 1929); reproduced in Alberti, *La arboleda perdida*, pp. 288–95.

PAGE 109

1 Alberti, *La arboleda perdida*, p. 149.
2 'Itinerarios jóvenes de España. Rafael Alberti', *La Gaceta Literaria*, no. 49 (January 1929).
3 Alberti, *La arboleda perdida*, p. 151.

PAGE 112

1 Alberti, *Teatro*, vol. I, p. 23.
2 Salinas, 'Aprecio y defensa del lenguaje', in *La responsabilidad del escritor y otros ensayos* (Barcelona, 1961), p. 70.
3 J. Cabre i Oliva, 'Parlant amb Pedro Salinas', *Mirador*, no. 255 (21 December 1933). Salinas, 'El poeta y las fases de la realidad', *Ínsula*, no. 146 (January 1959).

PAGE 113

1 Salinas, 'El poeta y las fases de la realidad', *Ínsula*, no. 146 (January 1959). The words of Thompson—whom Salinas mentioned in the above essay and in J. Cabre i Oliva, 'Parlant amb Pedro Salinas', *Mirador*, no. 255 (21 December 1933)—are reproduced in J. Walsh, *Strange Harp, Strange Symphony* (London, 1968), p. 90.
2 Gómez de la Serna, *Greguerías*, p. 23.
3 Guillén, 'El atento', *Asomante*, vol. VIII (1952), no. 2, p. 28.

PAGE 114

1 'Itinerarios jóvenes de España. Rafael Alberti', *La Gaceta Literaria*, no. 49 (January 1929).
2 Salinas, 'Lamparilla a Paul Valéry', *Sur*, nos. 129–34 (1945), pp. 46–7.
3 Salinas, *Víspera del gozo*, pp. 36–7.
4 Salinas, 'Lamparilla a Paul Valéry', *Sur*, nos. 129–34 (1945), p. 47.

PAGE 115

1 Salinas, *Reality and the Poet*, p. 3.
2 Salinas, *El desnudo impecable*, p. 170.
3 Salinas, *Víspera del gozo*, p. 56.
4 Salinas, 'Poética', in Diego, *Antología*, p. 318.
5 A. Quesada, 'Poema truncado de Madrid (Entrevisión de un insulario)', *España*, no. 288 (6 November 1920), p. 14.

PAGE 116

1 Salinas, *Teatro completo* (Madrid, 1957), p. 402.
2 Guillén, 'El atento', *Asomante*, vol. VIII (1952), no. 2, p. 29. See too Guillén, 'Introduction: Pedro Salinas', in Salinas, *Reality and the Poet*, pp. xvi–xvii.
3 Salinas, 'Voz de jugar', *La Pluma*, no. 1 (June 1920), pp. 23–4.
4 Salinas, *Víspera del gozo*, pp. 63–4.
5 Joyce, *Ulysses*, p. 623.
6 Salinas, 'Aprecio y defensa del lenguaje', in *La responsabilidad del escritor*, p. 68.

NOTES, PP. 117–127

PAGE 117

1 Aleixandre, 'En casa de Pedro Salinas', *Ínsula*, no. 127 (June 1957).
2 A. Valbuena Prat, *La poesía española contemporánea* (Madrid, 1930), p. 111.
3 Freud, 'The Relation of the Poet to Day-Dreaming', in *Collected Papers* (London, 1925), vol. IV, p. 174.

PAGE 118

1 Espina, *Signario*, p. 76.

Chapter 3: In Praise of Creation

PAGE 119

1 Guillén, 'Cinco florinatas', *España*, no. 354 (27 January 1923), p. 8.
2 Guillén, *El argumento de la obra* (Milan, 1961), p. 12; largely reproduced as the 'Prólogo' to Guillén, *Selección de poemas* (Madrid, 1965), pp. 7–18.

PAGE 120

1 Guillén, *El argumento de la obra*, p. 39; 'Anatole France', *España*, no. 303 (14 January 1922).
2 A. Monterde, *La poesía pura en la lírica española* (Mexico, 1953), p. 122.
3 Guillén, *Language and Poetry*, p. 208.
4 'Les grenades', *Verso y Prosa*, no. 4 (April 1927); 'El cementerio marino', *Revista de Occidente*, vol. XXIV (1929), no. LXXII, pp. 340–53.
5 V., 'Para acompañar a una traducción', *Revista de Occidente*, vol. XXIV (1929), no. LXXII, p. 397.
6 Valéry, 'Carta inédita', *La Verdad*, no. 55 (4 July 1926).

PAGE 121

1 Monterde, *La poesía pura en la lírica española*, p. 124.
2 Guillén, 'Poética', in Diego, *Antología*, p. 344.
3 Guillén, *Federico en persona*, pp. 115 (January 1927), 86 (2 March 1926), 99 (9 September 1926).

PAGE 122

1 Salinas, 'Preface' to *Lost Angel and Other Poems* (Baltimore, 1938), p. xii; Guillén, *El argumento de la obra*, p. 18.

PAGE 124

1 Guillén, *Federico en persona*, p. 112.

PAGE 126

1 G. E. McSpadden, 'New Light on Speech Rhythms from Jorge Guillén's Reading of his Poem *Gran Silencio*', *Hispanic Review*, vol. XXX (1962), p. 218.
2 Guillén, *El argumento de la obra*, p. 12.

PAGE 127

1 Guillén, *El argumento de la obra*, p. 22.

261

PAGE 128
1 Guillén, *El argumento de la obra*. p. 10.
2 C. Couffon, *Dos encuentros con Jorge Guillén*, p. 13; Guillén, *Selección de poemas*, p. 7.
3 Guillén, *Language and Poetry*, pp. 54, 88.
4 C. Couffon, *Dos encuentros con Jorge Guillén*, p. 13.

PAGE 129
1 Guillén, *El argumento de la obra*, p. 9.
2 Valéry, *Poésies*, 83rd ed. (Paris, 1942), p. 88.
3 Guillén, *Language and Poetry*, p. 204.
4 Guillén, *Federico en persona*, p. 105.
5 Guillén, *Language and Poetry*, pp. 39, 169.

PAGE 130
1 Guillén, *El argumento de la obra*, p. 36.

PAGE 131
1 Guillén, *El argumento de la obra*, p. 18.
2 Guillén, *Federico en persona*, p. 129.

PAGE 132
1 Guillén, 'Aire-aura', *Revista de Occidente*, vol. II (1923), no. IV, p. 4.
2 Guillén, 'Los aires', *Carmen*, nos. 6–7 (June 1928).
3 Guillén, *El argumento de la obra*, p. 21.

PAGE 133
1 Guillén, *Language and Poetry*, p. 24.

PAGE 134
1 Domenchina, *Crónicas de 'Gerardo Rivera'* (Madrid, 1935), p. 78.
2 Guillén, *Language and Poetry*, p. 96.   3 *Ibid.* pp. 23–4.
4 Cernuda, 'Anotaciones', *La Verdad*, no. 59 (October 1926).

PAGE 135
1 Cernuda, 'El crítico, el amigo y el poeta', in *Poesía y literatura*, pp. 214–15.
2 Cernuda, *Perfil del aire*, p. 36; Guillén, 'Poesía', *España*, no. 386 (8 September 1923), p. 4; Mallarmé, *Poésies* (Paris, 1945), pp. 121, 127.
3 Guillén, 'Poesías', *España*, no. 395 (10 November 1923), p. 9.

PAGE 136
1 Mallarmé, *Poésies*, p. 40.
2 Cernuda, *Perfil del aire*, pp. 22, 32, 36.
3 *Ibid.* p. 18.   4 *Ibid.* p. 47.

PAGE 137
1 Cernuda, *Perfil del aire*, p. 19.
2 Cernuda, 'El crítico, el amigo y el poeta', in *Poesía y literatura*, p. 214.

PAGE 138

1 Chabás, 'Vicente Aleixandre: *Ámbito*', *Revista de Occidente*, vol. XXI (1928), no. LXII, p. 248.

PAGE 140

1 Aleixandre, 'Mundo poético', *Verso y Prosa*, no. 12 (October 1928).

PAGE 142

1 Guillén, *El argumento de la obra*, p. 13.

Chapter 4: The Closed Door

PAGE 143

1 Proust, *À l'ombre des jeunes filles en fleur*, in *À la recherche du temps perdu* (Paris, 1955), vol. I, p. 863.
2 Bergamín, 'Carmen: enigma y soledad', *Carmen*, no. 2 (January 1928); Serrano Plaja, 'Arte de soledad y silencio', *Hoja Literaria* (May 1933), p. 3.
3 E. Azcoaga, 'Sentido antisocial del poeta', *Hoja Literaria* (May 1933), pp. 3–4.
4 Bécquer, *Obras completas*, 11th ed., p. 181.
5 A. Machado, *Poesías completas*, 6th ed., p. 148.
6 Jiménez, 'Diario vital y estético de "Estética y ética estética" (1914–1924)', *España*, no. 408 (9 February 1924), p. 6.
7 Jiménez, *Tercera antolojía poética*, p. 110.

PAGE 144

1 A. Machado, '¿Cómo veo la nueva juventud española?', in *Los complementarios*, p. 156.
2 Jiménez, *Tercera antolojía poética*, pp. 963, 348.
3 *Ibid.* p. 385.
4 Altolaguirre, 'Poética', in Diego, *Antología*, p. 536; reproduced in *Poesías completas*, p. 9.
5 Altolaguirre, 'Inocencia y misterio', *Revista de Occidente*, vol. XXXV (1932), no. CV, p. 357.
6 Jiménez, *Tercera antolojía poética*, p. 623.
7 Jiménez, 'Diario vital y estético de "Estética y ética estética" (1914–1924)', *España*, no. 408 (9 February 1924), p. 6.
8 Altolaguirre, 'Poética', in Diego, *Antología*, p. 536.

PAGE 146

1 A. Machado, *Poesías completas*, 6th ed., p. 26.
2 Altolaguirre, *Antología de la poesía romántica española* (Buenos Aires, 1954), p. 9.

PAGE 147

1 Bergamín, 'Homenaje y recuerdo', *Índice de Artes y Letras*, no. 128 (August 1959), p. 5.

PAGE 148

1 Altolaguirre, 'Poética', in Diego, *Antología*, p. 537; also in *Poesías completas*, p. 9.

PAGE 149

1 Gide, *Le traité du Narcisse* (*Théorie du symbole*), in *Œuvres complètes* (Paris, 1913), vol. I, p. 209.
2 Blanco Aguinaga, 'La aventura poética de Emilio Prados', *Revista Mejicana de Literatura*, no. 8 (1956), p. 73.

PAGE 151

1 Prados, *Diario íntimo* (Málaga, 1966), p. 19.
2 *Ibid*. p. 22.

PAGE 152

1 Cernuda, 'El magnolio', in *Ocnos*, 3rd ed., pp. 63–4.
2 Prados, *Diario íntimo*, p. 22.
3 Prados, unpublished notes now in the Library of Congress, Washington; listed in C. Blanco Aguinaga, *Lista de los papeles de Emilio Prados en la Biblioteca del Congreso de Los Estados Unidos de América* (Baltimore, 1967).
4 Jiménez, *Tercera antolojía poética*, p. 603.

PAGE 153

1 P. Guiraud, *Index du vocabulaire du symbolisme. III. Index des mots des Poésies de Stéphane Mallarmé* (Paris, 1953); nos. 4, 7, 8 and 10 of 'Les mots-clés'.
2 Darío, 'Prefacio' to *Prosas profanas*, in *Poesías completas*, p. 612.

PAGE 154

1 Prados, *Diario íntimo*, pp. 38, 19, 43; 23, 21, 42, 30.
2 Alberti, *La arboleda perdida*, p. 237.
3 Prados, *Diario íntimo*, pp. 17, 18, 28.
4 *Ibid*. p. 34.   5 Prados, unpublished notes.
6 Cernuda, *Perfil del aire*, p. 22.

PAGE 155

1 Cernuda, 'Gregorio Prieto', in *Gregorio Prieto. Paintings and Drawings* (London, 1947), p. 5.
2 Cernuda, 'Palabras antes de una lectura', in *Poesía y literatura*, p. 199.
3 Cernuda, 'Historial de un libro'; originally published in *Papeles de Son Armadans*, vol. XII (1959), no. XXXV, pp. 121–72; reproduced in *Poesía y literatura*, pp. 231–80.
4 Cernuda, 'Hölderlin' [with translations by Cernuda and Hans Gebser], *Cruz y Raya*, no. 32 (November 1935), pp. 113–34; 'El poeta y los mitos', in *Ocnos*, 3rd ed., pp. 35–6.
5 Cernuda, 'Divagación sobre la Andalucía romántica', *Cruz y Raya*, no. 37 (April 1936), p. 10.
6 Cernuda, 'Trozos', *Verso y Prosa*, vol. I (1927), no. 3.

7 Cernuda, *Perfil del aire*, p. 51.
8 Cernuda, *Variaciones sobre tema mexicano*, p. 46.
9 Cernuda, 'El indolente', *La Verdad*, no. 56 (18 July 1926); letter to Capote of 31 August 1929 in 'Cartas de Luis Cernuda (1926–1929)', *Ínsula*, no. 207 (February 1964).

PAGE 156

1 Cernuda, *Perfil del aire*, pp. 51, 22.
2 Postcards to Capote of 19 November 1927, 12 November 1928, in 'Cartas de Luis Cernuda (1926–1929)', *Ínsula*, no. 207 (February 1964).
3 Letter to Capote of 4 December 1929, in 'Cartas de Luis Cernuda (1926–1929)', *Ínsula*, no. 207 (February 1964).

PAGE 157

1 Cernuda, *Variaciones sobre tema mexicano*, p. 80.
2 Cernuda, 'Paul Eluard', *Litoral*, no. 9 (1929), p. 26.
3 Cernuda, 'Anotaciones', *La Verdad*, no. 59 (October 1926); 'Poética', in Diego, *Antología*, p. 691.

PAGE 158

1 Cernuda, 'La soledad', in *Ocnos*, 3rd ed., p. 163.
2 Letter to Capote of 6 September 1928, in 'Cartas de Luis Cernuda (1926–1929)', *Ínsula*, no. 207 (February 1964).
3 Cernuda, 'Pedro Salinas y su poesía', *Revista de Occidente*, vol. XXXV (1929), no. LXXIV, pp. 251–4; 'Pedro Salinas', in *Estudios*, p. 202.
4 Cernuda, 'El escándalo', in *Ocnos*, 3rd ed., pp. 37–8; 'Vicente Aleixandre', *Orígenes*, no. 26 (1950), p. 9.
5 See for example: 'Bécquer y el romanticismo español', *Cruz y Raya*, no. 26 (May 1935), pp. 45–73; 'Gustavo Adolfo Bécquer', in *Estudios*, pp. 43–55; 'Bécquer y el poema en prosa español', *Papeles de Son Armadans*, vol. XVI (1960), no. XLVII, pp. 233–45 (reproduced in *Poesía y literatura II*, pp. 59–72).

PAGE 159

1 Cernuda, *Perfil del aire*, p. 51.
2 Cernuda, 'El poeta y los mitos', in *Ocnos*, 3rd ed., p. 36.

PAGE 160

1 Cernuda, 'Historial', in *Poesía y literatura*, p. 236; 'Rilke', in *Poesía y literatura*, p. 168, note 1.
2 Cernuda, *Perfil del aire*, p. 22; Mallarmé, *Poésies*, p. 39.
3 Cernuda, 'El indolente', *La Verdad*, no. 56 (18 July 1926).
4 Cernuda, 'Juan Ramón Jiménez', in *Estudios*, pp. 121, 123.

PAGE 162

1 Cernuda, *Variaciones sobre tema mexicano*, p. 69.
2 Bécquer, 'El rayo de luna', in *Obras completas*, 11th ed., pp. 180–93.
3 Salinas, *Víspera del gozo*, p. 136.
4 Gide, *Le traité du Narcisse*, p. 213; Salinas, *Reality and the Poet*, p. 3.

PAGE 163

1   Salinas, *El desnudo impecable*, p. 226.
2   Salinas, 'Poética', in Diego, *Antología*, p. 319.
3   Bécquer, *Obras completas*, 11th ed., p. 449.
4   Domenchina, *Crónicas de 'Gerardo Rivera'*, pp. 242–3.

PAGE 167

1   Proust, *Du côté de chez Swann*, in *À la recherche du temps perdu*, vol. I, pp. 399–400.

PAGE 168

1   Salinas, *Teatro*, p. 167.

PAGE 169

1   Proust, *Du côté de chez Swann*, in *À la recherche du temps perdu*, vol. I, p. 410.
2   Á. del Río, 'El poeta Pedro Salinas: Vida y obra', *Revista Hispánica Moderna*, vol. VII (1941), p. 25.

PAGE 171

1   Cernuda, 'Palabras antes de una lectura', in *Poesía y literatura*, p. 195.

Chapter 5: The Broken Rhythm

PAGE 172

1   Joyce, *Ulysses*, p. 928.
2   R. Durgnat, *Luis Buñuel* (London, 1967), p. 22. See for example J. R. Masoliver, 'Un chien andalou (Film de Luis Buñuel y Salvador Dalí)', *Hélix*, no. 7 (November 1929), p. 7.
3   W. S. Lieberman, *Max Ernst* (New York, 1961), p. 12.

PAGE 173

1   Aragon, *Le paysan de Paris*, 10th ed. (Paris, 1926), p. 12.
2   Breton, *Manifestes du surréalisme* (Paris, 1946), pp. 38, 149.
3   Breton, *What is Surrealism?* [tr. D. Gascoyne] (London, 1936), p. 25.
4   Dalí, *The Secret Life of Salvador Dalí* (London, 1961), p. 330.
5   Breton, *Poèmes* (Paris, 1948), p. 65.

PAGE 174

1   Aragon, *Le paysan de Paris*, 10th ed., p. 81; Diego, 'Posibilidades creacionistas', *Cervantes* (October 1919), p. 24.
2   J. Ferraté, *La operación de leer y otros ensayos* (Barcelona, 1962), p. 210.
3   A. Machado, *Juan de Mairena*, 3rd ed., vol. II, p. 51.
4   Guillén, *Language and Poetry*, p. 204.
5   *Ibid.* p. 204.
6   J. Albi, 'Introducción' to a selection of poems in *Verbo*, nos. 23–24–25 (February 1952), p. 5.
7   Cernuda, 'Historial', in *Poesía y literatura*, pp. 241–2.

8 See G. Díaz-Plaja, *Memoria de una generación destruída (1930–1936)* (Barcelona, 1966), pp. 61, 63–4, 74.
9 Alberti, *La poesía popular,* p. 14.

PAGE 175

1 Alberti, *La arboleda perdida*, pp. 269, 270.
2 Cernuda, 'Vicente Aleixandre', *Orígenes*, no. 26 (1950), p. 12.
3 See for example: Breton, 'Texto super-realista' and Eluard, 'Entre peu d'autres', in *Alfar*, no. 58 (June 1926), p. 17; Breton, 'Poisson soluble', *Hélix*, no. 1 (February 1929), p. 8; P. Picón, 'La revolución super-realista', *Alfar*, no. 52 (September 1925), pp. 9–12; Aristo, ¿'Qué es el superrealismo?', *La Gaceta Literaria*, no. 9 (May 1927); L. Montanyà, 'Superrealismo', *L'Amic de les Arts*, vol. II (1927), no. 10, pp. 3–4; G. Díaz-Plaja, 'Notes', *Hélix*, no. 4 (May 1929), p. 4; G. Díaz-Plaja, 'Dues notes' and C. Casanova, 'Conversa', in *Hélix*, no. 5 (June 1929), pp. 6 and 8; Dalí, 'Posició moral del surrealisme' [Lecture read at Ateneo Barcelonés on 22 March 1930], *Hélix*, no. 10 (March 1930), pp. 4–6.

PAGE 176

1 Alberti, *Imagen primera de...*, p. 21.
2 Aragon, 'Fragments d'une conférence', *La Révolution Surréaliste*, Première année, 15 July 1925, pp. 24–5.
3 Espina, *Luna de copas*, p. 156.
4 Sánchez Mejías, *Sinrazón. Juguete trágico en tres actos y en prosa* (Madrid, 1928), p. 16.
5 Espina, *Luna de copas*, pp. 48, 79.
6 Domenchina, *La túnica de Neso* (Madrid, 1929), p. 81.
7 *Ibid.* p. 298.   8 *Ibid.* p. 36.
9 *Ibid.* p. 82.
10 Domenchina, *Poesías completas (1915–1934)* (Madrid, 1936), p. 168.

PAGE 177

1 Domenchina, *Poesías completas*, p. 196.
2 Moreno Villa, *La música que llevaba*, p. 254.
3 Giménez Caballero, *Yo, inspector de alcantarillas*, p. 156.
4 Alonso, 'Cédula de eternidad', *Revista de Occidente*, vol. XX (1928), no. LVIII, p. 2.
5 Moreno Villa, *Vida en claro*, p. 197; 'Autocrítica', *Revista de Occidente*, vol. VI (1924), no. XVIII, p. 437.
6 Moreno Villa, *La música que llevaba*, pp. 231, 282.
7 *Ibid.* pp. 171–2.

PAGE 178

1 Domenchina, *La túnica de Neso*, p. 323.
2 *Ibid.* p. 37.
3 Jiménez, *Cartas (primera serie)*, p. 382.
4 Cernuda, 'Generación de 1925', in *Estudios*, p. 184.
5 Hinojosa, *La flor de California*, p. 117.

6   See Foix, *Obres poètiques* (Barcelona, 1965) and the Castilian versions of
    E. Badosa in Foix, *Antología lírica* (Madrid, 1963).
7   Hinojosa, 'Estos dos corazones', *Litoral* (June 1929), p. 12.
8   *Ibid.* p. 11.
9   Hinojosa, *La flor de California*, p. 21.

PAGE 179

1   Cernuda, 'Generación de 1925', in *Estudios*, p. 194.
2   Guillén, *Language and Poetry*, p. 206.
3   Aleixandre, *Mis poemas mejores*, p. 9.
4   *Ibid.* p. 8.   5   *Ibid.* p. 10.
6   *Ibid.* pp. 30, 10.

PAGE 180

1   Aleixandre, *Mis poemas mejores*, p. 10.

PAGE 181

1   Aleixandre, 'Poesía, moral, público', *Ínsula*, no. 59 (November 1950);
    E. Canito, 'Diálogo con Vicente Aleixandre', *Ínsula*, no. 50 (February 1950).

PAGE 182

1   Aleixandre, 'Poética', in Diego, *Antología*, p. 494.
2   Aleixandre, *Mis poemas mejores*, p. 9.

PAGE 184

1   Aleixandre, *Mis poemas mejores*, p. 33.

PAGE 185

1   Aleixandre, 'Poética', in Diego, *Antología*, p. 495.
2   Neruda, *Veinte poemas de amor y una canción desesperada*, 5th ed. (Buenos Aires,
    1954), p. 12.

PAGE 186

1   Breton, *Manifestes du surréalisme*, p. 38.
2   Whitman, 'A Woman Waits for Me', *Leaves of Grass* (New York, 1954),
    p. 105.
3   Domenchina, *Poesías completas*, p. 173.

PAGE 187

1   Domenchina, *La túnica de Neso*, p. 23.

PAGE 188

1   Aleixandre, *Mis poemas mejores*, p. 49.
2   C. Bousoño, *La poesía de Vicente Aleixandre. Imagen. Estilo. Mundo poético*, 2nd
    ed., p. 118.

PAGE 189

1   Aleixandre, *Mis poemas mejores*, p. 8.

PAGE 191

1 Cernuda, *Ocnos*, 3rd ed., p. 186.
2 Cernuda, 'Gregorio Prieto', in *Gregorio Prieto. Paintings and Drawings*, p. 5.
3 Cernuda, 'Historial', in *Poesía y literatura*, p. 240.
4 *Ibid.* pp. 247, 245.
5 *Ibid.* p. 242. See too letter to Capote of 4 December 1929 in 'Cartas de Luis Cernuda (1926–1929)', *Ínsula*, no. 207 (February 1964).
6 Cernuda, 'Historial', in *Poesía y literatura*, p. 249.

PAGE 193

1 Cernuda, 'Historial', in *Poesía y literatura*, p. 242.
2 Cernuda, 'Baudelaire en el centenario de "Las flores de mal"', in *Poesía y literatura II*, p. 144.
3 *Ibid.*

PAGE 194

1 Cernuda, 'Historial', in *Poesía y literatura*, p. 267. See 'Experimento en Rubén Darío', in *Poesía y literatura II*, pp. 73–89, particularly pp. 76, 78, 79.
2 Cernuda, 'Historial', in *Poesía y literatura*, p. 267.
3 Cernuda, *Perfil del aire*, pp. 28, 17.

PAGE 195

1 Bécquer, 'Tres fechas', in *Obras completas*, 11th ed., p. 392.
2 Cernuda, 'Vicente Aleixandre', *Orígenes*, no. 26 (1950), p. 12; O. Paz, 'La palabra edificante', *Papeles de Son Armadans*, vol. XXXV (1964), no. CIII, p. 50.

PAGE 198

1 Paz, 'La palabra edificante', *Papeles de Son Armadans*, vol. XXXV (1964), no. CIII, p. 57.

PAGE 200

1 C. Day Lewis, *The Poetic Image* (London, 1947), p. 74.

PAGE 202

1 Alberti, *La arboleda perdida*, p. 271.
2 Jiménez, 'Acento. Satanismo inverso', *La Gaceta Literaria*, no. 98 (January 1931).
3 Salinas, 'Nueve o diez poetas', in *Ensayos de literatura hispánica*, 3rd ed., p. 368.
4 Alberti, *La arboleda perdida*, pp. 268–9.

PAGE 203

1 J. L. Salado, 'Rafael Alberti, de niño, quería ser pintor', *Cervantes*, vol. VII (March–April 1934), p. 40.

PAGE 204

1 Alberti, *La arboleda perdida*, p. 269.

PAGE 207

1 Rimbaud, *Une saison en enfer*, in *Œuvres complètes* (Paris, 1946), p. 213.
2 Alberti, 'Miedo y vigilia de Gustavo Adolfo Bécquer', *El Sol* (6 September 1931), p. 3.

PAGE 209

1 Rimbaud, *Œuvres complètes*, p. 205.

PAGE 211

1 Alberti, *Teatro*, vol. I, p. 37.

PAGE 213

1 Alberti, *Teatro*, vol. II, p. 100.

PAGE 214

1 J.G.O., 'El estreno de "El hombre deshabitado", de Rafael Alberti', *Heraldo de Madrid* (27 February 1931), p. 5.

PAGE 215

1 Alberti, 'Índice de familia burguesa española (Mis otros tíos, tías, tías y tíos segundos)', *Hoja Literaria* (May 1933), p. 5.

PAGE 216

1 Alberti, 'Federico García Lorca: *Poeta en Nueva York*', *Sur*, vol. IX (1940), no. 75, p. 148.

PAGE 217

1 Alberti, 'Federico García Lorca: *Poeta en Nueva York*', *Sur*, vol. IX (1940), no. 75, p. 148.
2 Lorca, 'Trip to the Moon. A Filmscript' [tr. B. G. Duncan], *New Directions*, vol. XVIII (1964), pp. 35–41. See too V. Higginbotham, 'El viaje de García Lorca a la luna', *Ínsula*, no. 254 (January 1968).
3 Guillén, *Federico en persona*, p. 114; letter to Guillén of January 1927.
4 A. Barea, 'Las raíces del lenguaje poético de Lorca', *Bulletin of Spanish Studies*, vol. XXII (1945), p. 13; G. Correa, 'Significado de "Poeta en Nueva York" de Federico García Lorca', *Cuadernos Americanos*, vol. CII (1959), p. 224.
5 Alberti, 'Federico García Lorca: *Poeta en Nueva York*', *Sur*, vol. IX (1940), no. 75, p. 148.

PAGE 218

1 Guillén, *Federico en persona*, p. 103.

PAGE 219

1 Lorca, 'Oda al Santísimo Sacramento del Altar', *Revista de Occidente*, vol. XXII (1928), no. LXVI, pp. 294–8.

PAGE 221

1 Lorca, *Cartas a sus amigos* (Barcelona, 1950), p. 28.

PAGE 222

1 Larrea, 'Asesinado por el cielo', *España Peregrina*, vol. I (1940), p. 252.
2 Á. del Río, '*Poet in New York*: Twenty-Five Years After', in *Poet in New York* [tr. Ben Belitt] (London, 1955), p. xxx.

PAGE 223

1 Remarque, *All Quiet on the Western Front* (London, 1960), p. 229.

PAGE 224

1 Remarque, *All Quiet on the Western Front*, p. 90.

PAGE 227

1 Guillén, *Federico en persona*, p. 73.

PAGE 228

1 Aragon, *Le Paysan de Paris*, 10th ed., p. 248.
2 Larrea, 'Asesinado por el cielo', *España Peregrina*, vol. I (1940), p. 252; M. E. Añez, 'Interpretación de algunos aspectos de *Poeta en Nueva York*', *Anuario de Filología*, vol. IV (1965), p. 307.

PAGE 229

1 Guillén, *Federico en persona*, p. 31.
2 R. Diers, 'Introductory Note' to Lorca, 'Trip to the Moon', *New Directions*, vol. XVIII (1964), p. 34. Examples of Dalí's verse are: 'Poema', *La Gaceta Literaria*, no. 28 (February 1928); 'Con el sol', *La Gaceta Literaria*, no. 54 (March 1929); 'UNA PLUMA, que no es tal PLUMA...', *La Gaceta Literaria*, no. 56 (April 1929). As for Buñuel's verse, see: 'Poemas' ['Redentora' and 'Bacanal'], *La Gaceta Literaria*, no. 50 (January 1929); 'Poema. Olor de santidad', *La Gaceta Literaria*, no. 51 (February 1929); 'Palacio de hielo' and 'Pájaro de angustia', *Hélix*, no. 4 (May 1929), p. 5.
3 C. Marcilly, 'Notes pour l'étude de la pensée religieuse de F. García Lorca: *Crucifixión*', *Mélanges offerts à Marcel Bataillon par les hispanistes français* (Bordeaux, 1962), p. 512.

PAGE 230

1 Alberti, 'Federico García Lorca: *Poeta en Nueva York*', *Sur*, vol. IX (1940), no. 75, p. 148.

PAGE 231

1 C. Day Lewis, *The Poetic Image*, p. 72.

Epilogue: After the War

PAGE 235

1 Aleixandre, *En un vasto dominio* (Madrid, 1962), p. 13.
2 Aleixandre, *Retratos con nombre* (Barcelona, 1965), p. 45.

PAGE 237

1   Prados, *Signos del ser* (Madrid–Palma de Mallorca, 1962), p. 60.
2   Prados, *La piedra escrita* (Mexico, 1961), p. 127.
3   Prados, *Signos del ser*, p. 20.

PAGE 238

1   Cernuda, *Ocnos*, 3rd ed., p. 175.
2   Cernuda, *Desolación de la quimera* (Mexico, 1962), p. 68.

PAGE 239

1   Alberti, *Poemas escénicos (primera serie)* [1961–2] (Buenos Aires, 1962), p. 75.

PAGE 240

1   Alberti, *Poemas escénicos*, p. 95.

PAGE 241

1   Guillén, *A la altura de las circunstancias* (Buenos Aires, 1963), p. 35.

PAGE 242

1   Guillén, . . .*Que van a dar en la mar* (Buenos Aires, 1960), p. 185.
2   C. Couffon, *Dos encuentros con Jorge Guillén*, p. 24.
3   Guillén, *A la altura de las circunstancias*, p. 134.
4   Guillén, . . .*Que van a dar en la mar*, p. 120; 'Aire-aura', *Revista de Occidente*, vol. II (1923), no. IV, pp. 1–8.
5   Guillén, *Maremágnum* (Buenos Aires, 1957), pp. 124, 181.
6   *Ibid.* p. 17.
7   Guillén, *A la altura de las circunstancias*, p. 52.

PAGE 243

1   Guillén, *A la altura de las circunstancias*, p. 73.
2   Guillén, *Maremágnum*, p. 125.
3   *Ibid.* p. 144; *A la altura de las circunstancias*, p. 89.
4   Guillén, . . .*Que van a dar en la mar*, p. 148; *A la altura de las circunstancias*, p. 150; *Homenaje. Reunión de vidas* (Milan, 1967), p. 526.
5   Guillén, . . .*Que van a dar en la mar*, p. 136.

PAGE 244

1   Guillén, . . .*Que van a dar en la mar*, p. 131.
2   Salinas, 'La gran cabeza de turco o la minoría literaria', in *La responsabilidad del escritor*, p. 133.

PAGE 245

1   Guillén, *A la altura de las circunstancias*, p. 137.
2   D. Alonso, 'España en las cartas de Pedro Salinas', *Ínsula*, no. 74 (February 1952).

BIO-BIBLIOGRAPHICAL
APPENDIX

An exhaustive bibliography of Alberti, Aleixandre, Altolaguirre, Cernuda, García Lorca, Guillén, Prados and Salinas would need a volume to itself. The books and essays I list, after specifying the major titles and collections of the eight poets who dominate this book, is a necessarily selective guide to a group of writers who, with the exception of Altolaguirre and Prados, have received generous critical attention. A number of the books I quote are collections of previously published essays; to save space, I have not mentioned these essays individually.

THE GENERATION AS A WHOLE
ANTHOLOGIES

Aguirre, J. M. *Antología de la poesía española contemporánea*. 2nd ed. Saragossa, 1966.

Diego, G. *Poesía española contemporánea (1901–1934)*. Nueva edición completa. Madrid, 1959.

Gaos, V. *Antología del grupo poético de 1927*. Madrid, 1965.

González Muela, J. and Rozas, J. M. *La generación poética de 1927. Estudio, antología y documentación*. Madrid, 1966.

Turnbull, E. L. *Contemporary Spanish Poetry: Selections from Ten Poets*. Baltimore, 1945.

SELECT CRITICAL BIBLIOGRAPHY

Alberti, R. *La poesía popular en la lírica española contemporánea*. Jena and Leipzig, 1933.

 Lope de Vega y la poesía española contemporánea, seguido de La pájara pinta. Paris, 1964.

Alonso, D. *Poetas españoles contemporáneos*. Tercera edición aumentada. Madrid, 1965.

Aub, M. *La poesía española contemporánea*. Mexico, 1954.

Cano, J. L. *De Machado a Bousoño. Notas sobre poesía española contemporánea*. Madrid, 1955.

 Poesía española del siglo XX: de Unamuno a Blas de Otero. Madrid, 1960.

Cernuda, L. *Estudios sobre poesía española contemporánea*. Madrid, 1957.

Ciplijauskaité, B. *La soledad y la poesía española contemporánea.* Madrid, 1962.

Cirre, J. F. *Forma y espíritu de una lírica española (1920–1935).* 2nd ed. Madrid, 1966.

Debicki, A. P. *Estudios sobre poesía española contemporánea. La generación de 1924–25.* Madrid, 1968.

Dehennin, E. *La résurgence de Góngora et la génération poétique de 1927.* Paris, 1962.

Diego, G. 'Crónica del centenario de Góngora (1627–1927)'. *Lola,* no. 1, 1927; no. 2, 1928.

Díez Canedo, E. *Estudios de poesía española contemporánea.* Mexico, 1965.

González Muela, J. *El lenguaje poético de la generación Guillén–Lorca.* Madrid, 1954.

Guillén, J. 'The Language of the Poem. One Generation'. In *Language and Poetry. Some Poets of Spain.* Cambridge, Mass., 1961.

Salinas, P. *Literatura española siglo XX.* Segunda edición aumentada. Mexico, 1949.

Ensayos de literatura hispánica (Del ' Cantar de Mio Cid' a García Lorca). 3rd ed. Madrid, 1967.

Santos Torroella, R. *Medio siglo de publicaciones de poesía en España. Catálogo de revistas.* Segovia-Madrid, 1952.

Torre, G. de. *Literaturas europeas de vanguardia.* Madrid, 1923.

Historia de las literaturas de vanguardia. Madrid, 1965.

Vivanco, L. F. *Introducción a la poesía española contemporánea.* Madrid, 1957.

Zardoya, C. *Poesía española contemporánea: estudios temáticos y estilísticos.* Madrid, 1961.

Poesía española del 98 y del 27. (Estudios temáticos y estilísticos.) Madrid, 1968.

RAFAEL ALBERTI
(1902–   )

Born Puerto de Santa María, Cádiz, 16 January 1902. Educated at Jesuit Colegio de San Luis Gonzaga, 1912–17. 1917: Moved to Madrid. Took up painting. 1922: Exhibited paintings at Ateneo, Madrid. 1923–4: Lived in Sierra de Guadarrama for health reasons. 1925: Awarded Premio Nacional de Literatura for *Marinero en tierra.* 1929: Joined student demonstrations against the dictatorship of Primo de Rivera. 1930: Married María Teresa León. 1931–2: Travelled widely in

Europe, visited Russia. 1934: Founded with his wife the revolutionary left-wing periodical *Octubre*. Travelled in Europe and Russia. 1935: Gave lectures and recitals in New York and Havana. 1936: Returned to Spain and campaigned for Popular Front. 1936–8: Helped to organize Second International Congress of Writers. 1939: Fled Spain. Worked in Paris as radio announcer. 1940: Left France for Argentina. 1951–5: Visited Poland, Rumania, Czechoslovakia and East Germany. 1955: Visited China. 1960: Travelled in Venezuela, Cuba, Colombia, Peru. 1966: Visited Paris.

WORKS

Poetry

Poesías completas. Buenos Aires, 1961.
Poemas escénicos (primera serie) [1961–1962]. Buenos Aires, 1962.
Abierto a todas horas (1960–1963). Madrid, 1964.
Selected Poems. Tr. Lloyd Malan. New York, 1944.
Selected Poems. Tr. Ben Belitt. Berkeley and Los Angeles, 1966.
Concerning the Angels. Tr. Geoffrey Connell. London, 1967.

Drama

Fermín Galán. Romance de ciego en tres actos. Madrid, 1931.
Bazar de la Providencia (Negocio). Dos farsas revolucionarias. Madrid, 1934.
Teatro. 2 vols. Buenos Aires, 1959–64.

Prose

La poesía popular en la lírica española contemporánea. Jena and Leipzig, 1933.
Imagen primera de... Buenos Aires, 1945.
La arboleda perdida. Libros I y II de memorias. Buenos Aires, 1959.
Lope de Vega y la poesía española contemporánea, seguido de La pájara pinta. Paris, 1964.

SELECT CRITICAL BIBLIOGRAPHY

Anon. 'An Andalusian Poet'. *The Times Literary Supplement*, no. 2405. 1948.
Bergamín, J. 'De veras y de burlas'. *La Gaceta Literaria*, no. 71. 1929.
Bowra, C. M. 'Rafael Alberti, *Sobre los ángeles*'. In *The Creative Experiment*. London, 1949.

Connell, G. W. 'The Autobiographical Element in *Sobre los ángeles*'. *Bulletin of Hispanic Studies*, vol. XL. 1963.

Connell, G. W. 'The End of a Quest: Alberti's *Sermones y Moradas* and Three Uncollected Poems'. *Hispanic Review*, vol. XXXIII. 1965.

Couffon, C. *Rafael Alberti*. Paris, 1966.

González Muela, J. '¿ Poesía amorosa en *Sobre los ángeles*?' *Ínsula*, no. 80. 1952.

Grant, H. F. 'La poesía de Rafael Alberti'. *Boletín del Instituto Español*, no. 8. 1949.

Horst, R. ter. 'The Angelic Prehistory of *Sobre los ángeles*'. *Modern Language Notes*, vol. LXXXI. 1966.

Morris, C. B. *Rafael Alberti's 'Sobre los ángeles': Four Major Themes*. Hull, 1966.

'Parallel Imagery in Quevedo and Alberti'. *Bulletin of Hispanic Studies*, vol. XXXVI. 1959.

'*Sobre los ángeles*: A Poet's Apostasy'. *Bulletin of Hispanic Studies*, vol. XXXVII. 1960.

Pérez, C. A. 'Rafael Alberti: Sobre los tontos'. *Revista Hispánica Moderna*, vol. XXXII. 1966.

Proll, E. 'The Surrealist Element in Rafael Alberti'. *Bulletin of Spanish Studies*, vol. XVIII. 1941.

'Popularismo and Barroquismo in the Poetry of Rafael Alberti'. *Bulletin of Spanish Studies*, vol. XIX. 1942.

Quiroga Plá, J. M. 'Ulises adolescente'. *Revista de Occidente*, vol. XXIII, no. LXIX. 1929.

Salado, J. L. 'Rafael Alberti, de niño, quería ser pintor'. *Cervantes*, vol. VII. 1934.

VICENTE ALEIXANDRE

(1898–   )

Born Seville, 26 April 1898. 1900–9: Lived in Málaga. 1909: Family moved to Madrid. Education: Colegio Teresiano, Madrid, 1909–13; studied law and commerce, 1913–20. 1920–2: Taught in Escuela de Intendentes Mercantiles, Madrid. Published several articles on railways. 1925–7: Through illness, lived in countryside outside Madrid. Wrote poems of *Ámbito*. 1927: Returned to Madrid. 1932: Seriously ill. Convalesced in Miraflores de la Sierra. 1933: Returned to Madrid. Awarded Premio Nacional de Literatura for unpublished *La destrucción o el amor.* 1936–8: Rest enforced by illness. Ill again. 1949: Elected member of Real Academia Española. Lives in Madrid, spends summers in Miraflores de la Sierra.

WORKS
Poetry

Poesías completas. Madrid, 1960.
Mis poemas mejores. Madrid, 1956.
En un vasto dominio. Madrid, 1962.
Retratos con nombre. Barcelona, 1965.

Prose

Vida del poeta: el amor y la poesía. [Discurso de ingreso en la Real Academia Española.] Madrid, 1950.
Algunos caracteres de la nueva poesía española. Madrid, 1955.
Los encuentros. Madrid, 1958.

SELECT CRITICAL BIBLIOGRAPHY

Alonso, D. '*Espadas como labios,* por Vicente Aleixandre'. *Revista de Occidente,* vol. XXXVIII, no. CXIV. 1932.
'Vicente Aleixandre: *La destrucción o el amor*'. *Revista de Occidente,* vol. XLVIII, no. CXLIV. 1935.
Álvarez Villar, A. 'El panteísmo en la obra poética de Vicente Aleixandre'. *Cuadernos Hispanoamericanos,* vol. LIV, nos. 175–6. 1964.
Bousoño, C. *La poesía de Vicente Aleixandre. Imagen. Estilo. Mundo poético.* 2nd ed. Madrid, 1956.
Canito, E. 'Diálogo con Vicente Aleixandre'. *Ínsula,* no. 50. 1950.
Cano, J. L. 'Entrevista con Aleixandre'. *Cuadernos del Congreso por la libertad de la cultura,* no. 39. 1959.
Cernuda, L. 'Vicente Aleixandre'. *Orígenes,* no. 26. 1950.
Chabás, J. 'Vicente Aleixandre: *Ámbito*'. *Revista de Occidente,* vol. XXI, no. LXII. 1928.
Gaos, V. 'Fray Luis de León, "fuente" de Aleixandre'. *Papeles de Son Armadans,* vol. XI, nos. XXXII–XXXIII. 1958.
Río, Á. del. 'La poesía surrealista de Aleixandre'. *Revista Hispánica Moderna,* vol. II. 1935–6.
Zardoya, C. 'Los tres mundos de Vicente Aleixandre'. *Revista Hispánica Moderna,* vol. XX. 1954.

MANUEL ALTOLAGUIRRE
(1905–59)

Born Málaga, 29 July 1905. Education: Colegio de Jesuítas de Miraflores del Palo, Málaga, 1914(?)–20; graduated in law from University of Granada, 1922. 1923: Founded 'Imprenta Sur' in Málaga with Emilio Prados; in it published magazines *Litoral* (1926–9) and *Poesía* (1930–1). 1930: Visited Paris. Lived in Madrid. 1931: Returned to Paris. 1932: Married Concha Méndez Cuesta. 1933: Visited London. Lectured in Oxford and Cambridge. Published magazine *1616* (1934–5). 1935: Returned to Madrid. Published magazines *Héroe* and *El Caballo Verde*. 1936: Directed university theatre group 'La Barraca'. Collaborated in Alianza de Intelectuales Antifascistas. 1939: Escaped to Paris. 1939–43: Lived in Havana. Published magazine *La Verónica*. 1943–59: Lived in Mexico. 1950: Visited Spain. 1952: Wrote screenplay of film *Subida al cielo*, directed by Buñuel. 1958: Wrote and directed film *El cantar de los cantares*. 1959: Attended San Sebastián Film Festival. Died after road accident in Burgos.

WORKS

Poetry

Poesías completas [1926–1959]. México, 1960.
Vida poética. Málaga, 1962.

Prose

Garcilaso de la Vega. Madrid, 1933.
'El caballo griego'. [Chapter of unpublished novel of that title written in 1939.] *Papeles de Son Armadans*, vol. x, no. xxx. 1958.

SELECT CRITICAL BIBLIOGRAPHY

Aleixandre, V. 'La poesía y *Soledades juntas*'. *Revista de Occidente*, vol. XXXV, no. CIII. 1932.
Bergamín, J. 'Homenaje y recuerdo'. *Índice de Artes y Letras*, no. 128. 1959.
'Silencio y soledad'. In *Al volver*. Barcelona, 1962.
Cano, J. L. 'Manuel Altolaguirre, poeta de la nube'. *Caracola*, nos. 90–4. 1960.

Cernuda, L. 'Manuel Altolaguirre'. *Caracola*, nos. 90–4. 1960.
'Altolaguirre'. In *Poesía y literatura II*. Barcelona, 1964.
Fernández Almagro, M. 'La escalera para subir sin alas'. *Caracola*, nos.
90–4. 1960.

LUIS CERNUDA
(1902–63)

Born Seville, 21 September 1902. Education: University of Seville,
1919–25; graduated in law. 1928: Left Seville for Madrid. 1928–9:
Lector in Spanish in the University of Toulouse. 1929–38: Lived mostly
in Madrid. 1931: Worked with Misiones Pedagógicas founded by
Republican government. 1936: Went to Paris as secretary to Ambas-
sador to France in July. Returned to Madrid in September. 1936–7:
Lived in Madrid and Valencia. 1938: Left to give a lecture-tour in
England. Became Assistant Master at Cranleigh School, Surrey. 1939–
43: Lector in Spanish at the University of Glasgow. 1943–5: Lector in
Spanish at the University of Cambridge. 1945–7: Lecturer at the Insti-
tuto de España, London. 1947–52: Taught at Mount Holyoke College,
Massachusetts. 1952: Moved to Mexico. 1960: Visiting Professor at
University of California at San Francisco. 1962: Visiting Professor at
University of California at Los Angeles. 1963: Died in Mexico City.

WORKS
Poetry
Perfil del aire. Málaga, 1927.
La realidad y el deseo [1924–1956]. Tercera edición, corregida y aumen-
tada. Mexico, 1958.
Desolación de la quimera [1956–1962]. Mexico, 1962.

Prose
Variaciones sobre tema mexicano. Mexico, 1952.
Estudios sobre poesía española contemporánea. Madrid, 1957.
Pensamiento poético en la lírica inglesa (siglo XIX). Mexico, 1958.
Poesía y literatura. Barcelona, 1960.
Ocnos. Tercera edición aumentada. Xalapa, Mexico, 1963.
Poesía y literatura II. Barcelona, 1964.
'Cartas de Luis Cernuda (1926–1929)'. *Ínsula*, no. 207. 1964.

SELECT CRITICAL BIBLIOGRAPHY

Aguirre, J. M. 'La poesía primera de Luis Cernuda'. *Hispanic Review*, vol. XXXIV. 1966.

Brines, F. 'Ante unas poesías completas'. *La Caña Gris*, nos. 6–8. 1962.

Cano, J. L. 'Bécquer y Cernuda'. *Asomante*, vol. IX. 1953.

'Notas sobre el tema del amor en la poesía de Luis Cernuda'. *Revista Nacional de Cultura*, vol. XX, no. 129. 1958.

'Un personaje en la poesía de Cernuda: el demonio'. *Papeles de Son Armadans*, vol. XVII, no. LI. 1960.

Córdova Infante, J. 'Estudio lingüístico de la poesía de Luis Cernuda'. *Asomante*, vol. I. 1945.

Ferraté, J. 'Luis Cernuda y el poder de las palabras'. In *La operación de leer y otros ensayos*. Barcelona, 1962.

Gullón, R. 'La poesía de Luis Cernuda'. *Asomante*, vol. VI. 1950.

Harris, D. R. 'Ejemplo de fidelidad poética: el superrealismo de Luis Cernuda'. *La Caña Gris*, nos. 6–8. 1962.

Jiménez, J. O. 'Emoción y trascendencia del tiempo en la poesía de Luis Cernuda'. In *Cinco poetas del tiempo*. Madrid, 1964.

Newman, R. K. 'Primeras poesías'. *La Caña Gris*, nos. 6–8. 1962.

Otero, C. 'La tercera salida de *La realidad y el deseo*'. *Papeles de Son Armadans*, vol. XVII, no. LI. 1960.

'Poeta de Europa'. *Papeles de Son Armadans*, vol. XXIX, no. LXXV. 1963.

Paz, O. 'La palabra edificante'. *Papeles de Son Armadans*, vol. XXXV, no. CIII. 1964.

Silver, P. W. '*Et in Arcadia Ego*'. *A Study of the Poetry of Luis Cernuda*. London, 1965.

Valencia, J. 'El "cansancio" en la poesía de Luis Cernuda'. *Clavileño*, no. 30. 1954.

Valente, J. A. 'Luis Cernuda y la poesía de la meditación'. *La Caña Gris*, nos. 6–8. 1962.

FEDERICO GARCÍA LORCA
(1898–1936)

Born Fuentevaqueros, Granada, 5 June 1898. 1898–1908: Lived in Fuentevaqueros. Education: Instituto de Almería, 1908; Colegio del Sagrado Corazón de Jesús, Granada, 1909–15; studied law and letters in

University of Granada, 1915–20, whence he graduated in law in 1923. 1916: Travelled widely in Andalusia and Castile. 1919–28: Lived in the Residencia de Estudiantes, Madrid. 1922: In Granada lectured on *cante jondo* and helped to organize the Fiesta del Cante Jondo held on 13–14 June. 1926: Lectured in Granada on Góngora and on Soto de Rojas. 1927: Exhibited drawings in Barcelona, 25 June–2 July. 1928: Lectured in Granada. 1929: Lectured in Madrid. Went to New York *via* Paris, London, Oxford, Scotland. 1929: In Columbia University, New York. Visited Vermont, Catskill Mountains. Lectured in Columbia University and Vassar College. 1930: Lectured in Cuba. Returned to Spain. 1932: Collaborated in foundation of university theatre group 'La Barraca', which he directed on its tours of Spain. Lectured widely in Spain. 1933: Toured with 'La Barraca'. Lectured in Madrid. 1933–4: Visited Argentina, Uruguay. 1934: Toured with 'La Barraca'. 1936: Murdered on 19 August in Granada.

WORKS

Obras completas. 3rd ed. Madrid, 1957.
Cartas a sus amigos. Barcelona, 1950.
Poet in New York. Tr. Ben Belitt. London, 1955.
Lorca. Tr. J. L. Gili. Harmondsworth, 1960.

SELECT CRITICAL BIBLIOGRAPHY

Aguirre, J. M. 'El sonambulismo de Federico García Lorca'. *Bulletin of Hispanic Studies*, vol. XLIV. 1967.

Alberti, R. 'Federico García Lorca: *Poeta en Nueva York*'. *Sur*, vol. IX, no. 75. 1940.

Añez, M. E. 'Interpretación de algunos aspectos de *Poeta en Nueva York*'. *Anuario de Filología*, vol. IV. 1965.

Barea, A. *Lorca, the Poet and his People.* London. 1944.
'Las raíces del lenguaje poético de Lorca'. *Bulletin of Spanish Studies*, vol. XXII. 1945.

Bosch, R. 'Los poemas paralelísticos de García Lorca'. *Revista Hispánica Moderna*, vol. XXVIII. 1962.

Bowra, C. M. 'Federico García Lorca, *Romancero gitano*'. In *The Creative Experiment.* London, 1949.

Campbell, R. *Lorca: An Appreciation of his Poetry.* 2nd ed. London, 1961.

Cannon, C. 'Lorca's *Llanto por Ignacio Sánchez Mejías* and the Elegiac Tradition'. *Hispanic Review*, vol. XXXI. 1963.

Cano Ballesta, J. 'Una veta reveladora en la poesía de García Lorca (Los tiempos del verbo y sus matices expresivos)'. *Romanische Forschungen*, vol. LXXVII. 1965.

Castro, J. A. 'Poeta en Nueva York'. *Cultura Universitaria*, vols. LXXIV–LXXV. 1961.

Correa, G. *La poesía mítica de Federico García Lorca*. Eugene, Oregon, 1957.

'El simbolismo religioso en la poesía de Federico García Lorca'. *Hispania*, vol. XXXIX. 1956.

El simbolismo de la luna en la poesía de Federico García Lorca'. *Publications of the Modern Language Association of America*, vol. LXXII. 1957.

'Significado de *Poeta en Nueva York* de Federico García Lorca'. *Cuadernos Americanos*, vol. CII. 1959.

'El simbolismo del sol en la poesía de Federico García Lorca'. *Nueva Revista de Filología Hispánica*, vol. XIV. 1960.

Devoto, D. 'Notas sobre el elemento tradicional en la obra de García Lorca'. *Filología*, vol. II. 1950.

'Lecturas de García Lorca'. *Revue de Littérature Comparée*, vol. XXXIII. 1959.

'García Lorca y Darío'. *Asomante*, vol. XXIII. 1967.

Durán, M. (ed.). *Lorca. A Collection of Critical Essays*. Englewood Cliffs, New Jersey, 1962.

Flys, J. M. *El lenguaje poético de Federico García Lorca*. Madrid, 1955.

Guillén, J. *Federico en persona: semblanza y epistolario*. Buenos Aires, 1959.

Laffranque, M. *Les idées esthétiques de Federico García Lorca*. Paris, 1967.

'Pour l'étude de Federico García Lorca. Bases chronologiques'. *Bulletin Hispanique*, vol. LXV. 1963.

López Morillas, J. 'García Lorca y el primitivismo lírico: Reflexiones sobre el *Romancero gitano*'. In *Intelectuales y espirituales*. Madrid, 1961.

Marcilly, C. *Ronde et fable de la solitude à New York: prélude à 'Poeta en Nueva York' de F. G. Lorca*. Paris, 1962.

'Notes pour l'étude de la pensée religieuse de F. García Lorca: *Crucifixión*'. In *Mélanges offerts à Marcel Bataillon par les hispanistes français*. Bordeaux, 1962.

Morla Lynch, C. *En España con Federico García Lorca* (*Páginas de un diario íntimo. 1928–36*). Madrid, 1958.

Riley, E. C. 'Considerations on the Poetry of García Lorca'. *The Dublin Magazine*, vol. XXVII. 1952.

Río, Á. del. '*Poet in New York*: Twenty-five Years After'. In Lorca, *Poet in New York*. London, 1955.

Rizzo, G. L. 'Poesía de Federico García Lorca y poesía popular'. *Clavileño*, no. 36. 1955.

Turcato, B. 'Struttura ed evoluzione delle prime metafore lorchiane'. *Quaderni Ibero-Americani*, vol. IV, no. 27. 1961–2.

JORGE GUILLÉN
(1893–   )

Born Valladolid, 18 January 1893. Education: Instituto de Valladolid, 1903–9; Maison Ferreyve of the French Fathers of the Oratory, Fribourg, 1909–11; Faculty of Philosophy and Letters at the Residencia de Estudiantes, Madrid, 1911–13; graduated from the University of Granada, 1913; awarded doctorate of letters by University of Madrid, 1924. 1913–14: Visited Germany. 1914–17: Lived in Madrid and Valladolid. 1917–23: Lector in Spanish at the Sorbonne. 1921: Married Germaine Cahen. 1925–6: Professor of Spanish Literature in the University of Murcia. 1929–31: Lector in Spanish at University of Oxford. 1931–8: Professor of Spanish literature at the University of Seville. 1938–9: Taught at Middlebury College, Vermont. 1939–40: Taught at McGill University. 1940–57: Professor at Wellesley College, Massachusetts. 1947: Visiting Professor at Yale University. Wife died. 1949: Spent summer in Valladolid. 1950: Professor at the Colegio de México, Mexico City. 1951: Visiting Professor at the University of California at Berkeley. Travelled in Europe. 1952: Visiting Professor at Ohio State University. 1954: Spent summer in Italy. 1955: In France, Minorca and Italy. 1957: Appointed Charles Eliot Norton Professor of Poetry at Harvard University for 1957–8. 1958–9: In Greece, Spain, France and Italy. 1960: In America, Puerto Rico and Italy. 1961: In Italy and Bogotá. Married Irene Mochi-Sismondi. 1962: Visiting Professor at the University of Puerto Rico. 1963: In Italy and America. Lives in America.

WORKS
Poetry

Cántico. Primera edición completa. Buenos Aires, 1950.
Clamor: Maremágnum. Buenos Aires, 1957.
   ...*Que van a dar en la mar.* Buenos Aires, 1960.
   A la altura de las circunstancias. Buenos Aires, 1963.
Selección de poemas. Madrid, 1965.
Cántico. A Selection. Ed. N. T. di Giovanni. London, 1965.
Homenaje. Reunión de vidas. Milan, 1967.

Prose

Federico en persona: semblanza y epistolario. Buenos Aires, 1959.
El argumento de la obra. Milan, 1961.
Language and Poetry. Some Poets of Spain. Cambridge, Mass., 1961.

SELECT CRITICAL BIBLIOGRAPHY

Alonso, A. 'Jorge Guillén, poeta esencial'. In *Materia y forma en poesía.* Madrid, 1955.
Alonso, D. 'Pasión elemental en la poesía de Jorge Guillén'. *Ínsula,* no. 26. 1948.
Blecua, J. M. and Gullón, R. *La poesía de Jorge Guillén.* Saragossa, 1949.
Casalduero, J. *Cántico de Jorge Guillén,* Madrid, 1953.
Castro, A. '"Cántico" de Jorge Guillén'. *Ínsula* [Buenos Aires], vol. I. 1943.
Cervera Tomás, J. 'La concepción del mundo en la obra de Jorge Guillén'. *Monteagudo,* no. 2. 1953.
Ciplijauskaité, B. 'Jorge Guillén y Paul Valéry, al despertar'. *Papeles de Son Armadans,* vol. XXXIII, no. XCIX. 1964.
Couffon, C. *Dos encuentros con Jorge Guillén.* Paris [1963].
Darmangeat, P. *Jorge Guillén ou le cantique émerveillé.* Paris, 1958.
Frutos, E. 'El existencialismo jubiloso de Jorge Guillén'. *Cuadernos Hispanoamericanos,* no. 18. 1950.
González Muela, J. *La realidad y Jorge Guillén.* Madrid, 1962.
   'Sobre el Cántico de Jorge Guillén'. *Bulletin of Hispanic Studies,* vol. XXXII. 1955.
   'Poesía y amistad: Jorge Guillén y Pedro Salinas'. *Bulletin of Hispanic Studies,* vol. XXXV. 1958.

Lida, R. 'Sobre las décimas de Jorge Guillén'. *Cuadernos Americanos*, vol. c. 1958.

Valverde, J. M. 'Plenitud crítica de la poesía de Jorge Guillén'. In *Estudios sobre la palabra poética*. Madrid, 1952.

Whittredge, R. 'The Poetic World of Jorge Guillén'. *Romanic Review*, vol. XXXIX. 1948.

Wilson, E. M. 'Studies in Modern Spanish Poetry. I. Guillén and Quevedo on Death'. *Atlante*, vol. I. 1953.

'Studies in Modern Spanish Poetry. I. Guillén and Quevedo on Death. Postscript'. *Atlante*, vol. II. 1954.

Xirau, R. 'Lectura a "Cántico"'. In *Poetas de México y España*. Madrid, 1962.

EMILIO PRADOS
(1899–1962)

Born Málaga, 4 March 1899. Education: Residencia de Estudiantes, Madrid, 1915–20; studied natural sciences at University of Madrid, studied philosophy at Fribourg, 1920–1. 1911: Through illness lived for a year in countryside outside Málaga. 1920: Ill. Returned to mountains around Málaga. 1920–1: Spent a year at sanatorium in Davos. 1921: Visited Paris. Settled in Málaga. 1925: Founded with Manuel Altolaguirre 'Imprenta Sur', where they published the magazine *Litoral* (1926–9). 1929: Went into retreat in mountains. 1936: Went to Madrid. Collaborated in Alianza de Intelectuales Antifascistas. 1939: Escaped to Paris. Went to Mexico, where he taught at the Instituto Luis Vives. 1962: Died in Mexico.

WORKS
Poetry

Antología [1923–1953]. Buenos Aires, 1954.
La circuncisión del sueño. Mexico, 1957.
Jardín cerrado. Buenos Aires, 1960.
La piedra escrita. Mexico, 1961.
Signos del ser. Madrid–Palma de Mallorca, 1962.
Últimos poemas. Málaga, 1965.

Prose

Diario íntimo. Málaga, 1966.

SELECT CRITICAL BIBLIOGRAPHY

Blanco Aguinaga, C. *Emilio Prados: Vida y obra. Bibliografía. Antología.* New York, 1960.

'La aventura poética de Emilio Prados'. *Revista Mejicana de Literatura,* no. 8. 1956.

Diego, G. 'Emilio Prados: *Vuelta*'. *Revista de Occidente,* vol. XVII, no. LI. 1927.

Gil-Albert, J. 'Emilio Prados de la "Constelación Rosicler"'. *Taller,* vol. II, no. II. 1940.

Xirau, R. 'El poema de Emilio Prados'. In *Poetas de México y España.* Madrid, 1962.

PEDRO SALINAS

(1892–1951)

Born Madrid, 27 November 1892. Education: Instituto de San Isidro, Madrid, 1904(?)–9; studied letters and law at University of Madrid, 1909–13; graduated in letters, 1913; received doctorate in letters, 1917. 1914–17: Lector in Spanish at the Sorbonne. 1915: Married Margarita Bonmatí. 1918–26: Professor of Spanish Literature at the University of Seville. 1922–3: Lector in Spanish at the University of Cambridge. 1926–36: Lived in Madrid. Collaborated in Centro de Estudios Históricos. Secretary of Universidad Internacional de Santander. Lectured in Spain, Austria, Belgium, Germany, Holland, Hungary and Italy. 1936–9: Professor at Wellesley College, Massachusetts. 1940–51: Professor of Spanish Literature at The Johns Hopkins University, Baltimore. Taught in summer schools at Middlebury College, Vermont, and at the University of Puerto Rico from 1942 to 1945. 1951: Died in Boston.

WORKS

Poetry

Poesías completas. Madrid, 1955.
Volverse sombra y otros poemas. Milan, 1957.

Drama

Teatro completo. Madrid, 1957.

Prose

Víspera del gozo. Madrid, 1926.
Jorge Manrique o tradición y originalidad. Buenos Aires, 1947.
La poesía de Rubén Darío. Buenos Aires, 1948.
Literatura española siglo XX. Segunda edición aumentada. Mexico, 1949.
La bomba increíble. Fabulación. Buenos Aires, 1950.
El desnudo impecable y otras narraciones. Mexico, 1951.
La responsabilidad del escritor y otros ensayos. Barcelona, 1961.
Reality and the Poet in Spanish Poetry. 2nd ed. Baltimore, 1966.
El defensor, 2nd ed. Madrid, 1967.
Ensayos de literatura hispánica (Del 'Cantar de Mio Cid' a García Lorca).
3rd ed. Madrid, 1967.

SELECT CRITICAL BIBLIOGRAPHY

Alonso, D. 'Un poeta y un libro (*Fábula y signo*, por Pedro Salinas)'.
Revista de Occidente, vol. XXXIII, no. XCVIII. 1931.
Blecua, J. M. 'Una charla con Pedro Salinas'. *Ínsula*, no. 70. 1951.
Bravo-Villasante, C. 'La poesía de Pedro Salinas'. *Clavileño*, no. 21.
1953.
Cernuda, L. 'Pedro Salinas y su poesía'. *Revista de Occidente*, vol. XXV,
no. LXXIV. 1929.
Costa Viva, O. 'Pedro Salinas, exaltación de la realidad'. *Revista de la
Universidad de Buenos Aires* [5ª época], no. 3. 1960.
Darmangeat, P. *Pedro Salinas et La voz a ti debida*. Paris, 1955.
Dehennin, E. *Passion d'absolu et tension expressive dans l'œuvre poétique de
Pedro Salinas*. Ghent, 1957.
Feal Deibe, C. *La poesía de Pedro Salinas*. Madrid, 1965.
Feldbaum, J. 'El trasmundo de la obra poética de Pedro Salinas'.
Revista Hispánica Moderna, vol. XXII. 1956.
Gilman, S. 'The Proem to *La voz a ti debida*'. *Modern Language Quarterly*,
vol. XXIII. 1962.
González Muela, J. 'Poesía y amistad: Jorge Guillén y Pedro Salinas'.
Bulletin of Hispanic Studies, vol. XXXV. 1958.
Guillén, J. 'El atento'. *Asomante*, vol. VIII. 1952.
'Introduction: Pedro Salinas'. In Salinas, *Reality and the Poet in
Spanish Poetry*. 2nd ed. Baltimore, 1966.
Murciano, C. *Las sombras en la poesía de Pedro Salinas*. Santander, 1962.
Palley, J. *La luz no usada. La poesía de Pedro Salinas*. Mexico, 1966.

Quiroga Plá, J. M. 'El espejo ardiendo'. *Cruz y Raya*, no. 11. 1934.

Río, Á. del. 'El poeta Pedro Salinas: Vida y obra'. *Revista Hispánica Moderna*, vol. VII. 1941.

Rogers, D. 'Espejos y reflejos en la poesía de Pedro Salinas'. *Revista de Literatura*, vol. XXIX, nos. 57–8. 1966.

Rosales, L. 'Dulce sueño donde hay luz'. *Cruz y Raya*, no. 11. 1934.

Spitzer, L. 'El conceptismo interior de Pedro Salinas'. *Revista Hispánica Moderna*, vol. VII. 1941.

GLOSSARY OF
SPANISH TERMS

anaglifo: A type of nonsense verse composed in their ebullient youth by Alberti, Buñuel, Dalí, Lorca and others in accordance with a rigid pattern: three nouns in four lines, the second of which had to be 'la gallina' and the third of which had to have no connection with the first.

auto: An early one-act play.

auto sacramental: In vogue from the mid-sixteenth to the mid-eighteenth century, the *auto sacramental* is a one-act play that presented allegorically some moral and doctrinal lesson and culminated in a display or exaltation of the Sacrament.

cancionero: A collection of songs or poems.

cante jondo: Andalusian song, also called *cante flamenco*.

cantiga de amigo: A Galician–Portuguese song, current in the thirteenth and fourteenth centuries, that recorded in lines intertwined by repetition and parallelism a girl's feelings for her lover.

copla: Although loosely applied in the sixteenth and seventeenth centuries to all kinds of stanzas, the *copla* in its popular form is an octosyllabic quatrain whose second and fourth lines rhyme.

costumbrismo: The description of contemporary customs in literature.

creacionismo: A poetic movement of the early 1920s, introduced into Spain by the Chilean Vicente Huidobro and nurtured by Gerardo Diego, which, disdaining anecdote, description and emotion, aimed to transform poetry into an autonomous organism of melodies and images that would ideally complement rather than represent creation.

culto: In its broadest sense *culto* poetry was the opposite of *poesía popular*: poetry written by educated men for cultured readers. In the seventeenth century *culto*, as well as retaining its true sense, came to be used synonymously with *culterano* to mean the densely textured poetry cultivated by Góngora and his followers, who used learned and resonant words, audaciously coined images, classical allusions and syntactically complex periods to create an elegant, stylized poetic world remote from common experience and banal expression.

décima: A cultured poem composed of ten octosyllables whose authentic Spanish form, the *décima espinela*, has the following rhyme scheme: a b b a a c c d d c.

deshumanización: A word popularized by Ortega y Gasset, who attempted to diagnose in his essay *La deshumanización del arte*, published in 1925, the playfulness and levity characterizing life and literature in the early 1920s.

esdrújulo: A *palabra esdrújula* is a word accentuated on the antepenultimate syllable.

glosa: A gloss.

gongorismo: The conscious imitation of Góngora's manner (see *culto*).

greguería: A waggish, ironic and at times extravagantly fanciful epigram composed by Ramón Gómez de la Serna according to his formula: 'Humour + metaphor = *greguería*.'

letrilla: Akin to the *glosa*, the *letrilla* is essentially a stylization of popular forms like the *villancico* (see); generally of a religious, amorous or satiric nature, its stanzas are linked by a refrain.

lira: A stanza of Italian origin, composed in its more common form of three heptasyllables and two hendecasyllables according to the following rhyme scheme:

$$7 - a,$$
$$11 - b,$$
$$7 - a,$$
$$7 - b,$$
$$11 - b.$$

nana: A lullaby.

novelización: The process frequently encountered in traditional Spanish ballads of subordinating factual accuracy to poetic effect by the introduction of fictitious, fanciful or lyrical elements.

octava: A stanza of Italian origin, consisting of eight hendecasyllables that rhyme according to the following scheme: a b a b a b c c.

rima infantil: A nursery rhyme or a children's song.

romance: The Spanish ballad, composed of octosyllables with assonance on every even line.

romancero: A collection of Spanish ballads; or the corpus of Spain's traditional ballads.

saeta: A song generally consisting of two, three or four octosyllables that in Andalusia was improvised and sung spontaneously by spectators of religious processions, especially during Holy Week.

seguidilla: A popular song formed with heptasyllables and pentasyllables, consisting of either four lines (the *copla*) or seven lines (the *copla* plus a refrain) linked with assonance which recurs in the following way:

7
5 – a,
7
5 – a,
5 – b,
7
5 – b.

serranilla: Deriving its form from the *villancico* (see), the *serrana* or *serranilla* is a poetic composition that related the encounter of a traveller with a shepherdess or cow-girl.

solear: The *solear*, an Andalusian corruption of *soledad*, is a popular Andalusian poem of a melancholy nature, composed of three octosyllables with assonance on the first and third lines.

ultraísmo: A poetic movement, founded by Guillermo de Torre, which celebrated the technical advances and the mechanical vitality of the early 1920s with the enthusiasm and abrasive belligerence displayed by Marinetti in his advocacy of futurism. Scorning the orthodox disciplines of form, emotion and narrative, the *ultraístas* wrote deliberately disjointed and artificially patterned verses that purported to give visible shape to their theme; tenaciously observing the formula of 'Words in liberty', they packed their poems with images coined indiscriminately and repetitively out of technical words.

verbena: Popular celebrations held on the eve of certain religious festivals.

villancico: A popular song or carol of a fresh and simple lyricism, comprising an initial lyrical statement of one, two, three or four lines (usually heptasyllables or octosyllables), which is glossed in successive stanzas and sometimes repeated at the end of each stanza. At times only this first part, the *cabeza* or *estribillo* survives; at others, the *cabeza* is followed by another section, the *pie*, of six lines.

INDEX

Bold type is used to denote the eight major figures of the book and the sections devoted to them.